SO-DSP-023

VENEZUELA
AT THE POLLS

AEI's AT THE POLLS STUDIES

The American Enterprise Institute
has initiated this series in order to promote
an understanding of the electoral process as it functions in
democracies around the world. The series will include studies
of at least two national elections in each of nineteen countries
on five continents, by scholars from the United States and
abroad who are recognized as experts in their field.
More information on the titles in this series can
be found at the back of this book.

A15043 823292

VENEZUELA AT THE POLLS
THE NATIONAL ELECTIONS OF 1978

Edited by Howard R. Penniman

JL
3892
. V46
West

American Enterprise Institute for Public Policy Research
Washington and London

Library of Congress Cataloging in Publication Data
Main entry under title:

Venezuela at the polls.

(AEI studies ; 286)

1. Elections—Venezuela—Addresses, essays, lectures.
2. Political parties—Venezuela—Addresses, essays,
lectures. 3. Venezuela—Politics and government—
1958-   —Addresses, essays, lectures. I. Penniman,
Howard Rae, 1916-   II. Series: American Enterprise Institute for Public Policy Research. AEI
studies ; 286.
JL3892.V46   324.987′0633   80-21506
ISBN 0-8447-3418-7
ISBN 0-8447-3391-3 pbk.

AEI Studies 286

© 1980 by the American Enterprise Institute for Public Policy Research,
Washington, D.C., and London. All rights reserved. No part of this
publication may be used or reproduced in any manner whatsoever without
permission in writing from the American Enterprise Institute except in the
case of brief quotations embodied in news articles, critical articles,
or reviews.

The views expressed in the publications of the American Enterprise Institute
are those of the authors and do not necessarily reflect the views of the staff,
advisory panels, officers, or trustees of AEI.

"American Enterprise Institute" and (ʀʒ) are registered service marks of
the American Enterprise Institute for Public Policy Research.

Printed in the United States of America

The American Enterprise Institute for Public Policy Research, established in 1943, is a publicly supported, nonpartisan, research and educational organization. Its purpose is to assist policy makers, scholars, businessmen, the press, and the public by providing objective analysis of national and international issues. Views expressed in the institute's publications are those of the authors and do not necessarily reflect the views of the staff, advisory panels, officers, or trustees of AEI.

Council of Academic Advisers

Paul W. McCracken, *Chairman, Edmund Ezra Day University Professor of Business Administration, University of Michigan*

Robert H. Bork, *Alexander M. Bickel Professor of Public Law, Yale Law School*

Kenneth W. Dam, *Harold J. and Marion F. Green Professor of Law and Provost, University of Chicago*

Donald C. Hellmann, *Professor of Political Science and International Studies, University of Washington*

D. Gale Johnson, *Eliakim Hastings Moore Distinguished Service Professor of Economics and Chairman, Department of Economics, University of Chicago*

Robert A. Nisbet, *Adjunct Scholar, American Enterprise Institute*

Herbert Stein, *A. Willis Robertson Professor of Economics, University of Virginia*

James Q. Wilson, *Henry Lee Shattuck Professor of Government, Harvard University*

Executive Committee

Richard B. Madden, *Chairman of the Board*

William J. Baroody, Jr., *President*

Herman J. Schmidt

Richard J. Farrell

Charles T. Fisher III

Richard D. Wood

Edward Styles, *Director of Publications*

Program Directors

Russell Chapin, *Legislative Analyses*

Robert B. Helms, *Health Policy Studies*

Thomas F. Johnson, *Economic Policy Studies*

Sidney L. Jones, *Seminar Programs*

Lawrence J. Korb, *Defense Policy Studies*

Marvin H. Kosters/James C. Miller III, *Government Regulation Studies*

W. S. Moore, *Legal Policy Studies*

Rudolph G. Penner, *Tax Policy Studies*

Howard R. Penniman/Austin Ranney, *Political and Social Processes*

Robert J. Pranger, *International Programs*

Periodicals

AEI Economist, Herbert Stein, Editor

AEI Foreign Policy and Defense Review, Lawrence J. Korb and Robert J. Pranger, *Co-Editors;* James W. Abellera, *Managing Editor*

Public Opinion, Seymour Martin Lipset, Ben J. Wattenberg, *Co-Editors;* David R. Gergen, *Managing Editor*

Regulation, Antonin Scalia and Murray L. Weidenbaum, *Co-Editors;* Anne Brunsdale, *Managing Editor*

Contents

Preface

Venezuela at the Polls: The National Elections of 1978 is the first study of a national election in Latin America to be published in the American Enterprise Institute's *At the Polls* series. A volume on the 1978 elections in Colombia is in process.

Comparable studies of national elections in some twenty-four democracies have been published, are in progress, or are planned, making the AEI project the largest and most comprehensive examination of national elections ever undertaken by a private research organization. AEI expects to publish volumes on two or more elections in each of the countries included in the series. The books already published and those scheduled for completion in the near future are listed at the back of this volume.

Venezuela at the Polls follows the pattern typical of books in the series. It provides a historical context for the 1978 elections, a description of the electoral process and the rules for candidate selection, a discussion of the characteristics of the electorate and its political attitudes, analyses of the political parties and their campaigns, a discussion of the role of the media, an analysis of the financing of campaigns, and reflections on the outcome. What I would like to do here, drawing on material in this and other books in the *At the Polls* series, is to highlight several aspects of Venezuela's electoral experience and relate them to the experience of other nations.

Prosperity is very unevenly distributed among the Venezuelan people in spite of a large national return from oil production and recent government efforts to ameliorate the social and economic conditions of the underprivileged. John D. Martz states that in 1978, "with the rise of new sectors, the continuing migration from rural to urban settings, and the rapid population increase, it remained to be proved that the political and economic progress that had taken place could be translated into benefits for the great mass of the citizenry." Robert O'Connor notes that 73 percent of Venezuelans are working class or poor. More than 45 percent of the adults in his survey sample had "not completed primary school [and] many . . . were illiterate." Housing is at best marginal for many rural dwellers and for thousands of those who have left the farms and small towns and now occupy rude buildings jammed together on the mountainsides from Caracas to the sea fifteen miles away. The government has provided heavy financial support to develop new industries and expand agricultural production, but progress in both areas has been slow, and the results have not yet greatly increased the number of jobs to be had or decreased the cost of food .

In the political realm advances have been clearer. Despite recurring internal problems, including leftist guerrilla activity in the mountains and terrorist violence in the cities as late as 1969 and occasional limited threats from the military, democratization has increased. Since the overthrow of dictator Marcos Pérez Jiménez in 1958, the Venezuelan people have freely chosen their national and state government officials in five elections—and in 1978 for the third consecutive time they shifted power from one major party to the other. During the same period, campaign violence has declined. Commenting on the conduct of the 1978 elections, Martz writes: "In a hemisphere characterized . . . by a preponderance of military and authoritarian regimes, Venezuela once again demonstrated a public vigor and political vibrancy unparallelled in Latin America."

The role of the military in the restoration and development of democracy in Venezuela is worth pausing over. Most military leaders, like most business and church leaders, supported the ouster of Pérez Jiménez, and officers who were thought to oppose the new democratic regime were forced to resign. Though there is still skepticism in some quarters about the military's commitment to democracy, most Venezuelans have come to see the military as essential to the nation's internal well-being. The electoral arrangements reflect both this reliance on the military and an underlying wariness. On the one hand, military personnel, who are well paid on the job and in retirement, have been given responsibility for guaranteeing the peaceful conduct of elections and the integrity of the count; in particular, they search everyone who enters a polling place—a precaution taken only in Venezuela. (Voters I talked to in 1978 insisted that they did not object to being searched. The assurance of safety, they said, was worth the inconvenience.) On the other hand, members of the armed forces are denied the right to vote—a provision that is in striking contrast to the special efforts many democracies make to facilitate voting for those on active duty in the military.[1]

Turnout in 1978, according to unofficial figures, was 87.1 percent of the registered voters. This figure, high by world standards, was the lowest ever recorded in Venezuela. It was also lower than recent turnout in any other country (except Greece) where registration and voting are compulsory; and it was below the usual turnout of West Germany, Sweden, and Italy, where voting is not compulsory. In Venezuela persons failing to register and vote may be refused certificates of candidacy, passports, licenses, or other official documents, but for most of the more than 750,000 nonvoters in 1978, the threat of penalties apparently carried little weight.

Elections in Venezuela come at the end of a six- to eight-month campaign—the longest in any modern democracy. This legal time frame, according to Henry Wells, was established in July 1977 to *reduce* the length of campaigns. In 1978 the official campaign began on April 1, when the Supreme Electoral Council (CSE) announced that the elections would be held on December 3. All of the parties except one had already chosen their presidential nominees—six to ten months before the CSE announcement. The incumbent Democratic Action party (AD) had selected Luis Piñerúa Ordaz in a party-conducted presidential primary in June 1977 after an acrimonious contest between representatives of the party's two major factions; the contenders had begun their primary campaign in December 1976, almost twenty-four months before the general elections. The AD primary opened wounds that had not altogether healed by December 1978. It was the second time that AD had experimented with the primary and the second time that the party had lost the presidency. Luis Herrera Campíns was the unanimous choice of the Social Christian party (COPEI) convention. Candidates of most small parties were either self-selected or merely endorsed by what Wells calls "mock conventions."

In many ways Venezuelan general election campaigns are similar to those of North America and Western Europe, but they are longer and more expensive. Though some of the "participatory practices" of an earlier era survive, as Martz points out, there is a "heavy and

---

[1] According to a recent study by Ivor Crewe, Colombia also denies members of the armed forces the right to vote, while France, India, Ireland, Israel, Italy, Switzerland, the United Kingdom, and the United States all make special arrangements to facilitate their voting. See Ivor Crewe, "Electoral Participation," in David Butler, Howard R. Penniman, and Austin Ranney, eds., *Democracy at the Polls* (Washington, D.C.: American Enterprise Institute, forthcoming).

sophisticated reliance on the media; extensive use of polling and public opinion surveys," and nearly constant traveling by the candidates. In 1978 the major parties hired internationally known American managers to assist in directing their efforts. According to David J. Myers and Donald L. Herman, AD employed Joseph Napolitan and Clifton White while COPEI named David Garth after rejecting the proffered assistance of European campaign advisers. The Italian Communist party, Myers says, was "particularly generous in providing the MAS with expertise in the areas of publicity and party organization." MAS candidate José Vicente Rangel, who finished third with 5.15 percent of the valid vote, also enjoys "important support among Venezuelan social scientists [who] invest considerable time and effort in MAS election campaigns."

Venezuela's campaigns are the most expensive in the democratic world. It is clear that the parties together spent far more money for each vote cast in 1978 than has been spent in any other reasonably free and honest election in recent history. Exact figures, on the other hand, are hard to come by. The parties received generous financial assistance from the national treasury, and the law allowed them to spend as much more as they could raise. But full reporting of receipts and expenditures is not required by law, and the figures mentioned in the press—estimates generally based on private statements of the ubiquitous "well-informed party source"—vary widely. Some of these variations are due to differences in the comprehensiveness of the totals provided. Wells points out that the government gave not only direct and indirect aid to the parties but also subsidies in kind. Of the latter, the most important is the free radio and television time available to any party obtaining at least 10 percent of the valid votes in the legislative race (in practice, only AD and COPEI). If the value of this airtime is included, total campaign costs rise.

Whatever the reason, the estimates of campaign expenditures in 1978 quoted in reputable publications ranged from $80 million to $200 million. One source Myers quotes insisted that AD alone spent $103 million, and estimates I was given in Caracas immediately after the election, purportedly coming from advisers close to a major party, mentioned $180 to $200 million as the total for all of the parties. If $103 million was in fact the cost of the AD campaign, then the party spent $44.63 for each of the 2,308,096 votes Piñerúa received. If all the parties together spent $180 million, their combined expenditure for each of the 5,325,305 valid votes cast in the election was $33.80. Both figures are far above those for West Germany's campaigns, which are generally thought to be the most expensive in Europe.

Each German party receiving at least 0.5 percent of the second ballot vote is eligible for a subsidy of DM3.5 (about $2.00 in 1980) per vote; in 1976 total government subsidies, excluding free radio and television time, amounted to about DM150 million. Michael Pinto-Duschinsky has estimated the total cost of the 1979 campaign in Britain at approximately $1.05 per valid vote. And total candidate and party expenditures in the 1976 American presidential race—including the funds given by the government to the major parties, money spent by private persons for major party candidates, and expenditures of lesser party candidates—amounted to less than $0.60 per valid vote, a per vote rate lower than in virtually any other Western democracy.

In most countries with proportional representation (PR) electoral systems, there is a separate ballot for each party. Depending on the country's rules, it may simply give the party's name or symbol or it may provide a full list of the candidates for the district. Voters select their preferred party's ballot, put it in an envelope, and drop it into the ballot box. This arrangement existed in Venezuela through the 1968 election. But in 1973 Venezuela acquired yet another electoral superlative: the largest and most colorful ballot. Henry Wells explains the history and mechanics of this gorgeous ballot, which is reproduced (unfortunately, in black and white) in appendix A. I will only point out that it shows the winner's picture in eight places: Luis Herrera Campíns was endorsed for president by three parties in addition to his own COPEI, and each of them ran his picture in both its legislative slot and its presidential slot on the ballot.

The rule allowing multiple party endorsement of presidential candidates and legislative slates has undoubtedly helped narrow the number of serious contenders. In 1978 COPEI's Herrera received 46.63 percent of the valid votes and AD's Piñerúa 43.34 percent. The total of 89.97 percent for the major party candidates was the highest two-party total since the return of democracy to Venezuela and thirty percentage points above the low of 57 percent in 1963. In the 1978 legislative race the COPEI and AD slates finished in a virtual tie. COPEI's 39.72 percent and AD's 39.71 percent gave them the same number of elected seats in each house—eighty-six in the Chamber of Deputies and twenty-one in the Senate. The lesser parties won twenty-seven Chamber seats in 1978 as compared with thirty-four in 1973 and ninety-one in 1968. Their rate of decline in Senate seats was roughly comparable. The parties of the left took 7.7 percent of the presidential vote and 13.1 percent of the legislative support. They cannot seriously contest the presidency or expect to win more than 10 to 20 percent of the legislative vote, according to Myers; Venezuela has a two-and-a-quarter-party system, he says, and only a disaster that destroys one or both of the parties can bring the left to power in the foreseeable future. This defractionalization of the party system is unusual in a country employing a PR system—especially one where the law requires a party to win only 1 percent of the vote to retain legal status.

Venezuela continues to face social and political stresses. In 1979 there were dangers of serious national divisions, but the government weathered the storm. Once again, Samuel Huntington's generalization that a government that has survived 100 years is 100 times more likely to survive than a government that is only one year old seems to have been validated. As this book goes to press, Venezuelan democracy has survived twenty-two years, five elections, and three changes of party government. Its chances of continuing through the 1983 elections are more than reasonably good. As Martz and Baloyra have said, Venezuela has "evolved a political system which, despite many flaws, [stands] among the most representative and participatory in a region more noted for the absence of liberties and citizen involvement."

All the contributors to this volume are Latin American experts. John D. Martz provides the historical setting for the 1978 Venezuelan elections and a chapter on the nation's minor parties; Henry Wells discusses the electoral rules and the methods by which the parties select their candidates; David J. Myers analyzes the Democratic Action party and in the final chapter discusses the results of the elections and some later developments; Donald E. Herman describes the rise to power of the Social Christian party from its days of weakness in the 1940s to its presidential victories in 1968 and 1978; Robert E. O'Connor discusses the electorate and its political attitudes and provides basic information on the communications media and their role in the election; David Blank traces the changing impact of regionalism on the affairs of Venezuela; and Richard M. Scammon provides detailed returns for the 1973 and 1978 national elections.

HOWARD R. PENNIMAN

Abbreviations

AD	Acción Democrática, Democratic Action
CCN	Cruzada Cívica Nacionalista, Nationalist Civic Crusade
COPEI	Partido Socialcristiano, Social Christian or Christian Democratic party
FALN	Fuerzas Armadas de Liberación Nacional, National Liberation Army
FDP	Fuerza Democrática Popular, Popular Democratic Force
FE	Fuerza Emancipador, Emancipating Force
FND	Frente Nacional Democrático, National Democratic Front
FUN	Frente Unido Nacionalista, United Nationalist Front
IPFN	Independientes Pro-Frente Nacional, Independents for a National Front
JRC	Juventud Revolucionaria Copeyana, COPEI Revolutionary Youth
MAN	Movimiento de Acción Nacional, Movement for National Action
MAS	Movimiento al Socialismo, Movement toward Socialism
MDI	Movimiento Democrática Independiente, Independent Democratic Movement
MEP	Movimiento Electoral del Pueblo, People's Electoral Movement
MIN	Movimiento de Integridad Nacional, Movement for National Integrity
MIR	Movimiento de Izquierda Revolucionaria, Movement of the Revolutionary Left
MORENA	Movimiento Renovador Nacional, Movement for National Renewal
OPINA	Opinión Nacional, National Opinion

PCV	Partido Comunista de Venezuela, Communist party of Venezuela
PNI	Partido Nacional Integracionalista, National Integrationalist party
PRIN	Partido Revolucionaria de Integración Nacional, Revolutionary party of National Integration
PRN	Partido Revolucionaria Nacionalista, Nationalist Revolutionary party
PSD	Partido Socialista Democrática, Democratic Socialist party
UPA	Unión para Avanzar, Union for Progress
URD	Unión Republicana Democrática, Democratic Republican Union
VC, VUC	Vanguardia Comunista, Communist Vanguard

1

The Evolution of Democratic Politics in Venezuela

John D. Martz

Introduction

On Sunday, December 3, 1978, over 5 million Venezuelans went to the polls to choose their elected officials for the next five years. For the fifth time since the initiation of Venezuela's democratic system twenty years earlier,[1] some 90 percent of eligible voters cast their ballots for the presidency, both houses of Congress, and the state legislatures. The victory of Luis Herrera Campíns of the Social Christian party, COPEI,* marked the third successive election in which the opposition had defeated the candidate of the party in power. In a hemisphere characterized in recent years by a preponderance of military and authoritarian regimes, Venezuela once again demonstrated a public vigor and political vibrancy unparalleled in Latin America. At a time when the international press was preoccupied with turmoil in Nicaragua, Cuban involvement in Africa, and a potential military confrontation between Argentina and Chile, the continuation of the democratic experience in Venezuela may well have had greater importance in the broader historical perspective.

---

[1] For a survey of the post-1958 system by several authors, see John D. Martz and David J. Myers, eds., *Venezuela: The Democratic Experience* (New York: Praeger, 1977). Among other useful earlier surveys are David E. Blank, *Politics in Venezuela* (Boston: Little, Brown and Company, 1973); Daniel H. Levine, *Conflict and Political Change in Venezuela* (Princeton: Princeton University Press, 1973); and Leo B. Lott, *Venezuela and Paraguay: Political Modernity and Tradition in Conflict* (New York: Holt, Rinehart and Winston, Inc., 1972).

---

* EDITOR'S NOTE: COPEI stands for Comité de Organización Política Electoral Independiente, but the party commonly calls itself the Partido Socialcristiano. In English it is referred to more or less interchangeably as the Social Christian and the Christian Democratic party.

1

By the 1970s, Venezuela had assumed a position of leadership within the Latin American bloc. Rich natural resources provided bases for economic growth and expansion. Despite substantial social inequities, its population was mobile, active, participatory, and optimistic about the future.[2] In foreign policy, it occupied a position of leadership in hemispheric affairs and among Third World nations.[3] With the campaign and elections of 1978, Venezuela again testified to the fact that it "had evolved a political system which, despite many flaws, stood among the most representative and participatory in a region more noted for the absence of liberties and citizen involvement."[4] Given its historical background and traditions, moreover, the emergence of a consensual, party-based system was extraordinary.

The 1978 elections represented a continuation and extension of characteristics that had blossomed rapidly during the two preceding decades. A fragmented multiparty system once dominated by Acción Democrática (AD) had evolved into a two-party system—a rarity for Latin America—in which the AD and COPEI dominated party competition. For both, organization and the party *aparato* had played a decisive role in electoral contests and in the operation of government. Ideological considerations had declined in salience as the AD from the left and COPEI from the right had moved toward the political center. In both 1973 and 1978 the two parties' presidential candidates together had received more than 85 percent of the votes. The role of personalism and *caudillismo* had also declined as the generation of party founders gradually receded into history, although such figures as ex-presidents Rómulo Betancourt and Rafael Caldera remained highly influential.

In the realm of political campaigning, Venezuela in 1978 also reflected some of the characteristics of previous contests. Among the more evident were the intensity of the competition; its length (well over a year); extravagant expenditures; heavy and sophisticated reliance on the media; extensive use of polling and public opinion surveys, many of them designed and implemented by North American advisers; and the enduring practice of more traditional participatory

---

[2] An extended empirical study of opinion is Enrique A. Baloyra and John D. Martz, *Political Attitudes in Venezuela: Societal Cleavages and Political Opinion* (Austin: University of Texas Press, 1979).

[3] A recent compendium by six students of the country is Robert D. Bond, ed., *Contemporary Venezuela and Its Role in International Affairs* (New York: New York University Press, 1977).

[4] John D. Martz and Enrique A. Baloyra, *Electoral Mobilization and Public Opinion: The Venezuelan Campaign of 1973* (Chapel Hill: University of North Carolina Press, 1976), p. 3.

methods, with candidates traveling the country incessantly by air, by car, and on foot. These and other traits are analyzed in subsequent chapters. To set the stage, then, an overview of the historical setting and of the creation of the post-1958 democratic system is in order.

Sociopolitical Background. Mainland Venezuela, discovered in 1498 on Columbus's third Atlantic crossing, is an inverted triangle lying on the northern coast of the South American continental land mass. Approximately the size of Texas and Oklahoma with 352,150 square miles of territory, it is the seventh largest country in Latin America. Venezuela was relegated to a minor position throughout the 300 years of Spanish colonial rule; a pronounced rise of cacao production in the late eighteenth century produced somewhat greater attention from the Spaniards, but on the whole it remained a colonial backwater, predominantly rural and agricultural. With the outbreak of the wars of independence early in the nineteenth century, Venezuela's social order was itself at the point of collapse. The conflict not only pitted the native-born (*criollos*) against the Spanish-born (*peninsulares*), but also involved slaves and mixed-bloods (*pardos*) on both sides. Following the expulsion of royalist forces, the Liberator, Simón Bolívar, established the Gran Colombian federation, but in 1830, the year of his death, its three major components went their separate ways. Thus, with Colombia and Ecuador, Venezuela began its existence as an independent country.

Virtually a century passed before the effective institutionalization of national authority. Caracas itself was little more than one of many provincial market centers, and power devolved from one region to another: the nation's leaders were first plainsmen, then men from the east, the west, and, by the turn of the century, the Andes. One historian estimated that 39 major and 127 minor revolts occurred between 1830 and 1900, lasting a total of 8,847 days.[5] In the oft-quoted phrase of one nineteenth-century leader, Venezuela was "like a dry hide; you step on it on one end and it pops up on the other."[6] Still predominantly agricultural, the country had seen a decline in cacao followed by a boom in coffee production by the 1880s. By the early 1900s Venezuela possessed a constricted, one-crop economy and a political system characterized by violence, regionalism, and the frag-

[5] Antonio Arraiz, as cited by Juan Liscano, "Aspectos de la vida social y política de Venezuela" [Aspects of social and political life in Venezuela], in *150 Años de vida republicana (1811–1961)* [One hundred and fifty years of the republic (1811–1961)] (Caracas: Ediciones de la Presidencia de la República, 1963), p. 191.

[6] As cited by José Agustín Silva Michelena, *The Illusion of Democracy in Dependent Nations* (Cambridge: MIT Press, 1971), pp. 42-43.

3

mentation of power and authority. It was within this context that General Juan Vicente Gómez strode to center stage in 1908, remaining there until his death in 1935.

A cunning and unprincipled authoritarian, the so-called Tyrant of the Andes achieved a concentration of power previously unknown to Venezuela. Overwhelming his opponents and creating the country's first effective central government, he established a national military force, developed a bureaucratic structure, shattered traditional patterns of *latifundismo*, and developed an integrated internal market. After the first great oil strike, late in 1922, he began to erect an increasingly powerful bourgeois capitalist system. Vast reserves of oil in the Maracaibo Basin attracted international corporations, and Venezuela's commercial activities shifted from domestic agriculture to world trade. By the time of his death, Gómez had seen the flowering of the *criollo* oligarchy and the birth of a national industry. Despite periodic bursts of opposition, the political environment remained harshly repressive.

The next decade saw a gradual relaxation of authoritarianism under the rule of two more Andean military men, Generals Eleazar López Contreras (1935–1941) and Isaías Medina Angarita (1941–1945). It was during this period that modern political parties emerged in Venezuela. A movement headed by Rómulo Betancourt was permitted to organize legally in 1941 as Acción Democrática, as was the Partido Comunista de Venezuela (PCV). A subsequent crisis over presidential succession led ultimately to an armed uprising in October 1945 and the seizure of power by a provisional government headed by Betancourt. The resultant three-year period (commonly termed the *trienio*) was a watershed in Venezuelan political history, marking as it did the nation's first genuine experiment in democratic, party-based government. Supported by junior military officers, the AD-dominated regime undertook a major transformation of political life.[7]

The Failure of Fledgling Democracy. Impatient after years in the political wilderness which were marked by jailings, harassment, and persecution, the *adecos* (as Acción Democrática's supporters are called) were further buoyed by a series of electoral victories. Universal suffrage was instituted by decree, and the party swept the elections for a constituent assembly, taking 78.8 percent of the vote. The AD's candidate for the presidency, the eminent novelist Rómulo Gallegos, and those for the municipal offices did almost as well, with 74.4 and

---

[7] For further discussion of the *trienio* see John D. Martz, *Acción Democrática: Evolution of a Modern Political Party in Venezuela* (Princeton: Princeton University Press, 1966), pp. 62-80.

70.1 percent respectively. Drastic social and economic reforms were introduced in areas ranging from health, housing, and education to agriculture and industry, and a nationalistic petroleum policy was adopted. Important political sectors were alienated in the brusque, often arrogant race to remake the system and society. Landowners resented agrarian reform; business interests feared AD radicalism; international oil corporations resisted government policies; and the church was nervously apprehensive of anticlerical educational reforms. Furthermore, notwithstanding massive popular support enhanced by the AD's organizational domination of the national labor and peasant federations, the governing party ran roughshod over lesser, newly organized political groups.

Principal among these were COPEI and the Unión Republicana Democrática (URD). The first traced its origins to the 1936 Catholic student movement founded by Rafael Caldera. Initially a quasi-falangist, ultranationalistic group opposed to an equally immoderate leftist student federation, it had been converted into a Caracas electoral movement in 1938 and, after further changes in name, was officially founded on January 13, 1946. Caldera, for a time Betancourt's attorney general, angrily resigned following the disruption by AD followers of a COPEI rally. Drawing upon conservative forces and followers of former President López Contreras while creating a pocket of solid electoral strength in the three Andean states, COPEI ran a distant second during the *trienio*. It received 13.2 percent of the vote for the constituent assembly, and Caldera, at age thirty-one, polled 22.4 percent in the 1947 presidential race, which Gallegos won. Five months later COPEI received 21.1 percent in municipal elections.

The URD, legally founded on December 14, 1945, was initially constituted by sympathizers of former President Medina. In less than a year it fell under the sway of Jóvito Villalba, whose personal influence was still strong at the time of the 1978 elections. Villalba had been a leader of the 1928 student outburst against Gómez, one of those who later assumed near legendary fame as the "generation of '28." [8] A brilliant public speaker, he had for a time worked with Betancourt in building a democratic party. The two were personally incompatible, however, and in the early 1940s Villalba moved to public

---

[8] An account based on original documents and interviews with participants is John D. Martz, "Venezuela's 'Generation of '28': The Genesis of Political Democracy," *Journal of Inter-American Studies*, vol. 6, no. 1 (January 1964), pp. 17–33. A more detailed historical overview is found in María de Lourdes Acedo de Sucre and Carmen Margarita Nones Mendoza, *La generación venezolana de 1928: estudio de una élite política* [The Venezuelan generation of 1928: study of a political elite] (Caracas: Ediciones Ariel, 1967).

prominence as an independent senator. Having captured the leadership of the URD, he became an outspoken critic of the *trienio* Government, although his policy stance was basically similar to the Government's. Despite Villalba's soaring rhetoric, the URD received but 3.8 percent in the elections for the constituent assembly and 3.9 in the May 1948 municipal races.

Also in opposition to the AD regime was the Communist party of Venezuela, whose founding dated back to 1931.[9] Shunned by the other parties, it won only 3.6 percent for the constituent assembly and 3.2 percent in the 1947 presidential race, when its candidate was Gustavo Machado. Only 3.4 percent voted Communist in the 1948 municipal elections. Yet the PCV too was treated with arrogance by the dominant party. So it was that these parties, along with the sectors already cited, shed few tears in November 1948 when the armed forces, repeatedly rebuffed by the Government, deposed the Gallegos administration and assumed power. Given the context of the times, it was perhaps inevitable. In any event, the result was a decade of military dictatorship, dominated after 1950 by Colonel (later General) Marcos Pérez Jiménez. Under his pseudotechnocratic rule, Venezuela was to experience the darkest years of its political history.

Political persecution, murder, and concentration camps were the order of the day. Acción Democrática was the immediate target, but in time the other parties also fell victim to the regime's intolerance. In 1952 Pérez Jiménez attempted to legitimize his rule by holding an election, but when it became clear that Villalba was ahead the vote counting was interrupted and the outcome reversed through massive fraud. URD and COPEI leaders were driven into exile, and all vestiges of party activity were mercilessly crushed. The dictatorship proceeded to shape its policies with little regard for the public. Social welfare and human needs were ignored in the rush for massive public works and flashy construction projects. With the economy fueled by booming oil production and the impetus of North American demands during the Korean fighting, government revenue doubled between 1951 and 1956. The dictator and his associates became wealthy, and the venality of the regime reached extraordinary proportions. In time, however, economic mismanagement and sagging oil prices caught up with it. Clandestine opposition spread, and a fraudulent plebiscite in December 1957, intended to solidify Pérez Jiménez's hegemony, instead fanned the flames of public opprobrium. A nationwide general strike led by young students and activists from the major political parties

---

[9] For an extended history see Robert J. Alexander, *The Communist Party of Venezuela* (Stanford: Hoover Institution Press, 1969).

ultimately forced the military itself to turn against its erstwhile leader. On January 23, 1958, Pérez Jiménez fled the country with suitcases filled with cash—one of which was left behind in the haste of the moment—and a caretaker regime took power under Vice Admiral Wolfgang Larrazábal. Betancourt, Caldera, Villalba, and their associates returned to Venezuela and initiated the discussions that were to shape the foundations of today's democratic system.

The Democratic System

Parties and Elections. The experience of the *trienio* and the subsequent decade of assassination, torture, and exile marked the psyche and outlook of *adeco* leaders. Upon returning home, they pursued a policy of consultation and cooperation with all of those whose support would be necessary for the implantation of a democratic system. The other parties equally recognized the necessity of identifying common policies and interests. All viewed the establishment and meaningful legitimization of the system as the highest priority. So it was that representatives of the AD, COPEI, and the URD negotiated and signed in October 1958 the Pact of Punto Fijo. The underlying commitment was later expressed with characteristic clarity by Rómulo Betancourt.

> Inter-party discord was kept to a minimum, and in this way leaders revealed that they had learned the harsh lesson which despotism had taught to all Venezuelans. Underground, in prison, in exile, or living a precarious liberty at home, we all understood that it was through the breach opened in the front of civility and culture that the conspiracy of November 24, 1948—unmistakably reactionary and supported by some with naive good faith—was able to pass, a conspiracy which overthrew the legitimate government of Rómulo Gallegos.[10]

Caldera, Villalba, and Betancourt—having consciously excluded the Communists from their group—recognized the separate identities of their parties and accepted a common program based on mutual interests. They agreed to collaborate in a multiparty Government after the elections of 1958, whatever the outcome. Furthermore, any partner withdrawing from the Government would remain committed to the

---

[10] Rómulo Betancourt, *Tres años de gobierno democrático* [Three years of democratic government] (Caracas: Imprenta Nacional, 1962), vol. 1, p. 13, as quoted by Daniel H. Levine, "Venezuela since 1958: The Consolidation of Democratic Politics," in Juan J. Linz and Alfred Stepan, eds., *The Breakdown of Democratic Regimes: Latin America* (Baltimore: Johns Hopkins University Press, 1978), p. 93.

defense of the democratic system. As Daniel Levine put it, the pact "was an attempt to begin building a set of rules of the game acceptable to major groups, committing each to the survival of all through acceptance of the same set of political processes."[11] Earlier in 1958 the three parties had discussed the possibility of backing a single candidate, but this had proved too much. Thus in 1958 the presidency was sought by Betancourt, Caldera, and—with the backing of both the URD and the Communists—Wolfgang Larrazábal, who resigned from the provisional presidency to become a candidate.

Drawing upon enduring *adeco* loyalties in the countryside, Betancourt won with 49.2 percent of the vote, followed by Larrazábal with 30.7 and Caldera with 15.2. Caracas's customary antipathy to the AD gave Larrazábal a wide margin in the capital, but, faced with demonstrators demanding the annulment of the results, the vice admiral made his own contribution to the fledgling system by calling for calm and recognizing Betancourt's victory. The three-party coalition survived for a year, until the URD withdrew from the Government over disagreements concerning policy toward Cuba. The impact of the Cuban Revolution was further dramatized by the initiation of guerrilla insurgency in Venezuela by revolutionary leftists. Members of the AD's own youth movement were among the insurgents, breaking from the party in 1960. The first of three divisions suffered by Acción Democrática in the 1960s, this reflected both ideological and generational conflict.

The left wing of the AD, constituted largely by its youth and student leaders, advocated rapid and drastic change and couched its policy in neo-Marxist terms. The senior leadership, having learned the lesson of the *trienio*, was unresponsive to demands for rapid and basic structural changes. In addition, youth leaders who had been active in the underground and prominent in the climactic street battles to topple Pérez Jiménez were at best reluctant to see party and governmental leadership in the hands of the party founders. Organizing the Movimiento de Izquierda Revolucionaria (MIR), they took their inspiration from Fidel Castro and dedicated themselves to immediate national transformation. In their initial stress on rural revolt and radicalizing the peasantry, the radicals' vision and their understanding of national political realities were severely flawed.

The Venezuela of the early 1960s had little in common with the Cuba of the late 1950s. The very heart and soul of Acción Democrática lay in the countryside, where Betancourt had traveled and recruited for a quarter of a century. The peasants resisted the young

---

[11] Levine in Linz and Stepan, *Breakdown*, p. 94.

revolutionaries, denied their appeals, reported them to the authorities, and upon occasion fired back. Only belatedly did the self-styled Fuerzas Armadas de Liberación Nacional (FALN, which incorporated many members of MIR) recognize the folly of their tactics and reorient their campaign toward urban terrorism; this was far more effective and, but for the extraordinary acumen and tenacity of Betancourt, might ultimately have succeeded. The revolutionaries' redirected campaign called for sowing unrest in the cities, which would culminate in a breakdown of authority and the intervention of the armed forces. The resulting military dictatorship, it was assumed, would inevitably grow repressive, ultimately to be toppled by a massive popular uprising in which the revolutionaries could emerge as the vanguard of the proletariat.

FALN's tactics were imaginative and diverse. The indiscriminate planting of bombs in government buildings, the burning of warehouses and factories owned by subsidiaries of international corporations, and a series of bank robberies were intended to intimidate the citizenry and drive the Government toward repression and the violation of civil liberties. The terrorists achieved international media coverage by stealing paintings loaned by France to the Caracas art museum, kidnapping an internationally renowned Spanish soccer star, and hijacking a small freighter, which was sailed from Venezuelan waters to a Brazilian port. They also made mistakes, such as killing women and children in an attack on an excursion train. Most decisive of all was their widely publicized pledge to block the 1963 elections, which they denounced as a fraud perpetrated by the puppets of Yankee imperialism.

Defying the revolutionaries' threats to snipe at voters from the rooftops, over 90 percent of the electorate went to the polls. This massive endorsement of the democratic system dealt the revolutionaries a decisive blow. In the wake of the elections some leftists advocated a return to the mountains and countryside; others proposed a revival of urban violence; yet another group called for a cessation of armed hostilities and resumption of peaceful participation in politics. From that day to this the Venezuelan left has been badly fragmented. Offers of partial amnesty by Betancourt's successor helped wean many former revolutionaries back to civilian life, and, under the subsequent COPEI Government of Rafael Caldera, amnesty was extended to all who had taken up arms against the system.

By the time of the 1963 elections, the fragmentation of the party system had grown apace. While four parties and three candidates had contested the previous elections, in 1963 there were seven presidential candidates and twice as many parties on the ballot. Acción Democrática, which had suffered a second division, nominated Raúl Leoni, another member of its founding generation and a longtime colleague of Betancourt. Caldera and Villalba ran for COPEI and the URD respectively. Larrazábal became the candidate of his own new personalistic group, the Fuerza Democrática Popular (FDP), while the noted essayist and novelist Arturo Uslar Pietri headed an explicitly "nonparty" organization. Raúl Ramos Giménez ran for the former *adecos* who had failed to seize control of Acción Democrática in 1962. Leoni won by a comfortable margin, though he polled but 32.8 percent of the vote, while Caldera increased COPEI's vote to finish second, with 20.2 percent.

The lengthy discussions between the AD and COPEI concerning a continuation of their collaboration failed. COPEI, whose loyalty to the democratic system had been a major factor in the survival of the Betancourt presidency, chose instead to follow a so-called AA strategy—autonomy of action. From 1964 to 1969, under Leoni, COPEI worked at building its organizational base for the next elections and provided enlightened and constructive opposition. Leoni in turn constructed a new government coalition, securing the backing of the URD and of Uslar Pietri's party, renamed the Frente Nacional Democrático (FND). While the proliferation of new parties compounded the increasing complexity and dispersal of the system of partisanship, Leoni proved a tranquilizing successor to the combative Betancourt. Betancourt's basic policies were extended and more fully implemented: agrarian reform was carried forward, infrastructural development continued, the economy flourished, and the roots of democracy reached deeper into the soil. Guerrilla activity ground to a virtual halt, the interplay of partisanship was freely pursued, and formerly hostile sectors were increasingly coopted into the system. The Leoni years, in short, built constructively and incrementally upon Betancourt's beginnings.

With the approach of the 1968 elections, many expected that another AD victory might lead to the "Mexicanization" of the system, with the AD achieving the kind of one-party control exercised by the Revolutionary Institutional party (PRI) in Mexico. It was presumed that, after the two earlier schisms, the AD would not again divide. However, in 1967 a bitter and traumatic split rent the majority party. The two remaining members of the *adeco* founding generation—AD President Luis B. Prieto Figueroa and Secretary General Gonzalo Barrios—competed for the party's nomination, which they took to be a guarantee of the presidency. Their rivalry was complicated by competition between two of their second-generation lieutenants, Jesús Angel Paz Galarraga, supporting Prieto, and Carlos Andrés Pérez, favoring Barrios. Rómulo Betancourt, living in voluntary exile in Europe, strongly supported Paz.

Policy differences were also in evidence. The *betancourtistas* and Barrios favored continuation and extension of the Betancourt policies and their implementation under Leoni, which reflected a concern with further development of the economy and the infrastructure necessary for greater industrialization. Prieto and his followers argued that, after a decade of such policies, the self-styled "party of the people" should reorient its concerns toward social reforms and the amelioration of continuing inequities. New directions were also proposed for education, a highly personal topic for Prieto, founder and conscience of the Venezuelan teachers' movement. Following a disruptive and unprecedented party primary won by Prieto, labyrinthine internal politicking ultimately spurred Prieto to leave and establish his own Movimiento Electoral del Pueblo (MEP). Prieto for the MEP and Barrios for the AD became chief contenders for the presidency, with all the participants badly scarred by the experience. The AD had been dealt a devastating blow, and the door of opportunity was opened wider than ever before to the Social Christians.

Rafael Caldera was approaching the peak of his powers. He personally reshaped COPEI's apparatus in the process of mounting his fourth and presumably final presidential bid with a brilliantly conceived and executed campaign. The fourth serious candidate was a young political independent, Miguel Angel Burelli Rivas, representing the tripartite Frente de la Victoria constituted by Villalba's URD, Uslar Pietri's FND, and Larrazábal's FDP, and two minor candidates also entered the race. In all, there were sixteen separate presidential ballots, and an additional seventeen parties competed in the congressional and municipal races. The 1968 campaign marked a major step in the development of the party system. COPEI, its appetite for national power whetted by fortuitous circumstances, responded smoothly to Caldera's guidance. Barrios and the AD were aided by Betancourt's return to Venezuela late in the campaign and also benefited from the support of the Leoni administration. The MEP suffered from organizational weakness and financial limitations but enjoyed an asset in Prieto's attractive personal style. Finally, Burelli had both to establish his own credentials and to capitalize upon the popularity of his three political mentors, Villalba, Uslar Pietri, and Larrazábal.

The contest, which was close and intense, eventually narrowed to Caldera and Barrios. The turnout was customarily heavy (97 percent out of 4.24 million eligible voters), and Caldera eked out a victory by 31,000 votes over Barrios. His 29 percent of the vote put him a mere 0.8 percentage points ahead, while Burelli polled 22.2 and Prieto 19.3 percent. A singular surprise was the strong showing in the Federal District of the Cruzada Cívica Nacionalista (CCN), composed of followers of the exiled dictator Pérez Jiménez, which won eleven of the thirty-seven seats in the Chamber of Deputies. Despite some indications of electoral irregularity, both President Leoni and Acción Democrática acceded to the results, and in March 1969 Rafael Caldera was inaugurated president. The equanimity of the proceedings was an impressive indication of the system's maturity. Leoni had been the first duly elected president to succeed a democratically chosen predecessor. Caldera, in 1969, was the first leader of an opposition party to do so.[12]

Confounding all expectations, Caldera opted for a one-party administration, despite the narrowness of his victory. With Acción Democrática's hegemony destroyed, he chose to govern through transitory congressional alliances. While this prevented Caldera from fully realizing his campaign pledges, it further strengthened the democratic system. The AD collaborated with the Social Christian Government on several important issues, and the MEP was an important participant, especially in the realm of petroleum policy.[13] During his administration Caldera also carried to fruition the policy of accommodation toward the left. By the next electoral campaign, all the parties of the left had been legalized, even the once-insurgent MIR. Thus the political environment was more open and competitive than ever before when contending forces began to measure their strength for the 1973 campaign.

"Polarization" of the Vote. By this point, as I have written elsewhere, the

> Venezuelans had come to value and to defend democratic procedures. Having agreed upon norms which embraced the legitimacy of party competition for governmental authority, they were also concerned with substantive results.

---

[12] See David J. Myers, *Democratic Campaigning in Venezuela: Caldera's Victory* (Caracas: Fundación La Salle, 1973). A briefer analysis is found in Martz and Baloyra, *Electoral Mobilization*, pp. 11-31.

[13] See the definitive study by Franklin Tugwell, *The Politics of Oil* (Stanford: Stanford University Press, 1975). A polemical critique of the Venezuelan system is the provocative if flawed work of James F. Petras, Morris Morley, and Steven Smith, *The Nationalization of Venezuelan Oil* (New York: Praeger Publishers, 1977).

It was within this context that the 1973 contest presented an intensity of competition and expenditure of funds by COPEI and the AD which dwarfed even the 1968 experience.[14]

The 1973 race reflected an accentuation of the party fragmentation that had begun with the first *adeco* schism in 1960. There were no fewer than twelve presidential candidates, and opportunism, ambition, and personalism remained endemic to the party system. At the same time, this was to redound to the benefit of COPEI and Acción Democrática. The growing monopolization of the electorate by the two centrist parties would become even more pronounced in 1978.

On the political right, self-declared *perezjimenista* stand-ins vied for the personal approval of the ex-dictator—among others, Burelli Rivas, the electoral phenomenon of 1968. On the left, enduring dissension produced two candidates, José Vicente Rangel and Jesús Angel Paz Galarraga. The former carried the banner of the Movement toward Socialism (MAS), which was composed of former Communists who had broken with the PCV over the Soviet invasion of Czechoslovakia in 1968. MAS also numbered virtually the entire younger generation of pro-Moscow Communists, still headed by the Machado brothers, Gustavo and Eduardo. The MEP, under Paz but with Prieto's imprimatur, had attempted to construct a leftist coalition, the Nueva Fuerza, modeled on that of Chile's Salvador Allende in 1970. Paz even noted that, like Allende, he was a medical doctor. His Venezuelan version of Chile's Unidad Popular emerged from a multiparty convention at which he outmaneuvered Villalba and the URD to secure the nomination. In later months Villalba, still mesmerized by the chimera of one final presidential bid, broke his word and launched his own candidacy. Paz was thus left with only the MEP and the minuscule PCV backing him.

In the face of such diverse and dispersed opposition, COPEI and Acción Democrática undertook a decisive struggle for control of the enlarged political center. At COPEI's convention, where pressure from the Caldera administration was powerful and unnecessarily blatant, a longtime confidant of Caldera and his former minister of interior, Lorenzo Fernández, was selected. Significantly for 1978, the aspirations of Luis Herrera Campíns were summarily dismissed in the process. In the AD, both former President Betancourt—eligible for another term after two terms out of power—and Gonzalo Barrios agreed to step aside in favor of AD Secretary General Carlos Andrés

---

[14] John D. Martz, "The Party System: Toward Institutionalization," in Martz and Myers, *Venezuela*, p. 98.

Pérez, a member of the party's second generation. The AD entered the campaign united while COPEI was weakened by the traumas of its convention.

As the competition progressed, the question of "polarization" was repeatedly raised—meaning in the Venezuelan political vernacular the monopolization of the electorate by two parties. The AD in particular stressed the economy-of-the-vote argument, urging voters not to waste their ballots on candidates with no chance of winning. Pérez, Betancourt's minister of interior during the worst of the FALN guerrilla activities in 1962–1963, projected the image of a tough, no-nonsense leader. A man of exceptional physical vigor, he stumped the country tirelessly under the banner "Democracia con energía"—democracy with energy. His unified and smooth-running campaign organization also benefited from the quiet efforts of Betancourt, who attracted to the fold a number of former party loyalists who had defected with the MEP in 1968. In his famous phrase, "Adeco es adeco hasta que se muera"—an *adeco* is an *adeco* till he dies.

Lorenzo Fernández promised to extend the policies and principles of the Caldera administration. As had been the case in 1963 and 1968, the Government was a meaningful participant in the race. Caldera himself toured the country, dedicating and rededicating public works, just as Leoni and Betancourt had before him. COPEI strategists, handicapped by the limited physical strength of the avuncular Fernández, relied heavily on propaganda and the media. Their candidate was presented as a paternalistic figure, often termed the "presidente amigo"—the president-friend. COPEI also attempted to attract voters from the left, at the same time attacking Pérez and Acción Democrática as rightists who had long since lost their reformist ardor.

On the left, Paz doggedly maintained his two-party Unidad Popular coalition despite the electoral and organizational insignificance of the Communist party and the dominance of the MEP. His campaign was dealt a deadly blow with the bloody overthrow of Allende in Chile on September 13, 1973. This was also damaging to José Vicente Rangel and his backers from the MAS and the MIR, although the candidate consistently argued that his was a distinctively Venezuelan road to socialism. Jóvito Villalba, his URD a tattered remnant of a once-powerful party, attracted scant attention with his characteristic rhetorical vagueness in calling for a Bolivarian nationalist revolution. At the other end of the spectrum the candidates were even less active and lacked both organizational resources and campaign appeals. They devoted more attention to soliciting endorsements from the exiled Pérez Jiménez in Madrid than to campaigning.

On December 9, 1973, some 4.3 million ballots were cast, representing 96.9 percent of all registered voters. The movement toward a two-party system was striking: Pérez and Fernández amassed 85.5 percent of the votes, and in the congressional race the AD and COPEI lists together took 74.6 percent. Thus the two centrist parties had established an unprecedented domination of the electorate, while such parties as the FDP, URD, and FND were decimated. On the left, Paz received but 5 percent of the vote, a shade ahead of Rangel. Quite clearly, the electorate was still reluctant to accept the return of former revolutionaries into the electoral fold. For the MEP, the support Prieto had won in 1968 had largely dissipated, with loyalists and sympathizers returning to Acción Democrática.

Equally dramatic was the magnitude of the AD's victory. Carlos Andrés Pérez received 48.8 percent of the national vote and more votes than any contender in nineteen of the twenty states, the Federal District, and the two federal territories. He surpassed 60 percent of the vote in two states and won over half the vote in another ten. Himself from the Andes, Pérez also broke COPEI's traditional domination of the three Andean states. Overall, the *adeco* sweep produced an outright AD majority in both houses of Congress, notwithstanding multiparty opposition and the application of proportional representation. The party also won a majority in over two-thirds of the nation's municipal councils. For COPEI, the one bright spot was the increase in its popular support, which reached 36.7 percent of the vote, some seven points higher than Caldera's winning total in 1968. With its 1.6 million votes, COPEI became the first governing party in Venezuela to gain rather than lose support between consecutive elections.

With the inauguration of Pérez in March 1974, Venezuela anticipated a one-party Government based on outright majorities in both houses of Congress. Its economic resources were at an unprecedented level. The four-fold increase of petroleum prices from 1973 to 1974 had more than tripled government revenues. The democratic system had been further strengthened through the second successive transfer of power from Government to opposition. The left had participated fully for the first time, and the Venezuelan electorate in fulfillment of its civic duty had been exemplary throughout a long, intensive, and costly campaign. The party system, ever more central to the operation of national affairs, was increasingly institutionalized. Clearly the performance of the Pérez administration, enjoying such pronounced political and economic strength, would influence the prospects for 1978. Before considering its accomplishments and failures, however,

15

we must direct our attention more closely toward the evolution of the parties since 1958.

The Dynamics of Venezuelan Parties

The Party System. The background to the electoral polarization that developed in 1973 was a history of factionalism, fragmentation, and the proliferation of parties beginning in 1958. A host of factors were involved, including conflicting personal ambitions, generational rivalries, policy disagreements, and ideological schisms. The three presidential candidates and four parties in 1958 had become twelve would-be presidents and over two dozen officially recognized parties by 1973 (see Figure 1–1). The consequences of factionalism are illustrated by the record of Acción Democrática, the third of whose divisions ultimately led to its loss of power in 1968.

In 1960 *adeco's* youth wing, responding to both generational and ideological forces, defected and produced the Movimiento de Izquierda Revolucionaria, which joined the guerrilla movement of the early 1960s, then entered a period of quiescence, and finally returned to the electoral battlefield in 1973. The second major split followed an unsuccessful effort by second-generation leaders to wrest control of the party from the old guard prior to the 1963 elections. After running a weak race that year, they joined with defectors from the URD. By 1973 their Partido Revolucionaria de Integración Nacional (PRIN) was at the point of extinction, its founders either retired from politics or reintegrated into Acción Democrática. Finally, the disastrous 1967 schism, from which the MEP was born, had reflected both differing policy orientations and the personality clashes revolving about Prieto, Barrios, Paz, Pérez, and Betancourt. The MEP took with it large numbers of party, labor, and peasant leaders from the AD, and Prieto's earthy appeal provided further momentum. After 1968, concluding that competition with the AD on similar policy grounds would be self-destructive, the MEP under Paz's guidance moved progressively toward the left, with the disappointing results already noted.

The trajectory of the URD after 1958 was a tale of unalloyed miscalculation. Jóvito Villalba, a fiery orator who consistently ignored organizational tasks, insisted upon remaining unchallenged party leader. Energetic and ambitious members of the URD left wing, known as the black wing, were expelled from the party. They soon joined defectors from the AD in the Partido Revolucionaria Nacionalista (PRN). Another would-be heir apparent, Alirio Ugarte Pelayo, was driven from the URD in 1966. The resultant Movimiento

FIGURE 1–1

PARTY FRAGMENTATION, 1958–1973

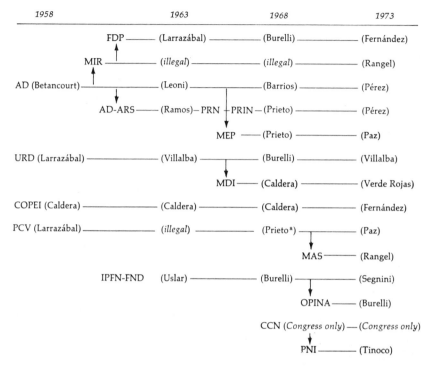

NOTE: Names of presidential candidates are given in parentheses. This figure is illustrative rather than exhaustive. It depicts parties (and their presidential candidates) that emerged from the original four parties competing in the 1958 elections, as well as Uslar Pietri's party and the *perezjimenista* CCN and their offshoots. [a] The PCV was still illegal in 1968. Its presidential candidate that year ran under the label UPA, Unidad para Avanzar.

Democrática Independiente (MDI) foundered upon Ugarte's suicide that same year, though it supported Caldera in 1968. In the wake of the 1973 debacle, URD Secretary General Leonardo Montiel Ortega was expelled. Villalba also made tactical mistakes. His withdrawal from the Betancourt coalition proved damaging; his own candidacy in 1963 was poorly organized; and collaboration with Leoni produced patronage opportunities that were not fully realized. Then, breaking his promise not to run after losing the Nueva Fuerza nomination to Paz and the MEP, Villalba finished in fifth place in 1973 with but 3.1 percent of the vote. The URD retained only one Senate seat and five deputies.

17

Other parties' histories also reflected personal ambition, vague or opportunistic policy positions, and an insensitivity to the importance of organization. The FDP became the personal vehicle for Admiral Larrazábal. Having received 9.4 percent of the vote in his fifth place finish in 1963, he joined the Frente de la Victoria to back Burelli in 1968. Five years later, having secured better terms from COPEI than from AD, he moved the FDP behind Lorenzo Fernández. The party won but 1.2 percent of the congressional vote that year, and Larrazábal retained his own Senate seat only through his inclusion on the COPEI list. Soon afterwards the minuscule FDP divided yet again, this time after a dispute between Larrazábal and his primary adviser, Jorge Dáger. Equally personalistic and diffuse was the FND of Uslar Pietri. Uslar ran fourth with 16.1 percent in 1963 and later joined the Leoni coalition. After backing Burelli in 1968, Uslar himself largely withdrew from politics. In 1973 his heir, Pedro Segnini La Cruz, won 0.5 percent of the vote and the FND was completely wiped out in Congress. Burelli won but 0.8 percent of the vote in 1973, receiving one seat in the lower chamber through the application of the electoral quotient.

Divisions within the Venezuelan Marxist movement have followed similar patterns. Ideological dispute over the proper road to socialism was evident from the early 1960s. The Communists only guardedly and weakly supported the FALN campaign, a source of resentment to members of the MIR. The PCV eagerly accepted partial amnesty from Raúl Leoni, supported Prieto in 1968 through the Unión para Avanzar (UPA), and then, legalized once more as the PCV under Rafael Caldera, fell behind Paz Galarraga in 1973. Yet its support was qualified, with some Communists quietly backing Fernández as the lesser of two evils. After 1973 the tiny PCV divided again, the followers of the two Machado brothers, the now septagenarian founders of the party, going their separate ways. Both ideological and generational conflict had already spawned the breakaway following the PCV-supported Soviet aggression in Czechoslovakia, culminating in 1970 in the founding of the Movement toward Socialism. Gaining greater strength than the PCV, the MAS in 1973 backed the independent leftist Rangel—himself once a member of the URD and later of the PRIN. The MAS rejected overtures for a united left from both the MEP and the MIR and only grudgingly acceded to MIR's endorsement of Rangel. After 1973 the parties went their separate ways.

Clearly, forces making for fragmentation characterized the party system after 1958. The only group to remain unaffected was COPEI, which successfully maintained its unity and coherence despite powerful centrifugal forces. As we shall see, its ideology proved powerful enough to cement the party together. The Social Christian organization was carefully and painstakingly built through the years, always under the guidance of Rafael Caldera. Having observed the central importance of the party apparatus to Acción Democrática, COPEI adjusted and fine-tuned its own machine. When opportunity beckoned in 1968, COPEI was ready. To be sure, there were doctrinal disputes; the party encompassed views ranging from hard-nosed conservatism to radical communitarianism. Caldera successfully bridged the chasm and, when faced in 1965–1967 by rebellion within the Juventud Revolucionaria Copeyana (JRC), the party's youth wing, negotiated a settlement with a minimum of bloodletting. Even his injudicious intervention to secure the presidential nomination for Fernández over Herrera Campíns in 1973, though it created tensions, did not divide the party.

The factors that most influenced the evolution of the party system after 1958 were leadership, organization, and ideology. The first proved perhaps the most disruptive and destabilizing to the individual parties. Villalba, Larrazábal, Uslar Pietri, Burelli, Ramos Giménez, Ugarte Pelayo, Segnini La Cruz—all were to fall from popularity and electoral strength through a combination of selfishness, unwillingness to compromise, personal interests, jealousy of possible rivals, generational rigidity, cavalier disregard for identifiable doctrinal positions, and insensitivity to the need for hard work at organizational tasks. It is scarcely coincidental that the leaders of both COPEI and the AD were more realistic and far-sighted. In both of the dominant parties a doctrinal orientation was established, but it was left sufficiently flexible to permit the cooptation of the broad political center by 1973. Beginning with Betancourt's dictum that every town, hamlet, and barrio[15] should have a party office, first the AD and then COPEI built a structure capable of year-round activity, recruitment, and political socialization. While most other party leaders tried to get along by merely resurrecting an electoral apparatus every fifth year, the leaders of the AD and COPEI recognized the necessity of constant work.

Personalism was not wanting, but it was restrained by pragmatic political judgment. Thus in 1962 Betancourt accepted the AD's nomination of Leoni even though he would have preferred an independent acceptable to COPEI. He also eschewed a second presidential candidacy of his own in 1973. That same year, Barrios recognized the

---

[15] *Barrios* are squatter settlements clustered in and about every Venezuelan city. These shantytowns bear a variety of names elsewhere in Latin America, such as *favelas* in Brazil, *callampas* in Chile, and *barriadas* in Peru.

emergence of the second generation by withdrawing in favor of Pérez, Herrera Campíns accepted the disappointment of being denied COPEI's nomination, and Caldera showed an ability to accept challenges to his hegemony. The rise of a new *adeco* generation, personified by Pérez and by collaborators in his Government after 1973, was matched by the prominence of young Social Christians who had cut their political teeth as student leaders in the JRC. And, to repeat, both parties adopted broad doctrinal commitments and tactical policies that proved congenial to large numbers of voters.

Ideology and Doctrine. The founders of Acción Democrática, the elder of the two dominant parties, had initially flirted with but then rejected Marxism.[16] By 1945, when the *trienio* began, the party was dedicated to a participatory, antiimperialist posture it termed "revolutionary," but it was in fact a reformist, basically Social Democratic, organization. Its objective was centralized state control within a democratic context. The economic system was thought of as fundamentally directed by the state. In the euphoria of those heady times, the AD's rhetoric often outran its policies. As a young party leader put it, "We are a multiclass party of the revolutionary left . . . called to fulfill the democratic and antiimperialist revolution with the participation of all political, economic and social forces interested in the transformation of the country."[17]

The chastening experience of a decade-long dictatorship was an impetus to doctrinal moderation. Following extended discussions inside the party, a new set of programmatic theses appeared in 1962; they have been revised only slightly since that time. Some of the opposing parties and dissenters from all three *adeco* schisms have charged that the party's ideological commitment has been dissipated— but the AD has retorted by citing its performance both in power and in opposition. The party has become more explicitly Social Democratic in recent years, as witness the meeting in Caracas in 1977 of Willy Brandt, Mário Soares, and the Scandinavian Social Democratic leaders, with Gonzalo Barrios presiding. In the words of a sympathetic Venezuelan observer,

---

[16] Summaries of AD and COPEI doctrine appear in Miguel Jorrín and John D. Martz, *Latin-American Political Thought and Ideology* (Chapel Hill: University of North Carolina Press, 1970), pp. 360-73 and 415-20.

[17] The author, later assassinated by the Pérez Jiménez dictatorship, was Leonardo Ruíz Pineda. For the citation, see his *Venezuela bajo el signo del terror; el libro negro de la dictadura* [Venezuela under the sign of terror: the black book of the dictatorship] (Santiago: Publicaciones Valmoré Rodríguez, Talleres Gráficos Astudillo, 1953), p. 26.

Acción Democrática is a party that responds to the theoretical postulates of social democracy. . . . Within the concept
of social democracy the party is committed to and fights for
the effectiveness of liberties, the profound modification and
democratization of the national economic structure, the
establishment of a government rule which permits the free
play of social forces, breaks the feudal relations of property
in the countryside.[18]

Both the 1973 AD program and subsequent policies of the Pérez
administration gave further testimony to the party's basic orientation.[19] However pragmatic, the *adecos* are not without an ideological
framework within which to operate. The Social Christians, of course,
have a more explicit philosophical base; their doctrinal evolution has
produced greater refinement and a more articulate exposition of basic
postulates than has that of Acción Democrática. Despite the falangist
elements of COPEI's early years as a student movement, the party's
doctrine soon took on progressive elements. Post–World War II
Christian Democratic movements in Western Europe encouraged
COPEI, as did the encyclicals of Pope John XXIII. Beginning in 1958,
the party moved perceptibly toward the political center. While Caldera
was perceived as representing business interests and standing to the
right of the AD, his performance after he took office in 1969 showed
otherwise. Observers would have been well advised to base their
judgments on the voluminous writings of Caldera, who stood with
Chile's Eduardo Frei in the front rank of Christian Democratic thinkers
in Latin America.[20]

In 1973, COPEI attempted to attract the support of the Venezuelan left, arguing that the AD had moved to the right. Yet the
Fernández candidacy reflected Caldera's centrist position within the
movement; he eschewed both the right and the youthful members
championing a communitarian dogma quite as revolutionary as that
of avowed Marxists. Fernández viewed industrialization as the driving motor of Venezuelan economic development and pledged pro-
tectionist state policies. He also promised to extend the "ideological
pluralism" and "international social justice" in the name of which

---

[18] Manuel Vicente Magallanes, *4 partidos nacionales* [Four national parties]
(Caracas: DIANA, 1973), p. 12.

[19] Extended treatments of the 1973 campaign platforms and promises appear
in Martz and Baloyra, *Electoral Mobilization;* for Pérez see pp. 144-51, for Fernández 135-42, and for the Marxists 156-69.

[20] In addition to Jorrín and Martz, *Ideology,* see Edward J. Williams, *Latin
American Christian Democratic Parties* (Knoxville: University of Tennessee
Press, 1967).

Caldera had granted diplomatic recognition to regimes of all ideological stripes. He characterized his position as "interventionist":

> Within the conception that I have, interventionism is the direct action of the state, by means of democratic planning, for the benefit, stimulus, protection, and development of private activity itself. . . . I believe that basic industries should be in state hands in order to guarantee to the private businesses that develop around them the best conditions and safeguards for their functioning, their growth, and their success.[21]

To this were added humanitarian concerns and commitments to the sanctity of the family and the chimera of unalloyed social justice and equity.

As the years unfolded following the restoration of constitutional rule, the AD and COPEI, both basically reformist, converged at the center of the spectrum. Internal party bureaucratization and growing entrenchment in power led their opponents, especially on the left, to characterize them as "El Status"—the status quo. While the term "establishment" might have been more apt, this attitude fit nicely with a Marxist interpretation of politics, at a time when Venezuelan Marxism was receiving a breath of fresh air with the founding of the Movement toward Socialism in 1970. MAS leaders like Teodoro Petkoff and Pompeyo Márquez attempted a diagnostic study of Venezuelan reality, freed from the rigidities of the PCV's orthodox Muscovite cant. Their objective was to develop detailed Marxist solutions to national problems, to be carried out through a popular, revolutionary struggle of the poor against the wealthy. Orthodox assumptions about the requisite stages of socialism were questioned, and labor, while considered a necessary element, was viewed as but one of several decisive sectors. The MAS candidate in 1973, Rangel, exemplified the commitment to internal dialogue, doctrinal flexibility, and the continuing dissection of national problems. Focusing on Venezuela's dependent capitalism, he insisted upon the need to create a participatory republic for and by the people. In the words of the leading MAS ideologue, "Understanding the reality of this decade of the 1970s . . . is an unpostponable task if we try to shape a contemporary revolutionary reply to contemporary problems and find a *Venezuelan* socialist solution to the many specific ills of Venezuela."[22]

---

[21] Fedecámaras, *Diálogo con los candidatos a la presidencia de la república* [Dialogue with the presidential candidates] (Caracas: Fedecámaras, 1973), p. 16.
[22] Teodoro Petkoff, *¿Socialismo para Venezuela?* [Socialism for Venezuela?], 3d ed. (Caracas: Editorial Fuentes, 1972), p. 163.

There was less vitality elsewhere on the left. The Communist party itself offered little of doctrinal substance, preferring to alter its tactics as appropriate for continued obeisance to Soviet dictates. Early in the 1970s MEP spokesmen sought a Marxist-based framework less radical in outlook than that of the MAS. Calling itself a "democratic socialist party of Venezuelan manual and intellectual workers," the MEP expressed a vision of the future centered on socialist democracy as embodied in the control of production and distribution by labor. In seeking national liberation, the party termed revolution "a means of accelerating the flowering of a new type of man, superior to the present in wisdom and in kindness."[23] MEP's efforts to develop a unique ideological position were dismissed as bourgeois reformism by many Marxists, and the party itself conceded that while Marxism was indispensable to revolutionary thought, it required discriminating and selective application. In any event, MEP declined rapidly in the 1970s, its eclecticism a passing curiosity.

While some critics have charged that contemporary Venezuelan politics is wholly issue oriented and lacking in doctrinal content, analyses of both COPEI and AD Governments show the relevance of the Social Christian and Social Democratic frameworks within which they work. For the Marxists, MAS's elaborations of socialist thought with reference to Venezuela progressively yielded to pragmatic reformulations of policy. In the final analysis, centrist reformism remains more attractive to the electorate than clarion calls for socialist transformation from the left.

The Prelude to 1978

Domestic Development. By the mid-1970s, Venezuela's population had passed the 12 million mark, with nearly 80 percent classified as urban. As the nation began to enjoy the fruits of the oil price bonanza, the Pérez administration undertook a massive program designed to lay the foundations for a modern industrialized society. Average government revenue per exported barrel of oil rose from $2.29 in 1973 to $9.45 in early 1975. Peréz sought to generate economic growth less dependent upon petroleum and to distribute more equitably the benefits thereby created. Between 1973 and 1974 current revenues increased by 150 percent; the next year was marked by stagnation, but current expenditures grew by 43 percent. In May 1974 the regime

---

[23] Movimiento Electoral del Pueblo, *Tesis política del MEP: liberación nacional y democracia socialista* [Political thesis of the MEP: national liberation and socialist democracy] (Caracas, 1970), p. 75.

created the Fondo de Inversiones de Venezuela (Venezuelan Investment Fund, FIV) as a means of freezing up to half of its petroleum income, increasing foreign reserves for the future, and providing a development bank for large and costly diversification projects in the public sector. Some $3 billion was allocated to the FIV during its first year, with an additional $2 billion in 1975. Such measures were also intended as a means of curbing inflation by withholding large sums from domestic spending. Through the FIV and other state agencies it was also hoped that major transfers of resources for productive private sector investment might stimulate further economic growth.

The largest portion of public investment was assigned to industry, notably steel, petrochemicals, aluminum, and electricity. Thus the development of the nation's abundant resources was to provide a foundation for an expanded manufacturing sector. Health, education, and social needs were to be financed by wealth accumulated after 1974. The framework that was to shape Venezuela's economic development was announced in the spring of 1976 with the introduction before Congress of the ambitious Fifth National Plan (1976–1980), double the size of the Fourth Plan (1970–1974). The handiwork of Planning Minister Gumersindo Rodríguez, it was sharply attacked by both COPEI and the left, but, after some adjustments, it was adopted and set into motion. This overarching attempt to achieve balanced development proved too optimistic on several counts. The 8.2 percent annual growth projected for the five years was high; during 1976 the growth rate was 7.4 percent, and it fluctuated little in 1977 and 1978. The projected expansion of key sectors also proved unrealistic. Manufacturing, while thriving, failed to reach the projected 13.1 percent expansion, while agriculture continued to stagnate. The Fifth Plan also mistakenly anticipated that nontraditional exports could expand rapidly. At the same time, imports continued to race ahead of government predictions.

In addition, a slackening of oil income by late 1976 threatened to weaken the financial base. While Venezuela held to its wisely conservative policy of limiting production to 2.2 million barrels per day, an increase in international resources produced difficulties for the industry. On the domestic market, oil was priced far below the break-even point, and any attempt to raise it would be politically explosive. An unprecedented domestic demand for oil hampered the work of the new state-operated Petróleos de Venezuela, created by the historic nationalization of the industry in 1976. An additional feature of the plan, hotly disputed by the opposition, was the call for extensive foreign borrowing to help finance its programs. Even Acción Democrática criticized the measure. Its defenders retorted that the external debt remained low and international reserves high; given the high liquidity of international capital markets, such extensive foreign borrowing was the most economical approach. Events were to prove the Venezuelans successful in negotiating favorable terms with a host of international lenders, who were optimistic about the long-range prospects of the economy.

The sector most stubbornly resistant to government stimulus was agriculture, which, since Betancourt's structural reforms, had stagnated despite the best efforts of both Leoni and Caldera. During his campaign Pérez had promised to give agriculture the highest developmental priority, and massive infusions of funds were initiated soon after he took office. In 1975 and 1976 some $700 million was invested to increase production and reduce imports, and the following year the rate of investment was increased. Yet by the close of Pérez's term the real problems of agriculture remained unresolved. In 1977, although the annual growth of the agricultural sector was averaging 5 percent, its share of gross domestic product had declined from 6.5 percent in 1971 to 5.9 percent—far short of the 9 percent anticipated by the Fifth National Plan. By May 1977 Venezuela faced a food crisis and an emergency airlift of supplies from Central America, Europe, and the United States. Though the Government had plowed a total of nearly $4 billion into agriculture, the basic situation remained unaltered.

The economic record was by no means without accomplishments, but in the aggregate it did not meet the unrealistically high expectations raised during the 1973 campaign. Venezuelans increasingly complained that their lives had not been materially improved despite the influx of such unprecedented income—an issue ready-made for the opposition in 1978. Furthermore, with the exception of major successes in the nationalized oil industry, government programs were plagued by inefficiency, waste, and an unparalleled level of corruption. Before the administration had reached its midpoint, discussions of dishonesty and graft were appearing almost daily in the press. Few were more vocal than Betancourt himself, who repeatedly denounced official corruption and called for bipartisan investigation and prosecution of its perpetrators. The growing outcry, accompanied by disappointment over domestic programs, overshadowed the administration's accomplishments and initiatives in the international realm.

Foreign Policy. President Pérez proved as peripatetic internationally as he had been domestically during the 1973 campaign. Seeking to become a leader of the Latin American nations, he visited the United Nations, Washington, Moscow, the Vatican, and the OPEC countries in addition to Latin America. Pérez projected himself as a spokesman for the Third World and assiduously championed the cause of North-South negotiations intended to restructure international trade and economic relationships. As the leader of one of the three Latin American democracies during much of his term, he defended freedom, human rights, and elected government. His Government spoke out sharply when dissident generals threatened to annul the Dominican elections in June 1978; he denounced the Somoza regime for its actions during the Nicaraguan domestic conflict the same year; and he treated cooly the military dictatorships of countries like Chile, Paraguay, and Argentina.

At the same time Pérez reversed the traditional *adeco* commitment to the Betancourt Doctrine, which called for severing diplomatic relations with nonelected regimes. Indeed, in this regard he followed the path of Rafael Caldera, whose concept of ideological pluralism had justified the maintenance of ties with regimes of varying ideologies and orientations. For Pérez, this approach also enhanced efforts to renew the ancient Bolivarian vision of a united hemisphere. With Mexican president Luis Echeverría he brought into being the Sistema Económica Latinoamericana (Latin American Economic System, SELA) to coordinate regional economic developmental policies and to create, implicitly, a counterweight to the U.S.-dominated Organization of American States. He was perhaps the single most influential foreign adviser to Panama's Omar Torrijos during the climactic negotiations with the United States over the canal. Early in his term Pérez reestablished diplomatic relations with Cuba and assumed a major role in promoting the reincorporation of Cuba into the hemispheric family of nations. There was irony in the prospect of a rapprochement between Venezuela and the revolutionary leader whose Venezuelan admirers had been frustrated some dozen years earlier by a tough and uncompromising interior minister named Pérez; but in the end the disclosure that Cuban troops were fighting in Angola cooled Pérez's ardor.

An important element in foreign policy was the increasing use of petrodollars to promote national interests. Recognizing the extreme budgetary problems created for its neighbors by the leap in oil prices, Venezuela devised a series of agreements whereby roughly half of a payment for oil imports remained in the purchasing country as a long-term loan to promote national development. Guatemala, Costa Rica, and several Caribbean nations were extended such assistance.

Venezuela also made major contributions to international and hemispheric organizations: $500 million apiece to the World Bank, the Inter-American Development Bank, and the International Monetary Fund; $60 million to the Andean Development Corporation; and $25 million to the Caribbean Development Bank. For the first time, moreover, Venezuela became heavily involved in the English-speaking Caribbean. Loans, investments, trade agreements—all were pursued vigorously, to such an extent that Trinidad-Tobago's prime minister eventually charged Venezuela with undertaking to recolonize the Caribbean.

It was a heady time for Venezuelan foreign policy. The international role which had grown progressively under Betancourt and Leoni and Rafael Caldera, himself among the hemisphere's most noted statesmen, found full expression in the combination of Pérez's irrepressible personal style and the nation's increased wealth. Venezuela did assume a position of greater prominence than in the past; its neighbors looked to Caracas for both economic and political support; democracy and individual freedom were ardently expounded; and Pérez established a warm relationship with Jimmy Carter, who called him "my chief adviser on Latin American affairs." Yet the more grandiose ambitions of hemispheric unity remained a chimera, and problems close to home resisted negotiation. Long-standing border disputes with Colombia and with Guyana went unresolved despite major diplomatic efforts, and the relationship with the Brazilian colossus to the south was never satisfactorily defined. For the Venezuelan public, pride at the enthusiastic welcomes Pérez received abroad was tempered with complaints that he should devote more time and attention to the domestic scene.

Prelude to the Election. As the Pérez years passed, it became evident that, despite the singular accomplishments of the democratic system, basic developmental challenges still confronted Venezuela.[24] The system had not yet extended its economic largesse and natural resources on an equitable basis to large numbers of the population. Both Venezuelans and foreigners agreed that the social agenda remained unfulfilled. With the rise of new sectors, the continuing migration from rural to urban settings, and the rapid population increase, it remained to be proved that the political and economic progress that had taken place could be translated into benefits for the great mass of the citizenry. This challenge remained as the parties moved toward candidate selection for the 1978 race.

---

[24] This argument is treated at length in John D. Martz and David J. Myers, "Venezuelan Democracy and the Future," *Venezuela*, pp. 359-92.

The shifting trajectory of the Pérez administration raised further questions that would have to be answered at the polls. During his early months in office Pérez had had a blank check from Congress and had issued a series of populistic decrees on wages, salaries, and price controls. Then there had been a shift toward measures more consistent with the preferences of the business and commercial sector. In all of Latin America, Venezuela's public sector is second only to Cuba's in the extent of its responsibilities and authority; in the context of Venezuela's state capitalism, the Government's economic policy decisions are crucial. In the latter part of his term, Pérez's policies seemed to benefit the wealthiest economic groups more than either the middle class or the lower sectors.[25] Such policies were predominantly the work of Gumersindo Rodríguez, sometime minister Carmelo Lauría, and wealthy advisers popularly and disparagingly known as the Twelve Apostles.

Pérez's reliance on nonparty technocrats and members of the business community exacerbated relations between the administration and Acción Democrática. In the wake of the party's decisive win, patronage positions were less numerous than party members had expected. Pérez gradually moved away from the more populistic promises outlined during his campaign, or so it seemed to the party. And he rubbed salt into wounds by making his confidant the unorthodox, publicity-seeking Federal District governor, Diego Arria, an ambitious and unpredictable figure who was not a party member. Eventually, in January 1977, Arria was moved to the less prestigious Ministry of Information and Tourism, but his proclivity for individual grandstanding and his close personal relationship with Pérez heightened the disharmony between Government and party.

As electoral planning began, Acción Democrática was in a more vulnerable position than might have been expected. Pérez, anxious to resume the party leadership in 1984 and eventually to launch a second presidential bid in 1988, found his ambitions opposed by his one-time mentor, Betancourt. Luis Herrera Campíns, meanwhile, loomed as COPEI's logical nominee for 1978, although that prospect remained unattractive to Rafael Caldera. On the left, the usual disunity seemed likely to produce multiple candidacies once again, with the MAS seemingly deaf to the possibility of alliance with its Marxist competitors. Even Rangel's candidacy was uncertain, given the conflict within the party itself. Rightist candidates were again a possibility,

---

[25] A searching treatment of public and private sectors and their relationship is José Antonio Gil Yepes, *El reto de las élites* [Challenge of the elites] (Madrid: Editorial Tecnos, 1978).

and veteran political observers speculated that some new figure might suddenly emerge in the fashion of Larrazábal, Uslar Pietri, and Burelli in earlier years. But at least a few predictions could be comfortably made as Venezuela braced itself for its fifth national election: the campaign would be long, intensive, and costly; electoral activity would grip the nation's attention for more than a full year; and nothing short of a split in one of the major parties could prevent the election of either the AD or the COPEI candidate.

2
The Conduct of Venezuelan Elections: Rules and Practice

Henry Wells

Electoral democracy did not take root in Venezuela until after the removal of the Pérez Jiménez dictatorship and the restoration of civil government in 1958. During all but three of the preceding 128 years of the country's existence as an independent republic, political conditions were not conducive to the emergence of democratic institutions and practices, though some semblance of representative government was maintained. Dictatorships alternated with periods of anarchy throughout the century that began in 1830 with the achievement of independence and ended in 1935 with the death of Juan Vicente Gómez. The Gómez dictatorship (1908–1935) had implacably repressed all attempts to organize resistance or opposition.

Under General Eleazar López Contreras, who assumed the presidency in 1936, the Congress remained dominated by Gómez conservatives. Responsible for adopting a new constitution, Congress used the opportunity to make the suffrage requirements even less democratic than they had been for the previous seventy-eight years. Since 1858 all males over twenty-one had been eligible to vote; but under the 1936 constitution only *literate* men could vote. The new constitution retained the previous constitution's limitations on the offices to be filled by direct election. Citizens eligible to vote could elect only the members of municipal councils and state legislative assemblies. The municipal and state legislators elected the members of the Congress, and the congressmen in turn elected the president.[1]

In 1945, following the overthrow of President López Contreras's successor, a revolutionary junta took power under the leadership of

[1] Daniel H. Levine, *Conflict and Political Change in Venezuela* (Princeton, N.J.: Princeton University Press, 1973), pp. 22-26; John D. Martz, *Acción Democrática: Evolution of a Modern Political Party in Venezuela* (Princeton, N.J.: Princeton University Press, 1966), pp. 31, 39.

Rómulo Betancourt. Serving as a provisional government until a new constitution could be adopted and a new president elected, the junta began to democratize the political system. Among its reform measures was Decree No. 216 of March 15, 1946, which it issued for the purpose of ensuring the free election of delegates to a constitutional convention. Among the innovations introduced by that decree were universal suffrage for all Venezuelans who had reached the age of eighteen, the direct involvement of parties in electoral administration, the proportional representation of parties in the convention, and the use of distinctive colors and symbols as a means of identifying parties and thus allowing illiterate voters to distinguish one party from another. On the basis of these provisions, universal suffrage, secrecy of the vote, proportional representation, party supervision of the electoral process, and other electoral reforms were enshrined in the constitution, which took effect in July 1947.

The election held under that constitution in December 1947 led to the inauguration of Rómulo Gallegos as president in February 1948 and also to the installation of directly elected senators and deputies in the Congress. But in November 1948 the military overthrew the Gallegos Government. Then followed nearly ten years of further repression—notably that of the Pérez Jiménez Government, which lasted from November 1950 until Pérez fled into exile in January 1958. During those years the electoral reforms of the 1945–1948 *trienio* were abrogated or ignored.

On May 24, 1958, the provisional government of Admiral Wolfgang Larrazábal issued Decree No. 234, which set the rules for holding the presidential and legislative elections of December 7, 1958. For the most part that decree reinstated the electoral innovations of the 1946 decree. Because the political realities of 1958 were considerably different from those of the mid-1940s, the reforms were widely accepted and quickly institutionalized.[2]

The main legal instruments undergirding the contemporary electoral system are the constitution of 1961 and the election law, known in Venezuela as the Organic Suffrage Act. Enacted in 1959, this law has undergone occasional revisions. The current version was enacted on August 13, 1977, in anticipation of the December 1978 election.

Election Administration

Responsibility for administering the electoral process in all its complexity rests in the Supreme Electoral Council (CSE), to which the

---

[2] Martz, *Acción Democrática*, pp. 64-77, 89-106.

Organic Suffrage Act grants "functional and administrative autonomy." The CSE performs such functions as registering new voters, keeping the Permanent Electoral Register up to date, setting the date of the election and of the opening of the campaign, regulating the conduct of parties and candidates during the campaign, preparing a list of voters for each polling place, preparing and distributing the ballots, issuing instructions, forms, and documents to election officials at all levels, determining the final result of the presidential election, and proclaiming the winner in that contest.[3]

The CSE consists of nine members elected by the two houses of Congress meeting in joint session in October of the year in which a new president takes office. The members of the CSE therefore serve a five-year term. Four of them must have no political affiliation. The other five are elected on the nomination of the five political parties that received the most votes in the preceding congressional election. Any other national party that received at least 3 percent of the valid votes cast in the last congressional election is entitled to send to the CSE one representative with the right to speak but not vote. Although a majority of the voting members owe their nomination to their party, the CSE has acquired a reputation for fairness and impartiality.[4]

The council heads a hierarchy of election boards, running from the CSE itself at the national level, through electoral boards at the state, district, and municipal levels, to polling places within each municipality. Immediately below the CSE are twenty-three Principal Election Boards—one in each of the twenty states, the two federal territories, and the Federal District. Each has seven members, all appointed by the CSE. Their main function is to represent the CSE at the state level and to carry out its decisions and regulations. They also receive election returns from lower-level election boards, determine the number of valid votes cast for each party's legislative candidates, apply the Venezuelan formula for proportional representation to those election results, and proclaim the winners. Another function of the Principal Election Board in each state is to elect a five-member board for each of the districts into which the state is divided. (The total number of such districts is currently 188.) In the Federal Dis-

---

[3] Venezuela, Consejo Supremo Electoral, *Ley orgánica del sufragio* [Organic suffrage act], arts. 38, 43.

[4] Ibid., art. 39. Seldom are the four members "without political affiliation" perceived to be independent voters. They tend to be identified more or less closely with one party or another—not surprisingly, since they have to be acceptable to party leaders in order to be elected by Congress. Like the five party representatives, however, they tend to act in a nonpartisan manner once they take up their CSE duties.

trict the principal board elects a board for each of its two departments; in the two federal territories, the principal boards each elect a single departmental board.

The major functions of a district or departmental board are to add up the votes cast within the district or department for each party's slate of legislative candidates and to report the results to the corresponding principal board. The district or departmental board also designates the five members of each municipal election board and of each polling place (*mesa electoral*) within its territorial jurisdiction.

Municipal boards are supposed to carry out the provisions of the Organic Suffrage Act and enforce the decisions of the CSE, the Principal Election Board, and the District Election Board above them in the hierarchy. They are also responsible for reporting to the CSE and the principal board the results of the voting at each *mesa electoral* within their jurisdiction. After the polls have closed, they take custody of each *mesa*'s records and other materials and forward them without delay to the district board.

The members of each *mesa electoral* must be appointed by the electoral board of its district or department at least thirty days before the election. The Supreme Electoral Council determines the number and location of the polling places. In deciding how many voters to allocate to each one, the CSE takes two guidelines into account: that electors should vote in the place where they reside, and that each center of population containing 100 or more voters should have at least one polling place.

The members of the *mesa electoral* are required to post on the doors of the polling place, at least five days before the election, a list of the registered voters assigned to that *mesa* and also a list of the candidates nominated by each party. The members and their alternates are required to be at the polling place at 5:30 A.M. on election day in order to prepare the voting materials before opening the polls. During the voting they are enjoined to adhere strictly to the rules and regulations set forth in the election law, and especially to safeguard the secrecy of the vote and maintain order within the polling place. When the polls close, they proceed immediately to counting the votes and drawing up the official report of the results. They then transmit the original of that document to the CSE and send copies and other materials to the Municipal Election Board, as specified in the election law.[5]

---

[5] Consejo Supremo Electoral, *Ley del sufragio*, arts. 47-57.

Elective Offices. In accordance with the 1961 constitution and the Organic Suffrage Act, the election of December 3, 1978, was contested by candidates for the presidency and for three sets of legislative bodies: the Senate, the Chamber of Deputies, and the state Legislative Assemblies. (State governors are appointed by the president of the republic.) In previous general elections members of a fourth set of legislative bodies, the municipal councils, were also elected. On August 18, 1978, however, Congress adopted a Municipal Organic Act which authorized the CSE to set the date of the municipal elections and thereby implied that it could schedule them separately from the national and state elections. On August 30 the CSE announced that the municipal elections would take place on June 3, 1979.[6]

The president is elected directly by popular suffrage, by a plurality of the votes cast. Anyone who has held the presidency for more than half of a regular five-year term is ineligible to be president again until ten years after leaving office. Ex-presidents automatically become members of the Senate for life.[7]

All senators, deputies, and state legislators are elected on the basis of proportional representation within their respective jurisdictions, in accordance with the system described in the next section. Two senators are elected from each of the twenty states and from the Federal District; no senators are assigned to the sparsely populated federal territories. Choosing each pair of senators by proportional representation makes it likely but not inevitable that the two winners will be the nominees of two different parties, given the evolution of the Venezuelan party system from multiparty pluralism to two-party dominance.[8]

The total of forty-two is known as the "fixed number of senators." In accordance with the 1961 constitution, additional representation is provided for "minorities" (in effect, for minority parties) after the results of the election have been ascertained. The process by which the additional Senate seats are awarded is the following: First, the

[6] "Ley orgánica de régimen municipal" [Municipal organic act], *Gaceta oficial de la República de Venezuela*, special no. 2,297, August 18, 1978, art. 33; *El Universal* (Caracas), August 31, 1978.

[7] *Constitution of the Republic of Venezuela, 1961* (Washington, D.C.: Pan American Union, 1963), arts. 148, 183, 185.

[8] Ibid., art. 148. In the 1978 election COPEI and AD each won twenty-one Senate seats; in the 1968 contest COPEI won seventeen and AD sixteen. In the AD sweep of 1973, however, the *adecos* won twenty-eight seats (including both senators in seven states), whereas the Social Christians won only twelve. See John D. Martz and Enrique A. Baloyra, *Electoral Mobilization and Public Opinion: The Venezuelan Campaign of 1973* (Chapel Hill: University of North Carolina Press, 1976), pp. 30, 227.

number of valid votes cast in the entire country for legislative candidates is divided by the fixed number of senators; the result is the "national electoral quotient" for the Senate. The number of valid votes obtained by each national political party is then divided by that quotient. If the difference between the result and the number of Senate seats a party won throughout the country is two or more, then the party is awarded two senators; if the difference is one, then it is awarded one senator. In no case, however, can a party be allocated more than two senators.[9]

There are also elected deputies and "additional" deputies. The number of elected deputies varies with the population of each of the twenty-three electoral jurisdictions, except that the twenty states and the Federal District must each have at least two deputies regardless of their population, and each cf the federal territories must have at least one. Not later than four months before the election the CSE must estimate the total population of the country and then calculate the "national population base"—defined by the Organic Suffrage Act as equal to 0.55 percent of the total population. The national population base then becomes the unit for determining the number of deputies to be elected in each jurisdiction by proportional representation. That number is arrived at by dividing the national population base into the population of a state, the Federal District, or a federal territory.

To illustrate: In 1978 the CSE estimated Venezuela's total population to be 13,285,751. The national population base (0.55 percent of that number) was therefore declared to be 73,072. Since the CSE estimated the population of the Federal District to be 2,281,423, dividing that number by 73,072 yielded 32 as the number of deputies to be elected in the Federal District. Similarly, given an estimated population of 494,118, the state of Bolívar was entitled to elect 7 deputies. Like calculations for the other jurisdictions brought the total to 183. This figure thus became the "fixed number of deputies" for the 1978 election.

As in the case of the additional senators, the CSE determines the number of additional deputies to be awarded to minority parties after the general election results become known and the number of Chamber seats won by each party on the basis of proportional representation has been determined. A national quotient of deputies is arrived at by dividing the fixed number of deputies into the total number of valid votes cast for legislative candidates in the election. Then the quotient is divided into the total number of valid votes obtained by each

---

[9] Consejo Supremo Electoral, Ley del sufragio, arts. 2, 14, 16; Constitution, art. 148.

national party. If the difference between the result of this calculation and the number of deputies won by a party through election is four or more, the party is awarded four additional deputies; if the difference is three, two, or one, it is awarded a corresponding number of deputies. But no national party may receive more than four additional seats in the Chamber of Deputies.[10]

Legislative Assemblies exist only in the states; neither the Federal District nor the federal territories have such bodies. All members of the Legislative Assemblies are elected by proportional representation. Their numbers vary from state to state in accordance with the following scale:

Up to 300,000 inhabitants	11 deputies
From 300,001 to 500,000	13 deputies
From 500,001 to 700,000	15 deputies
From 700,001 to 900,000	17 deputies
From 900,001 to 1,100,000	19 deputies
From 1,100,001 to 1,300,000	21 deputies
1,300,001 and above	23 deputies

Of the assemblies elected in 1978 the largest was that of Zulia, with twenty-three members. Next largest, at seventeen members, were the assemblies of Carabobo, Lara, and Miranda. Four state legislatures had fifteen members, six had thirteen, and six had eleven.[11]

Proportional Representation. Article 13 of the Organic Suffrage Act specifies that the principle of proportional representation be applied to the election of senators, deputies, state legislators, and members of municipal councils. The system used in Venezuela assumes that two or more seats are to be filled, that electors vote for party lists rather than for individual candidates, that the seats are distributed among the parties roughly in accordance with each party's share of the total vote, and that the order in which the names appear on the party list determines which candidates are elected from each party.

The method of proportional representation prescribed by the election law is a variation of the "highest average" formula invented by Victor d'Hondt, a Belgian university professor, in the nineteenth century. The number of valid votes cast for each of the party lists is successively divided by 1, 2, 3, 4, and so on until the number of

---

[10] Ibid., art. 151; Consejo Supremo Electoral, *Ley del sufragio*, arts. 3, 6, 14, 15; *El Nacional* (Caracas), December 1, 1978, p. D-2.

[11] Consejo Supremo Electoral, *Ley del sufragio*, art. 4; *El Nacional*, December 1, 1978, p. D-2.

TABLE 2–1

THE VENEZUELAN VARIANT OF THE D'HONDT SYSTEM OF PROPORTIONAL REPRESENTATION: A HYPOTHETICAL CASE

If seven seats are to be filled and the four parties contesting the election are Party A with 14,400 votes, Party B with 9,000 votes, Party C with 6,600 votes, and Party D with 12,000 votes, then the seats are distributed as follows:

	Political Party				Highest Quotient	Seat	Party Winning Seat
Divisor	A	B	C	D			
1	14,400	9,000	6,600	12,000	14,400	1st	A
2	7,200	4,500	3,300	6,000	12,000	2nd	D
3	4,800	3,000	2,200	4,000	9,000	3rd	B
4	3,600	2,250	1,650	3,000	7,200	4th	A
					6,600	5th	C
					6,000	6th	D
					4,800	7th	A

RESULTS: Party A receives three seats; Party D, two seats; Parties B and C, one seat each.

SOURCE: Author.

divisions equals not more than the number of seats to be filled. As the divisions take place, the quotients are listed in separate columns by party, in descending order, each column being headed by the number of valid votes cast for the party's list (the total number divided by 1). In an additional column the highest quotients in the party columns are listed in descending order, and alongside each is recorded the name of the party whose quotient it is. When the number of quotients so listed equals the number of seats to be filled, the process stops; for the allocation of seats among the parties has been accomplished.[12] Table 2–1 illustrates the method.

Qualifications for Voting. All Venezuelans who have reached the age of eighteen are eligible to vote unless they are subject to a prison sentence or some other conviction that carries with it the loss of political rights. The right to vote is also denied to members of the armed forces while on active duty. All other citizens between the ages of eighteen and seventy are required to register and vote unless a municipal judge has exempted them from having to do so. Although the election law declares that failure to register or vote is punishable

[12] Consejo Supremo Electoral, *Ley del sufragio*, art. 13.

by a fine of 1,000 to 2,000 bolívars* or by imprisonment, the provision is seldom enforced. According to CSE figures, 12.9 percent of the registered voters (some 800,000 persons) abstained from voting in the 1978 election without prior authorization. In 1973 the abstention rate was only 3.1 percent.[13]

Voter Registration. All eligible voters are required by law to enter their names in the Permanent Electoral Register, which they can do in the municipality where they live. (Venezuelans living abroad may register in any Venezuelan consulate or diplomatic post in the country in which they reside.) Each person seeking to register must present his or her personal identification card, sign the application form, and affix his or her fingerprints to it. The registration agent then gives the voter a duly signed copy of his or her entry in the Permanent Electoral Register; it includes the address of the voting center (for example, a school building) closest to the voter's residence and the number of the *mesa electoral* (for example, a particular classroom) to which the voter has been assigned. Other items of information in the permanent register are the full name, sex, date of birth, nationality, and occupation of the voter; indication of any physical defects; indication of whether the voter can read and write; the voter's identification card number, electoral-register number, and *mesa electoral* number (this last corresponding to the last digit of the identification card number); and the voter's complete home address.

The Permanent Electoral Register is the responsibility of the Supreme Electoral Council, which employs a director and staff to administer it. On the basis of information received from the Civil Registry, the courts, and other sources, the CSE continuously removes the names of registered voters who have died, lost their citizenship, lost their political rights, entered active military service, registered more than once, or registered fraudulently. Hence the register is constantly in process of being purged except during the ninety days before and thirty days after an election, when the only names stricken from the register are those of persons found to be fraudulently registered.

In addition the CSE undertakes an annual revision of the register, which occurs between January and June. Conducted by hundreds of

---

[13] *Constitution*, art. 111; Consejo Supremo Electoral, *Ley del sufragio*, arts. 7, 178; "Venezuela," *Latin America Political Report*, February 2, 1979, p. 35; Martz and Baloyra, *Electoral Mobilization*, p. 224.

* EDITOR's NOTE: At the time of the 1978 elections, one bolívar was worth 23.3 U.S. cents.

civil servants, such as municipal employees, court personnel, postal workers, and public-school teachers, who serve as registration agents, the revision attempts to incorporate into the permanent register all persons who have reached the age of eighteen, acquired Venezuelan citizenship, completed sentences that had disqualified them politically, or are no longer on active duty in the armed forces. It is during this period that registered voters who have changed their name or their address can request that the appropriate changes be made in the information concerning them in the permanent register.

During an election year, evidence of being a registered voter is an indispensable prerequisite for holding public office or government employment, for entering into a contract with any government agency, for enrolling in or receiving a degree or diploma from any public or private educational institution, for obtaining a driver's license, and for performing numerous other actions. Persons over seventy years of age are exempt from these limitations, as are those determined by a municipal judge to have sufficient cause to be exempt.[14]

The Ballot. At the elections of 1958, 1963, and 1968, the voter cast two separate party ballots, one for the presidency and the other for all legislative offices. The ballots consisted of two cards of unequal size, the larger being the presidential ballot. Each national party's pair of cards was distinctive in color and design. At the polling place the voter received a complete set of large and small cards. From these, he selected one card of each size, put them in an envelope, sealed the envelope, discarded the unused cards, and deposited the envelope in the ballot box.

This process was complicated and slow, given the large numbers of parties contesting the elections: in 1968 the voter had sixteen large cards and at least that many small cards from which to choose (in states where local parties had nominated legislative candidates, the voter received an additional small card for each list of local nominees).[15] By 1973, widespread demand for a better system of voting had led to reforms. The most important change was the adoption of the single ballot, used again in 1978. Instead of having to shuffle numerous cards of two different sizes, the voter has to cope with only one sheet of paper, on which all of the parties' large and small cards are printed. As before, each party's "cards" bear the color or colors

---

[14] The paragraphs above summarize the provisions of Title III, "The Permanent Electoral Register" (arts. 58-90), of the Organic Suffrage Act.

[15] Martz and Baloyra, *Electoral Mobilization*, pp. 37-38; Consejo Supremo Electoral, *Escrutinio de las elecciones* [Election results] (Caracas: Departamento de Relaciones Públicas, 1973), p. 42.

and symbol assigned to it by the Supreme Electoral Council.[16] As before, the larger one signifies the party's presidential candidate and the smaller its legislative lists. The Organic Suffrage Act specifies that the word "card" will continue to be used: "For the purposes of this law, card is to be understood as the colored square or box which is assigned on the ballot to each political party."[17] The difference is that the voter now expresses his or her preferences by striking one "large card" and one "small card" on the single ballot with an inked rubber stamp labeled CSE, instead of by putting real cards into an envelope for depositing in the ballot box.

Printed on black paper, the single ballot used in the 1978 election measured approximately fifteen by twenty inches and displayed in orderly rows and columns fifteen pairs of large and small cards and an additional nine small cards. The large card measured about two and three-eighths by one and one-half inches; the small card measured about one and five-eighths by one and one-eighth inches. In accordance with the election law, the parties themselves select the location of their cards on the ballot, choosing in order of their legislative vote in the previous general election: the party with the largest small-card vote in 1973 had first pick in 1978, and so on.[18] The CSE determines the size of the ballot, designs it, and orders enough copies to distribute to every polling place 20 percent more ballots than the number of registered voters assigned to it. The CSE also provides sample ballots for distribution in adequate numbers to all parties and groups that have nominated candidates.

---

[16] Martz and Baloyra, *Electoral Mobilization*, p. 40.

[17] Consejo Supremo Electoral, *Ley del sufragio*, art. 131, first paragraph.

[18] Ibid., art. 112 (1, 2). Since more votes were cast for the AD's small card in 1973 than for any other party's, the *adecos* had first choice of a position on the 1978 ballot and picked the upper left-hand corner. COPEI, which had second choice, picked the upper right-hand corner. The MAS had third place and selected the middle position in the top row, with the result that its two orange cards were flanked by the two white AD cards on the left and COPEI's two green ones on the right. Each pair contained the party's emblem and a picture of its presidential candidate. Beneath them from left to right on the second row were the large and small cards of the MEP, the Nationalist Crusade, and the URD. Five other parties (the FDP, PCV, MIR, OPINA, and FUN) completed the list of participants in the 1973 elections who were entitled to pick spaces on the 1978 ballot. Four new national parties—Vanguardia Comunista (VUC), the Labor Movement (MDT), the Movement for National Renewal (MORENA), and Common Cause (Causa Común)—also exercised the privilege of choosing ballot positions for their large and small cards. The nine parties running only legislative lists all figured on the lower half of the ballot.

Candidate Selection

Chapter II of Title IV of the Suffrage Act is entitled "Nominations," but it contains no information concerning the method or process that parties, coalitions, or other groups should use in selecting their presidential and legislative candidates. In the absence of statutory directives the parties have developed rules for candidate selection that are consistent with election-law requirements concerning other things— especially the form of the ballot, the process of voting, the first-past-the-post system of determining which presidential candidate gets elected, and the party-list system of proportional representation used in determining which legislative candidates get elected.

Nomination of Presidential Candidates. In September 1947 the Acción Democrática party held a national convention in order to nominate Rómulo Gallegos as its candidate for president in the first election to be conducted under the 1947 constitution. Ever since then the national convention has been the vehicle that the AD and COPEI have customarily used for selecting their presidential candidates. On two occasions, however, the AD has held a primary election for that purpose. Among the minor parties, only the MAS stages national conventions at which rival aspirants compete for the presidential nomination. The other minor parties tend to hold mock conventions that rubber-stamp the nomination of a candidate already chosen by the party leadership; or the leadership simply announces the nominee. The independent who forms his own mini-party often proclaims his own candidacy.

AD and COPEI national conventions. When the leaders of either major party are in substantial agreement concerning the person who should become its candidate, the national convention legitimizes their choice and may also contribute to the strengthening of party unity. This was true of the COPEI conventions of August 1963 and March 1967, both of which nominated Rafael Caldera for the presidency by acclamation. The AD conventions of July 1963 and August 1972 also had a legitimizing and unifying effect even though four prominent *adecos* sought the nomination in 1963 and three sought it in 1972. In each case the convention delegates gave a large majority of their first-ballot votes to only one of them (Raúl Leoni in 1963 and Carlos Andrés Pérez in 1972), whereupon the winner's erstwhile rivals closed ranks in support of the AD ticket in the ensuing campaign.[19] The

---

[19] Martz, *Acción Democrática*, pp. 338-41; Martz and Baloyra, *Electoral Mobilization*, pp. 11, 68-71.

COPEI national convention of August 1977 presented a similar situation: delegate support for Luis Herrera Campíns was so overwhelming (3,900 to 300) that his sole opponent, Arístides Beaujon, withdrew before the balloting began.

When either of the major parties is sharply divided by the struggles of party leaders for the presidential nomination, the selection of the candidate by a national convention can divide the party still further. COPEI's experience during the presidency of Rafael Caldera (1969–1974) illustrates this pattern. Caldera was ineligible to succeed himself. Four COPEI leaders competed strenuously for the nomination during the six months preceding the national convention of March 1972. The victory of one of them, Lorenzo Fernández, on the second ballot did not elicit the usual pledges of support from the losers. On the contrary, they and their followers remained resentful of the methods used by the pro-Fernández camp in seeking the votes of convention delegates and were therefore reluctant to participate in the 1973 campaign.[20]

AD primary elections. In September 1967 and July 1977 the AD resorted to primary elections in the hope of resolving bitter internal struggles for its presidential nomination—the only examples of the use of primaries in Venezuela's political history. Since the two primary contests weakened the party and contributed significantly to its loss of the presidency to COPEI in the elections of 1968 and 1978, there is some question whether the AD or any other Venezuelan party will choose to repeat the experiment in the foreseeable future.

The AD primary of 1967 pitted two powerful "old guard" leaders, Gonzalo Barrios and Luis B. Prieto Figueroa, and their respective wings of the party against each other. Although Prieto seems to have received about 70 percent of the total primary vote, violence prevented the votes in one district from being counted; moreover, Barrios supporters who controlled the AD national executive committee simply refused to countenance the Prieto candidacy. The hostility between the two camps intensified to such a degree that Prieto and his chief supporter, Jesús Angel Paz Galarraga, withdrew from the party and founded the People's Electoral Movement (MEP). As presidential nominee of the MEP, Prieto drew enough votes away from Barrios to allow Caldera, the COPEI candidate, to win the presidency.[21]

On the surface the second AD primary, that of July 17, 1977, was a contest between Luis Piñerúa Ordaz and Jaime Lusinchi for the

---

[20] Ibid., pp. 62-68, 84.

[21] Ibid., pp. 12-13.

presidential nomination. In reality, however, it was a test of strength between their respective sponsors, Rómulo Betancourt and President Carlos Andrés Pérez, who, once friends, were now political rivals. The Piñerúa-Betancourt faction won the primary with 62 percent of the votes, but it lost the election of December 3, 1978.

Nomination of Legislative Candidates. In accordance with Venezuela's system of proportional representation, the number of seats that a party wins in a national or state legislative body (Senate, Chamber of Deputies, state legislature) is proportional to its share of the total small-card vote within the appropriate jurisdiction. The party's seats are awarded to its candidates in the order in which their names appear on the party's list of candidates for each of the legislative bodies. As a result, not just the selection of candidates, but their ordering on the list is a vitally important political decision, which in most cases determines in advance which candidates will stand a serious chance of winning seats. It is all the more critical in that the demand of "deserving" party leaders and top-ranking political allies for places high on a party's list always far exceeds the supply of favored spots. A shrewd selection and ordering of candidates can increase the number of votes cast for a party's small card, whereas an inept selection or ordering can make politically significant enemies for the party and reduce its electoral support.

Little wonder, then, that every party's national executive committee (or its functional equivalent) reserves to itself the prerogative of making the final decision concerning the persons to be listed as legislative candidates and the position of each on the list. In the case of a minor party, the inner circle of party leaders usually assumes full responsibility for preparing the list. In the case of both COPEI and the AD, however, the national committee assigns district and regional committees the task of preparing preliminary lists of candidates for some or all of the available legislative seats within their respective jurisdictions. After receiving the regional committees' lists the national committee normally reviews and amends them as it sees fit. In preparing their lists for the 1978 election, however, both major parties departed slightly from this pattern. The COPEI national executive committee set up an ad hoc commission to review the regional committees' lists, consult national and regional leaders of the party, and prepare revised lists; the commission then submitted its revised list for each legislative body to the national committee for final approval or further amendment. In the AD case the national committee reviewed the regional committees' lists, consulted national and regional leaders, put together its own list, and then delegated to an informal group of top party leaders (the *cogollito*) the power to amend them and make the final selection. It should be added that the actual lists of names are published in the back pages of the big Caracas newspapers a few days before the election; otherwise they receive very little publicity or attention during the campaign.

Candidate Selection Provisions of the Election Law. Although the Organic Suffrage Act does not refer to the process of selecting candidates, it does require the parties and the CSE to take certain actions once the candidates have been nominated. The following deserve mention:

Any party or political group that nominates a presidential candidate must submit his name to the CSE between June 1 and July 30 of the year in which the election is held. If the CSE finds that the nominee meets the qualifications prescribed by the constitution and the suffrage act, it declares him to be a candidate for the presidency. It also assigns him a color or color combination different from that of any other nominee and publishes an announcement of his candidacy in the *Official Gazette* of the Republic of Venezuela.[22]

Any national or regional party or political group that wishes to obtain representation in legislative bodies must submit its lists of candidates to the appropriate Principal Electoral Boards between 120 and 90 days prior to the election. The names of its nominees for each legislative body must be listed, each with an alternate.[23]

No party or group can submit more than one list of nominees in each jurisdiction (state, Federal District, or territory) for the same legislative body. A party or group may nominate the same person for different elective offices within the same jurisdiction, and it may nominate the same person for the same legislative body in different jurisdictions. (In Venezuela a legislator does not have to be a resident of the jurisdiction from which he is elected.) But it cannot nominate the same person for the office of senator, deputy, or state legislator in more than two jurisdictions. Different parties or groups may nominate the same person for the same legislative body, but in that case the person's name should appear in the same position on the parties' lists.[24]

Within forty-eight hours after receiving the lists and accompanying documentation, a Principal Electoral Board must determine whether

---

22 Consejo Supremo Electoral, *Ley del sufragio*, arts. 94-97.
23 Ibid., arts. 100, 101.
24 Ibid., arts. 102, 103.

or not they comply with the relevant constitutional and statutory requirements. If everything is in order the board certifies the color and symbol chosen by the party or group submitting the lists. Within forty-eight hours following its approval of each list, the board must notify the CSE of the name of the party submitting it, the color or color combination and symbol assigned to it, and information concerning the candidates. A party, group, or candidate may appeal a board's decision to the CSE if it does so within three days of the announcement of the ruling. The CSE must act on the appeal within three days of its receipt. Once all these formalities are complied with, the Principal Electoral Board that received the nominations publishes all the lists in the *Official Gazette* of the state, Federal District, or territory, along with information concerning their respective colors and symbols. The board also posts this information for public inspection in the locality where it meets.[25]

The Campaign

In contemporary Venezuela many campaign procedures and practices are subject to regulation—some by the Organic Suffrage Act, which imposes certain restrictions on candidates and parties; others by the Supreme Electoral Council, to which the act grants regulatory authority over a variety of campaign matters. The limitations imposed by law, however, are not always enforced, and the powers granted to the CSE are not always fully exercised. Moreover, two of the most important of the parties' campaign activities, raising and spending money for campaign purposes, remain totally unregulated.

Article 154 of the election law not only requires the CSE to set the official opening date of the campaign but also specifies its duration: not less than six months and not more than eight months. Since Article 92 requires that the election be held on a Sunday during the first two weeks of December in the election year and Article 165 provides that campaigning must stop forty-eight hours before the voting begins, the campaign cannot officially start earlier than March 29 or later than June 13. The opening date set by the CSE for the campaign preceding the 1978 election was April 1, 1978.

Congress adopted the six-month minimum and eight-month maximum in July 1977 in order to shorten the campaign, but the reform came too late to have that effect in 1978. As in previous contests, the presidential aspirants in both COPEI and AD had been campaigning for their party's nomination since the first or second year

---

[25] Ibid., arts. 104-106.

of the constitutional term. By the end of 1975 the presidential campaign was in fact well under way, for each party had by that time chosen its secretary general and thereby indicated which of the contenders was the one most likely to obtain its presidential nomination. The AD candidate began full-scale campaigning as soon as he had won the July 1977 primary; COPEI's candidate followed suit once its August 1977 national convention had formally nominated him.

As soon as the campaign officially begins, all candidates, parties, and coalitions become entitled to "equitable" access to the communications media for the purpose of carrying out their publicity campaigns. Legally responsible for enforcing the parties' right to roughly equal time for promoting their programs and candidates on radio and television and roughly equal space for newspaper advertisements, the CSE attempts to accomplish this by limiting the number of lines of advertising that a party can place in newspapers and the amount of time it can devote to promotional broadcasts on television and radio.[26] Such regulations, however, fail to protect the small parties, for AD and COPEI regularly contract for media advertising up to (and beyond) the maximum allowed by the CSE, whereas the small parties usually lack the resources to do so. According to one estimate, the two big parties' heavy investment in television time during the 1978 campaign cost them about $8 million apiece out of an estimated total campaign outlay of some $40 million each. According to another estimate, the campaign expenditures of all the parties exceeded $100 million.[27]

During an election year the CSE contributes directly and indirectly to the financing of the parties' campaign advertising. It assists directly by making generous postelection grants to the parties that

---

[26] During the 1978 campaign, for example, the CSE decreed that each party or its presidential candidate was entitled to broadcast not more than ten minutes a day on each television channel and from each radio station, and to broadcast a program of only one half-hour on both radio and television not oftener than once a week. The programs could be used only for the purpose of presenting a party's governmental program or a candidate's campaign promises—not for attacking other parties or their candidates. The CSE rules for newspaper advertising limited each party to a maximum of 864 column-centimeters (equivalent to about 340 column-inches, or roughly two standard-size pages) per day, per newspaper; but such space could be accumulated for later use up to 1,296 centimeters (510 inches), or three pages. (Luis Rojas Vásquez, "El CSE apeló a todos los recursos que le concede la ley para frenar el nerviosismo de los partidos" [CSE had recourse to all the means the law gives it to check the parties' nervousness], El Nacional, November 27, 1978.)

[27] Time, December 18, 1978, p. 44; New York Times, December 3, 1978, p. 33, and December 4, 1978, p. A-8. Since there are no disclosure requirements, the parties' actual expenditures remain unknown and the estimates vary widely. See chaps. 4, 8.

have obtained at least 10 percent of the valid votes for congressional candidates. Subject to verification of claimed propaganda expenses and to the amount available in its budget for this purpose, the CSE distributes its funds among such parties in accordance with their respective percentages of the total number of valid small-card votes. It contributes indirectly to the financing of parties' campaign publicity by contracting for radio and television time and for advertising space in newspapers, and then distributing those time and space allotments on an equal basis to all parties that obtained more than 5 percent of the valid votes cast in the last previous congressional election.[28]

The election law forbids the use of political propaganda that is anonymous, disrespectful of human dignity, or offensive to public morals. It also prohibits advertising that encourages abstention from voting or other violations of law. Similarly proscribed are the use of any living person's name in campaign slogans without permission and the use of national symbols and pictures or likenesses of national heroes in any kind of electoral propaganda. To these legal restrictions the CSE has added its own rules banning defamatory, insulting, or otherwise injurious references to individuals, political parties, or public or private institutions in campaign publicity.[29]

Violations of such rules and regulations and of CSE limitations on the parties' use of the media occurred with increasing frequency toward the end of the 1978 campaign. They finally became so numerous and so blatant that the CSE resorted to unprecedented measures to stop them. On November 24, after having requested and received assurances of cooperation and support from the minister of defense on behalf of the armed forces and from the Venezuelan equivalent of the attorney general on behalf of the public prosecutors, the CSE decided that it would officially terminate the campaign and cut off all further electioneering if it learned of any new violations. Two days later public prosecutors, accompanied by the police, began appearing at newspaper offices armed with authority to prevent the distribution of any papers that violated CSE space limitations on political advertising. The CSE also ordered both COPEI and AD to cancel specific television commercials in which the other party's presidential candidate was held to be the object of false or belittling propaganda.[30]

[28] Consejo Supremo Electoral, *Ley del sufragio*, art. 155.

[29] Ibid., arts. 156, 160.

[30] See three articles by Luis Rojas Vásquez in *El Nacional:* "Enérgica advertencia hizo el CSE a los partidos y sus candidatos" [CSE issued vigorous warning to parties and candidates], November 25, 1978, p. D-1; "Dispuesto el CSE a dar por terminar la campaña electoral" [CSE disposed to terminate election campaign], November 26, 1978; and "El CSE apeló a todos" [The CSE made a general appeal], November 27, 1978.

Although the suffrage act forbids the posting of signs, placards, fliers, and similar forms of political advertising on public buildings and monuments, on churches, and on trees alongside streets or in public parks, no one pays much attention to the prohibition. Even the rule against placing such signs and posters on houses and other private buildings without the consent of their occupants is often ignored. Although the painting of political slogans, symbols, and other forms of partisan propaganda on the walls of houses, public buildings, plazas, and churches is "absolutely prohibited," the practice is widespread during every campaign, especially in urban areas. In fact, local party organizations have been known to distribute stencils and spray-paint cans to party activists. Less frequently violated is the rule that political banners, posters, and the like must not interfere with the flow of pedestrian or vehicular traffic; but the requirement that parties remove their posters and other propaganda from public places within thirty days after the election is seldom enforced.[31]

Finally, the act prohibits any governmental body—ministry, agency, institute, public enterprise, mixed enterprise, or any other organ of national, state, or municipal government—from propagandizing directly or indirectly on behalf of any party or candidate. It remains true, however, that the party in power has a decided advantage over its rivals during the campaign, precisely because governmental publications, services, and even personnel can do many things that give support to the party's presidential candidate. Skilled government employees, for example, can be lent to the party organization for all or part of the campaign—especially such personnel as media specialists and polling experts. Similarly, the president or a high-ranking spokesman may launch a well-prepared campaign in the national press and on television and radio to publicize the Government's activities and accomplishments. It has been estimated that during the 1978 campaign the Pérez administration spent $15 million praising its own achievements.[32]

The promoters of public meetings, rallies, parades, or demonstrations must give the municipal government of the locality and the appropriate municipal or district electoral board at least forty-eight hours' advance notice of the event they wish to put on. The local government cannot prevent the affair from taking place except for reasons of public order or to protect freedom of movement and other

---

[31] Consejo Supremo Electoral, *Ley del sufragio*, arts. 159, 161, 163, 168. In 1978, virtually all posters were down by the end of the third day, at least in Caracas.

[32] Ibid., art. 167; *Time*, December 18, 1978, p. 44.

rights of citizens. With the concurrence of the local authorities, the election board decides the places and locations where such events can take place, on the understanding that the parties are to use them on an equal basis and in the order in which they solicit their use. An adverse ruling by a local government can be appealed to the governor of the state, territory, or Federal District.[33]

The CSE strictly enforces Article 165, which requires all campaigning—including the publishing or broadcasting of advertisements or news concerning the parties or candidates—to come to a complete halt not later than forty-eight hours before the opening of the polls.[34] On election day, electioneering of any kind inside or outside the place where election boards are located is absolutely forbidden—a prohibition enforced by the CSE and the election boards themselves with the assistance of the armed forces.

Election Day and the Outcome

Setting the date of the election is one of the many responsibilities of the Supreme Electoral Council, as we have seen. At 5:30 A.M. on the day fixed, the five members of each *mesa electoral* assemble at the polling place, along with their respective alternates and two witnesses whom the board has appointed to serve as official poll-watchers. Witnesses appointed by political parties may also be present: the Organic Suffrage Act authorizes every party or group that has nominated candidates to station its own witness at each polling place.[35]

When the roster of *mesa* members, alternates, and official witnesses is complete, a member of the *mesa* announces that the polls are open and that voting is about to begin. The members then display the open ballot box to show all present that it is empty, whereupon they proceed to seal it with a strip of paper on which each of them and each official witness signs his or her name.[36]

---

[33] Consejo Supremo Electoral, *Ley del sufragio*, art. 164.

[34] In 1978 the CSE decreed that all electioneering would cease at 12 P.M. on Thursday, November 30.

[35] Consejo Supremo Electoral, *Ley del sufragio*, art. 115. On November 29, 1978, just four days before the election, the CSE decided to issue all parties a set of credentials for use by alternate witnesses. It took this action in response to the frequent complaint of minority parties that in case the witness of such a party for some reason could not be present on election day, that party would not have anyone at the *mesa electoral* to observe the proceedings and protect its interests. (Luis Rojas Vásquez, "Esta noche a las doce cesa toda propaganda electoral" [Tonight at midnight all electoral propaganda stops], *El Nacional*, November 30, 1978.)

[36] Consejo Supremo Electoral, *Ley del sufragio*, art. 112 (3).

The voter goes to the voting center (usually an educational institution) to which the Permanent Electoral Register has assigned him and enters the *mesa electoral* whose number corresponds to the last digit of the number on his identification card. The voter then presents the card to the members of the *mesa,* one of whom checks it against the list of voters assigned to that polling place and also checks to make sure that the person has not already voted. The *mesa* official then explains the process of voting and, before giving the voter a ballot, records in a notebook the serial number printed on the back of the ballot's lower left-hand corner. The official hands the voter a ballot and an inked rubber stamp that reads "CSE." The voter enters a booth or goes behind a curtain or screen in order to vote in secret. Using the inked CSE stamp, he votes for the presidential candidate of one of the parties by stamping its "large card," and for a party's legislative candidates by stamping its "small card." The voter then folds the ballot in such a way that its numbered corner, a perforated tab, can easily be removed. Returning to the *mesa* officials, the voter tears off the tab and shows it to them (thereby proving that the ballot is the one he had been given moments before), deposits the ballot in the ballot box, rips up the tab, and retrieves his identification card from the *mesa.* The members of the *mesa* conclude the process by having the voter place his fingerprint beside his name on the list of voters and by dipping the little finger of his right hand in indelible ink to show that he has voted.[37]

The *mesa* officials are authorized by law to evict a voter who spends more than two minutes in the polling booth or other place designated for voting in secret. No one can accompany a voter in the act of marking or casting the ballot, or attempt in any other way to influence his decision. In the case of blind voters, however, and of those unable to use their hands or feet, persons of their choice may accompany and assist them in the act of voting. The polls are supposed to close at 4 P.M. on election day but may remain open as long as voters are present and waiting to cast their ballots.[38] (At 6.30 P.M. on December 3, 1978, so many people were still waiting to vote that the CSE instructed the polling places to remain open until 10 P.M.)

No armed civilian, even if he is authorized to bear arms, may enter a polling place during voting hours or while the votes are being counted. Members of the armed forces charged with the responsibility

---

[37] Ibid., arts. 112 (4-6), 118, 122. See also the detailed, clearly illustrated instructions on how to vote published by the CSE in all daily newspapers during the week before the election of December 3, 1978; an example is to be found on p. D-19 of *El Nacional,* November 26, 1978.

[38] Consejo Supremo Electoral, *Ley del sufragio,* arts. 112 (7), 120, 121, 125.

of maintaining order can enter a polling place carrying a weapon only if called in by the officials of the *mesa*. On election day liquor stores must remain closed, no public meetings or demonstrations are permitted, and no other event that might interfere with the electoral process can be held. Theaters and other places of public entertainment must remain closed until 6 P.M. The transporting of voters in government-owned vehicles on election day is prohibited unless done by election boards.[39]

Counting the Votes. As soon as the polls have closed the president of the *mesa electoral* announces that the counting of the votes is about to begin. At least three members of the *mesa* must be present, and also the two witnesses it has appointed. If the witnesses are not present to observe the counting, the *mesa* members must appoint replacements. All parties or groups that nominated candidates have the right to have their own witnesses present at every stage of the vote-counting and vote-totaling process, and the proceedings themselves must be public. After making sure that the strip of paper sealing the ballot box has not been broken, the *mesa* members open the box, take out the ballots, and count them. The number of ballots must tally with the number of persons recorded on the *mesa*'s list of those who voted.[40]

Next, the board eliminates spoiled ballots and null votes. A ballot is invalid if it appears to be mutilated or if it does not have the *mesa*'s identifying stamp on the back. No vote can be counted for any presidential candidate if the voter has not stamped "CSE" on the large card, nor can a vote be recorded for any list of legislative candidates if no small card has been stamped. A vote for president is invalid if the voter stamps more than one large card, unless all the cards stamped are those of parties or groups that have nominated the same candidate. In that case one vote is recorded for the candidate, rather than for any of the parties or groups. Similarly, a vote for legislative candidates is null if two or more small cards have been stamped; however, if both or all of them are the cards of parties or groups that have formed a coalition and nominated identical lists of candidates, then a vote is recorded for the party of the coalition that has obtained the largest number of votes.

The counting of valid votes then takes place. First to be counted are the votes cast for each party's presidential candidate. When this operation is finished, the results are announced to all present in the

[39] Ibid., arts. 127-129.
[40] Ibid., arts. 130, 131 (1, 2), 139.

polling place and entered in the official record of election results. Next, the *mesa* members count the votes cast for each party's slate of legislative candidates, announce the results, and enter them into the record. The final tally sets forth the valid-vote and null-vote totals for the presidential contest and also for that of the legislators. The members of the *mesa* and the witnesses then place their signatures on the record, along with any observations or reservations they may wish to express. Finally, each *mesa* sends the original of the election-returns record to the CSE, and a copy of that document and all other official papers to its corresponding municipal election board.[41]

Each municipal board adds up the results from all of the polling places and sends the totals to its corresponding district board and also, by the fastest means possible, to the CSE and to the Principal Election Board of its state, territory, or Federal District.

Each principal board determines the total votes cast throughout its jurisdiction for the presidential candidate of each party, group, or coalition and likewise the total votes cast for their respective legislative candidates. It then sends its official record of the presidential election to the CSE. As for the total votes cast for legislative candidates, the principal board determines from them the allocation of seats in the legislative bodies among the parties or groups that nominated candidates. It makes that determination by applying the proportional-representation formula discussed above and then proclaims the results of the contests for the legislative bodies within its jurisdiction.[42]

The Supreme Electoral Council determines the total number of votes cast for the presidential candidates of all parties and groups and officially proclaims the winner—an action that it must take within twenty days of the election. After checking the returns received from all electoral boards for all offices, the CSE orders the election results to be published in the *Official Gazette* of the Republic of Venezuela within ten days of its proclamation of the elected candidates.[43]

Participation of the Armed Forces in the Electoral Process. Although members of the armed forces on active duty cannot vote, the four military services (army, navy, aviation, and national guard) play a not inconsiderable role in Venezuelan elections. In the first place, in recent elections the military establishment has strongly endorsed the

---

[41] Ibid., arts. 131 (3, 8, 9), 132.
[42] Ibid., arts. 133-136, 144.
[43] Ibid., art. 140.

electoral process and publicly supported the efforts of the Supreme Electoral Council to ensure the holding of free, honest, and peaceful elections. On November 28, 1978, for example, a full-page advertisement appeared in newspapers throughout the country announcing the beginning of "Operation Republic," by means of which the armed forces would guarantee to all voters "free participation in an exemplary electoral process." On December 2, over a nationwide network of radio and television stations, the minister of defense pledged on behalf of the armed forces that the election would take place "in a climate of normality, of public confidence, and of respect for the right of all electors to cast their votes freely."[44]

Second, the armed forces are in fact responsible for protecting voters and election officials against any disruption of the electoral process. The Military High Command, consisting of the inspector general of the armed forces, the chief of the Joint Chiefs of Staff, and the commander of each service, stations personnel of the four services at voting centers throughout the country, at CSE headquarters in Caracas, at other public buildings in the capital, and at newspaper offices, radio and television stations, and other installations providing essential services, in Caracas and elsewhere. As noted above, however, they cannot enter a polling place bearing arms unless called in by the *mesa* itself. In 1978 military units took up their guard duties at 5 A.M. on December 1, more than forty-eight hours before the opening of the polls, and remained at their posts until after the polls were closed and the votes counted during the night of December 3.

A related responsibility of the military is that of transferring official forms, records, and materials from the Supreme Electoral Council to the voting centers and *mesas* before the election, and of returning the official election returns, completed forms, and record books from the *mesas* to the CSE as rapidly as possible after the election. The process of delivering sealed packages of election materials to the *mesas* prior to the 1978 election also began in the early hours of December 1. Most of those deliveries were made in army trucks. On December 3 and 4, however, the military made use of air transport whenever possible in delivering the official returns and other materials to the CSE. Most of the flights were in military aircraft, but the armed forces also used private planes that had been volunteered for that

[44] "Operación república" [Operation Republic], *El Informador* (Barquisimeto), November 28, 1978, p. B-9; "Mensaje del alto mando militar: normalidad y seguridad en el proceso electoral garantizan fuerzas armadas" [Message of the Military High Command: armed forces guarantee normality and security in the electoral process], *El Universal*, December 2, 1978, p. A-1.

purpose, along with pilots and copilots, by civilians who belonged to the Aero Club.[45]

Contested Elections. Any registered voter above the age of twenty-one, any political party, or any election board can challenge the validity of an election on one or more of the following grounds: (1) that the election permitted the victory of a candidate who did not comply with the eligibility requirements or other conditions set forth in the election law; (2) that fraud, bribery, perjury, or violence occurred during registration, voting, or vote counting; (3) that the *mesa electoral* held the election on a day different from that set by the CSE or at a place different from that designated by the election board having jurisdiction over the *mesa*; (4) that the members of the *mesa* prevented a voter from enjoying the guarantees that the law provides anyone exercising the suffrage; (5) that the *mesa* illegally constituted itself; (6) that violence directed against members of the *mesa* during the voting or the vote counting could have changed the election results; (7) that voters were coerced into abstaining or forced to vote against their will; (8) that the official reports of election results were prepared by unauthorized persons; and (9) that the official documents or records of the *mesa* were altered or destroyed.

The voter, party, or board challenging an election on any of these grounds must bring the case before the Supreme Court of Justice within thirty days after the publication of the election results in the *Official Gazette*. In the case of elections challenged under (1) above, however, charges can be brought at any time. If the court declares an election invalid, the CSE must call a new election within thirty days.[46]

Conclusion

Ever since the election of 1963, which went off peacefully despite prior threats of violent disruption by guerrilla forces, Venezuelans have been able to go to the polls with confidence. They know from experience that the election is almost certain to be orderly, free, and honest. Among the factors that have contributed to the institutionalization of

---

[45] Luis Rojas Vásquez, "Absoluta normalidad dentro del plan República IV" [Absolute normality within the Republic IV plan], *El Nacional*, December 2, 1978, p. D-1; Rómulo Rodríguez, "Comenzó la distribución del material electoral" [The distribution of electoral material began], *El Nacional*, December 2, 1978, p. D-2; "Ayer se inició la segunda fase de la operación 'República IV'" [Yesterday the second phase of Operation Republic IV began], *El Universal*, December 2, 1978, p. 1.

[46] Consejo Supremo Electoral, *Ley del sufragio*, arts. 170-176.

a democratic electoral process in Venezuela have been a now wide-spread public awareness of and support for democratic norms, the quiet presence of the military in the background on election day, and the effective work of the Supreme Electoral Council, the agency legally responsible for regulating the campaign and conducting the election. An additional factor is undoubtedly the electoral system itself, which the electorate seems to perceive as resulting in the equitable representation of large and small parties in the legislative bodies, national, state, and local. That system, essentially the d'Hondt method of proportional representation, is well entrenched in Venezuela, as it is in a number of other Latin American countries, despite its seeming complexity.

3

The Electorate

Robert E. O'Connor

Composition

In Venezuela the electorate is essentially synonymous with the adult population. Voting is compulsory and turnout runs well over 90 percent.[1] Since 33 percent of the population is in the lowest social class,[2] we may assume that close to 33 percent of the electorate also falls in that class. Unlike candidates in the United States, who must devote great efforts to encouraging their likely supporters to vote on election day,[3] Venezuelan candidates can count on their supporters' turning up at the polls. The virtual isomorphism between the electorate and the adult population also means that an analysis of differences in turnout

---

[1] Nonvoters are subject to fine and some constraints in dealing with the government bureaucracy. Although the efforts to enforce compulsory voting seem weak, the infrequency of elections and the mere existence of the law encourage high turnout. Baloyra and Martz report that, if the law did not exist, only half of the adult population would vote. See Enrique A. Baloyra and John D. Martz, *Political Attitudes in Venezuela: Societal Cleavages and Political Opinion* (Austin: University of Texas Press, 1979), p. 71.

[2] This figure comes from the work of the polling firm DATOS. See DATOS, *Tablas sobre ciertos aspectos de la opinión pública en Venezuela* [Tables concerning certain aspects of public opinion in Venezuela], September 1978, p. 3. For a discussion in English of the class typology, see Baloyra and Martz, *Political Attitudes in Venezuela*, pp. 231-33.

[3] If voting were compulsory in the United States, many more poor and working-class Americans, the adults least likely to vote now, would be seen at the polls. Since these less privileged Americans usually vote disproportionately for candidates of the Democratic party, laws enhancing turnout usually aid Democrats. If all eligible Americans had voted in 1976, Jimmy Carter's narrow victory would have become a landslide. (See Gerald M. Pomper et al., *The Election of 1976* [New York: David McKay, 1977], p. 61.) As it is, Democratic candidates are especially active in attempting to persuade their often alienated supporters to vote.

rates among segments of the Venezuelan population is neither necessary nor possible. Everybody votes.

Four demographic characteristics—regionalism, urbanness, age, and economic status—are important for an understanding of the Venezuelan electorate in 1978 and how that electorate had changed since Carlos Andrés Pérez's victory in 1973. The significance of regionalism is examined at length in chapter 8. Here two trends must be noted: the continued growth of the Center Region and the decline of sharp regional differences. The first trend involves disproportionate increases in population in the industrialized areas close to Caracas, which now contain some 39 percent of the nation's total vote.[4] One political implication of this boom in the Federal District (Caracas) and the states of Aragua, Carabobo, and Miranda was that no candidate could hope to win the presidency while losing this area by a wide margin. Piñerúa based his hope of doing well here on Carlos Andrés Pérez's victory in the Center Region, while Herrera placed his faith in the fact that this had been an area of *adeco* weakness before Pérez's day. Herrera aspired to a majority in the Center Region large enough to offset expected Piñerúa victories in rural areas.

The other trend, the decline of sharp regional differences, was seen in Pérez's triumph over Lorenzo Fernández in every state except Zulia in 1973. This was quite a change from 1958, when Rómulo Betancourt had been elected in spite of receiving only 16 percent of the vote in Caracas. Further evidence of a decline in regional differences came from polls during the Pérez administration reporting declines in *adeco* support in areas, such as the east, that traditionally had had overwhelming AD majorities. One political implication of this decline in regional differences was that in 1978 neither candidate had many places where he could count on rolling up huge majorities. At the same time, there were very few areas in which either a Piñerúa or a Herrera victory was totally unthinkable. Both parties would have to work hard everywhere for their votes.

Venezuela is becoming a nation of city dwellers. In 1950, 27 percent of the population lived in cities of over 100,000. In 1971 the census reported that this figure had climbed to 41 percent.[5] In 1978, the polling firm DATOS estimated that 48 percent of the population lived in cities of over 100,000; 13 percent lived in cities of between 25,000 and 100,000; 15 percent lived in villages of between 2,500 and

---

[4] Venezuela, Central Office of Statistics and Information, *1976 Anuario estadístico* [1976 statistical annual], January 1979, p. 16.

[5] Venezuela, Ministry of Development, *X censo de población* [Tenth population census].

TABLE 3–1
AGE OF THE VENEZUELAN ELECTORATE, 1973 AND 1978
(in percentages)

Age Group	1973	1978
17-24	25	28
25-34	25	27
35-44	20	17
45-54	14	13
55-64	9	8
65+	6	6
Total	100	100

NOTE: Columns do not add to totals because of rounding.
SOURCE: Central Office of Statistics and Information, *1976 Anuario estadístico*, p. 22; DATOS, *Tables sobre la opinión pública*, p. 3.

25,000 people; and only 25 percent of Venezuelans lived in hamlets of under 2,500.[6] One political implication of urbanization is that a successful campaign for the presidency must respond to the demands of city people. This has posed a particular danger for Acción Democrática, which was traditionally the party of the *campesinos*, the rural poor. Piñerúa still hoped to win the votes of the *campesinos*, but he knew he needed to do so without sacrificing the support of the more numerous city dwellers.

The 1978 electorate was young, even younger than that of 1973 (see Table 3–1). The largest single cohort was the youngest even though it covered only seven years rather than ten: in 1978, 28 percent of the electorate was between seventeen and twenty-five years of age. The political implications were obvious: a focus on the needs of senior citizens would net few votes, while concern with the needs of the young was essential. Since Venezuelans typically marry at an early age and become parents shortly afterwards, young couples probably composed the largest single group of voters.

Economic Profile of the Electorate. Oil has introduced large quantities of money into the country, but Venezuela is still a developing nation with large numbers of extremely poor citizens. Although Venezuela has the highest per capita income in Latin America, the average family still must scrimp along on an income that would be considered meager in the United States. The polling firm DATOS has devised a typology of classes illustrating the economic condition of the electorate, which

[6] DATOS, *Tablas sobre la opinión pública*, p. 1.

is summarized here.[7] At the head of each class listing is the percentage of the population DATOS estimated fell within the stated class in 1978.

- *Class A (under 1 percent)*. The very rich.
- *Class B (3 percent)*. These people are secure and affluent, but they lack the great wealth of Class A. They include second-level managers, proprietors, technicians, and civilian and military officials. Many of them are in banking, insurance, and finance. Unlike people in Class A, they tend to have only one expensive car; if they have two cars, the second is used or inexpensive.
- *Class C (24 percent)*. The middle class. These people enjoy responsible jobs, some luxuries, and a degree of affluence. They are managers of small enterprises, small merchants, employees of large firms, salaried workers in government, industry, and commerce. Always with limited initiative, they are not leaders in their fields. They live in small houses or in apartment buildings where we also find Class B and Class D. They may have one servant. Often they own a car and appliances. Their furniture is not luxurious, but they may be able to afford rents as high as $233 if more than one person in the family has income.
- *Class D (40 percent)*. The working class. These people are distinguished from Class C in that their responsibilities are very limited. They are less skilled and earn lower salaries, as street vendors, domestic servants, sanitation workers, factory operatives, and so on. They live in government housing, small homes in the hills, or makeshift shacks.
- *Class E (33 percent)*. The poor. People in Class D normally have jobs; those in Class E—whether through instability, old age, illness, or some other handicap—have no security whatsoever. If employed, they work as messengers, janitors, street vendors. Otherwise they are beggars.

This distribution of income posed a dilemma for Luis Piñerúa, the Acción Democrática candidate. Piñerúa might be tempted to point with pride to the accomplishments of his fellow *adeco*, President Carlos Andrés Pérez, but he was aware that Class E still comprised one-third

---

[7] See footnote 2. DATOS calls the five categories classes, although respondent self-assignment or class consciousness is not involved. In fact, these categories should be viewed more as economic strata than as classes. When Venezuelans were asked in 1973 to place themselves in a class, a majority placed themselves in the middle class. See Baloyra and Martz, *Political Attitudes in Venezuela*, p. 15. On the concept of class, see Raymond Centers, *The Psychology of Social Classes: A Study of Class Consciousness* (Princeton, N.J.: Princeton University Press, 1949).

of the population. The polls also told Piñerúa that, although conditions for the large working class (Class D) were improving, the conspicuous presence of much oil-related wealth was a cause of dissatisfaction. For both candidates, these findings mandated populist appeals aimed at the people of less than middle-class status who constituted the bulk of the electorate.

In summary, the Venezuelan electorate in 1978 was disproportionately located in the Center Region, urban, young, and working class or poor. Before turning to a review of the political expectations of this electorate, the omission of race from this list of demographic factors deserves to be explained. Race is not a significant factor in Venezuelan politics, not because the society is racially homogeneous, but because its racial heterogeneity is so extreme that bigotry might be difficult to practice. Centuries of intermarrying among blacks, Indians, Orientals, and whites have produced a society where racial antagonisms are negligible.

Political Expectations

There is a consensus in the electorate in support of procedural democracy, development, and a very active state. Each of these three areas of consensus helps to define the Venezuelan electorate.

The first, support for democratic procedures, is noteworthy in a part of the world where elected governments are the exception. Nevertheless, the evidence is overwhelming that Venezuelans neither long for the return of right-wing dictatorships nor seek solutions through one-party "people's" democracies. In the election of 1978 the two parties that sought the return of *perezjimenismo* received well under 1 percent of the vote. DATOS, in its September 1978 poll, found that only 7 percent of respondents thought a one-party system desirable in Venezuela, and only 20 percent agreed that the same party always should govern—seemingly a clear rejection of some *adecos'* hopes for "Mexicanization."[8] Sixty-one percent agreed that it is good for the country that opposition parties criticize the government's mistakes. An earlier survey found an even higher level of support, 77 percent, for criticism by opposition parties.[9] The earlier survey also found that 73 percent of Venezuelans were opposed to military coups, the customary manner of changing governments in many developing nations. This high level of support for democratic procedures is remarkable in a country with so many poor people, who

---

[8] DATOS, *Tablas sobre la opinión pública*, p. 65.
[9] Baloyra and Martz, *Political Attitudes in Venezuela*, p. 211.

might have been thought susceptible to antidemocratic proposals for reform. However, survey results demonstrate that in Venezuela the poor are at least as committed to democratic norms as are more fortunate sectors. [10]

Economic development also is supported by a broad consensus of Venezuelans. When asked whether the government should give priority to accelerating development, maintaining the democratic system, or redistributing wealth, 61 percent chose development,[11] including a majority of every economic stratum, even the poor. Finally, there is "a solid consensus on the need for a very active state."[12] In the United States, Jefferson's dictum "that government is best which governs least" has a great deal of support,[13] but in Venezuela "no class or stratum deviates much from the 84 percent of the population who identify the public sector as the more idoneous agent for the solution of contemporary national problems."[14] Sixty-three percent of the population even identifies the government as the most likely source of assistance in solving personal problems.[15] In light of this consensus on the need for an active government, it is hardly surprising that Venezuelan politicians do not promise to "get the government off the people's backs" or to "reduce government interference in our lives." Instead, they promise to make the government a more effective force in bringing about economic development and solving citizens' problems.

The Issues Confronting the Electorate in 1978

Politicans may announce that certain subjects will be the issues in a given campaign, but the public may have other matters on its mind. In 1978, Luis Herrera, the COPEI candidate, regularly attacked the Pérez administration for corruption, in which he tried to implicate Piñerúa. The AD candidate in turn adopted "Correcto," a word denoting uprightness, as his slogan and promised that there would be no *sinvergüenzas*, those without shame, in his administration. Clearly,

---

[10] Ibid., p. 48, and DATOS, *Tablas sobre la opinión pública*, p. 24. For the classic statement of the supposed antidemocratic tendencies of poor masses, see Seymour Martin Lipset, *Political Man; The Social Bases of Politics* (Garden City, N.Y.: Doubleday, 1959).

[11] Baloyra and Martz, *Political Attitudes in Venezuela*, p. 59.

[12] Ibid., p. 58.

[13] See, for example, H. Mark Roelofs, *Ideology and Myth in American Politics* (Boston: Little, Brown, 1976).

[14] Baloyra and Martz, *Political Attitudes in Venezuela*, p. 58.

[15] Ibid.

TABLE 3–2

Voters' Perceptions of Change in the Quality of Life, 1978 Campaign

(in percentages)

Compared with Five Years Ago Life Today Is:	Nationwide Gallup Survey	Mycon Survey in Lara	Mycon Survey in Monagas
Better	39	23	31
The same	26	49	39
Worse	35	28	30
Total	100	100	100
N	(1,997)	(1,802)	(845)

Note: Mycon is a polling firm organized by David J. Myers and Robert E. O'Connor and hired by Acción Democrática to conduct surveys in Lara in September 1978 and Monagas in October 1978. Details of the sampling methodology are available from the author.
Source: Mycon and *Auténtico*, June 5, 1978, p. 16.

administrative corruption was an issue to the extent that the candidates were eager to denounce it. Yet this is not evidence that the voters cared about government corruption. In fact, other concerns seemed more salient to the Venezuelan electorate.

One of the question asked by the pollsters was whether people felt life had improved in the last five years. Table 3–2 reports Mycon's findings for Lara, a state in the Western Region carried by Herrera, and Monagas, an eastern state carried by Piñerúa, as well as Gallup's for Venezuela as a whole. The groups who felt that life had either improved or remained the same range from 65 to 72 percent; this suggests that the electorate was neither likely to endorse with wild enthusiasm a continuation of government policies nor likely to favor risking radical changes intended to improve conditions. People who felt that their lives had improved presumably would have tended to attribute this improvement to the *adeco* administration and to favor a continuation of *adeco* policies under Piñerúa. Conversely, people who felt that their lives had deteriorated presumably would have tended to favor change. In fact, as Table 3–3 reports, the percentage of voters intending to vote for Piñerúa declines as the belief that life has improved declines. Voters who considered themselves worse off than they had been five years before were less likely to support the *adeco* candidate than were voters who considered themselves better off.

TABLE 3-3

INTENDED VOTE FOR PRESIDENT, BY PERCEPTION OF CHANGE IN
THE QUALITY OF LIFE, 1978

(in percentages)

Intended Vote for President	Compared with Five Years Ago, Life Today Is:		
	Better	The same	Worse
Piñerúa (AD)	60	37	14
Herrera (COPEI)	16	27	48
The left	3	7	9
Other	1	2	2
Undecided[a]	19	27	26
Total	100	100	100
N	(654)	(1,188)	(748)

NOTE: Columns may not add to totals because of rounding.

[a] Here and in subsequent tables, this entry includes undecided respondents, non-voters, and those who intended to spoil their ballots. Most of the respondents in this category were undecided.

SOURCE: Mycon.

The relationship reported in Table 3-3 suggests that whether the quality of life was improving was a campaign issue for Venezuelan voters. If Piñerúa could convince more voters that their lives had become better over the past five years, presumably he would increase his proportion of the vote; similarly, Herrera would do better if he could convince voters that their lives had become worse under the *adecos*. As the two chapters on the AD and COPEI campaigns show, both parties paid great attention to this issue. The Government of Carlos Andrés Pérez unleashed an enormous advertising campaign using the slogans "Step by step we are doing the government's work" and "I am better off today." In contrast, COPEI proclaimed "Enough!" and "Venezuela has the wealth; Luis Herrera has the will," implying that Herrera would use the oil money to improve people's lives.[16] The results on election day suggest that more voters believed that their lives would improve more under the leadership of Luis Herrera than under another *adeco* administration.

---

[16] In Spanish these slogans are: "Paso a paso se cumple la acción del gobierno," "Hoy vivo mejor," "¡Ya basta!" and "Venezuela tiene la riqueza; Luis Herrera tiene la voluntad." The "paso a paso" slogan was followed in the advertisements by statistics showing advances such as increases in vegetable production and decreases in unemployment. One Caracas cynic painted a wall with his view: "Paso a paso somos un fracaso"—step by step, we are heading for disaster.

TABLE 3–4

PROBLEMS PERCEIVED AS VERY GRAVE BY VOTERS IN
LARA AND MONAGAS, 1978

	Lara		Monagas	
Problem	Percentage	Rank	Percentage	Rank
High cost of living	68	2	61	1
Housing shortages	61	4	55	3
Shortages of goods	60	5	51	4
Delinquency	63	3	47	5
Administrative corruption	48	11	39	10
Lack of medical services	57	6	41	8
Unemployment	49	10	45	6
Weaknesses in the educational system	40	12	27	12
Living conditions of the poor	74	1	56	2
Lack of public services such as water, light, garbage	51	9	39	10
Illegal aliens	33	13	27	12
Abandoned children	54	7	40	9
Lack of transportation, roads, mass transit	52	8	43	7

NOTE: Respondents were presented with the list of problems and asked to classify each as not grave, somewhat grave, very grave, or extremely grave. Responses in the last two categories are combined in the percentages given here. N varies from 634 to 811 for Monagas and from 1,464 to 1,831 for Lara according to the number of "don't know" responses excluded.
SOURCE: Mycon.

The Gallup organization followed up its question about whether life had improved by asking why things had become better or worse. The only response mentioned by at least 10 percent of respondents was inflation; 26 percent said that inflation had made their lives worse.[17] Other evidence also suggests that inflation was a significant issue. Table 3–4 gives the percentages of respondents who judged a number of problems to be very grave. In both Lara and Monagas the

[17] Gallup ran the survey for *Auténtico*, June 5, 1978, p. 19.

high cost of living was judged either the most or the second most serious of the thirteen problems listed.[18]

This evidence that Venezuelans were concerned with the high cost of living is still not grounds for concluding that inflation was an important issue determining how people would vote in 1978. After all, neither Herrera nor Piñerúa argued in favor of inflation, and their public statements on how they would treat the problem were similar and/or vague.[19] It is possible to conceive that voters felt the matter to be important yet could not differentiate between the positions of Piñerúa and Herrera, so based their votes on other issues. Figure 3–1 shows, however, that concern with the cost of living correlated with voting intentions. Of the voters who felt that the high cost of living was not a very grave problem, 52 percent planned to vote for Piñerúa; of the voters who viewed the problem as very grave, only 28 percent planned to vote for the *adeco* candidate. Conversely, only 19 percent of the voters less upset about the high cost of living intended to vote for Herrera, while 36 percent of those more upset about it planned to vote for Herrera. Among the first group of voters, Piñerúa beat Herrera by thirty-three percentage points; among the second group, Herrera was ahead by eight percentage points. One can hypothesize that, if fewer people had been upset about the high cost of living, Piñerúa would have won the election.

This concern with the cost of living is not a new development in Venezuela. In 1973 Baloyra and Martz asked voters what was the most important national problem.[20] Thirty-eight percent named the high cost of living. The next most frequently listed problems were unemployment (18 percent) and weaknesses in the educational system (10 percent). The decline in importance of these issues by 1978 may reflect both the Pérez administration's success in reducing unemployment and strengthening the educational system and the rising concern with housing shortages, crime, and poverty.

Besides confirming that inflation was an important issue, Table 3–4 provides four noteworthy bits of information concerning the Venezuelan electorate. First, the rankings of the issues in Lara, a

---

[18] Respondents were asked if each problem was *no grave, algo grave, muy grave,* or *gravísimo* (not grave, somewhat grave, very grave, or extremely grave). In this analysis—text, table, and figures—the responses have been dichotomized by combining the first two and second two categories.

[19] The Vietnam issue had a very similar effect in the presidential election of 1968 in the United States. See Benjamin I. Page and Richard A. Brody, "Policy Voting and the Electoral Process: The Vietnam War Issue," *American Political Science Review*, vol. 66 (September 1972), pp. 979-95.

[20] Baloyra and Martz, *Political Attitudes in Venezuela*, p. 216.

FIGURE 3–1
VOTING INTENTIONS AND VIEWS ON COST OF LIVING,
LARA AND MONAGAS, FALL 1978

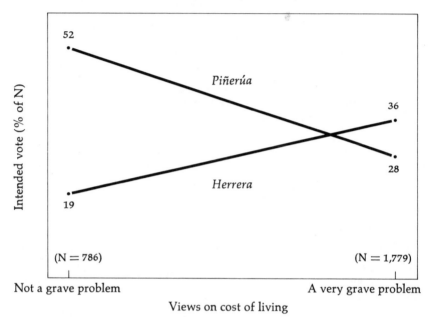

SOURCE: Mycon.

strong Herrera state in the west, and Monagas, a strong Piñerúa state
in the more traditional east, are almost identical. In both states poverty
and inflation are the problems seen as most severe and weaknesses in
the educational system and illegal aliens are the problems seen as the
least so. This is additional evidence of the breakdown of regional
differences.

Second, the percentages of respondents viewing each problem as
very grave are lower in Monagas than in Lara. This may be accounted
for by two factors: the greater reluctance of the *adeco* region to con-
demn the state of the nation during an *adeco* administration, and the
greater prevalence of fatalism in the more traditional east. Fatalists
presumably are less willing than others to judge any problem extremely
grave since for them the world always drifts along on a roughly even
keel. Lara, the more modern region, considered fewer problems only
moderately pressing.[21]

[21] A relationship between fatalism, a low expectation of change, and reluctance

Third, the living conditions of the poor ranked either first or second of the thirteen problems. In the United States, the cultural tradition usually places moral guilt on the poor for being poor, a form of blaming the victim,[22] but in Venezuela concern for the poor seemed widespread. Again, widespread concern about a problem need not make it an issue in a campaign; obviously, neither Herrera nor Piñerúa came out in favor of poverty. Figure 3–2 suggests, however, that concern with the living conditions of the poor was an issue. The Piñerúa vote drops from 49 percent among those who did not feel this to be a grave problem to 31 percent among those who did. While this eighteen-percentage-point drop is not as great as the twenty-four percentage points we found in the case of the cost of living, it is still substantial. Similarly, the increase in the Herrera vote, from 23 percent to 34 percent, is not as large as the seventeen-percentage-point increase for the cost-of-living issue, but it is marked. Among voters not as concerned about poverty, Piñerúa would have won a landslide victory, 49 percent to 23 percent; among voters very concerned about poverty, Herrera would have narrowly defeated Piñerúa, 34 percent to 31 percent.

Fourth, Table 3–4 suggests that administrative corruption may not have been as important an issue as some *adeco* leaders feared. Respondents in both Lara and Monagas ranked it near the bottom of the list; only weaknesses in the educational system and illegal aliens ranked lower. Nevertheless, substantial minorities (48 and 39 percent) found administrative corruption to be a grave or very grave problem. Since this is one problem which might be blamed entirely on the *adecos*, one might reasonably hypothesize that it would clearly divide AD and COPEI supporters. Figure 3–3 shows that this is only partly the case. Herrera scored better among those who considered corruption a very grave problem (36 percent) than among those who

---

to view problems as extremely grave may be found in industrialized democracies as well as in developing nations. See Peter Lupsha, "Explanation of Political Violence: Some Psychological Theories versus Indignation," *Politics and Society*, vol. 2 (Fall 1971), pp. 89-104; and Bernard N. Gorfman and Edward N. Muller, "The Strange Case of Relative Gratification and Potential for Political Violence: The V-Curve Hypothesis," *American Political Science Review*, vol. 67 (June 1973), pp. 514-39.

[22] For discussions of the ideological and psychological roots of lack of concern for the poor, see William Ryan, *Blaming the Victim* (New York: Pantheon, 1971); Roelofs, *Ideology and Myth*; Joe R. Feagin, "America's Welfare Stereotypes," *Social Science Quarterly*, vol. 52 (March 1972), pp. 921-33; and Joel F. Handler, *Reforming the Poor: Welfare Policy, Federalism, and Morality* (New York: Basic Books, 1972). For survey data on attitudes toward the poor, see Joe R. Feagin, *Subordinating the Poor: Welfare and American Beliefs* (Englewood Cliffs, N.J.: Prentice-Hall, 1975).

FIGURE 3–2
Voting Intentions and Views on Poverty, Lara and Monagas, Fall 1978

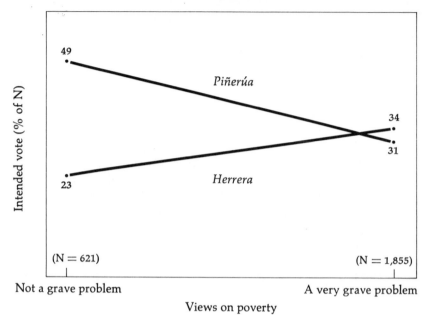

Source: Mycon.

did not (27 percent). Piñerúa, conversely, did better among those who were less concerned about corruption (43 percent) than those concerned with the problem (30 percent). However, these differences are not as great as the differences involving the issues of inflation and poverty. In light of the finding that only a minority of voters viewed the problem of administrative corruption as very grave, Herrera's margin (36 percent to 30 percent) among this group of voters is decidedly less significant than his similar margins among voters concerned about inflation and poverty. Perhaps the Piñerúa campaign was successful in its efforts to separate Piñerúa from the scandals of the Pérez administration.

Mycon also attempted to determine what issues were salient to voters by asking an open-ended question: "What are the principal problems which affect the people here?" Twenty-nine percent of the respondents mentioned problems with water, which is provided by INOS, the state-run water company. As Figure 3–4 shows, however, voters who said that water was a problem did not differ significantly

FIGURE 3-3

VOTING INTENTIONS AND VIEWS ON ADMINISTRATIVE CORRUPTION,
LARA AND MONAGAS, FALL 1978

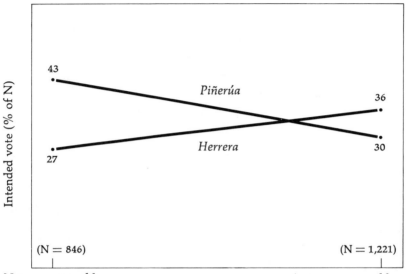

SOURCE: Mycon.

from voters who failed to mention water problems in their voting
intentions. The slight differences reported, although consistent with
the expectation that citizens who mentioned water as a problem would
be more likely to blame the *adecos* than anyone else, are within the
range of sampling error. The frequent interruptions of the water
supply in both Lara and Monagas did not become an issue separating
Piñerúa supporters from Herrera backers.

Up to this point we have seen that three issues—the quality of
life, the cost of living, and the living conditions of the poor—divide
Piñerúa's supporters from Herrera's. A fourth matter, administrative
corruption, also separates them, though less strongly than the other
three. In each instance the optimists, those who felt that their lives
had improved and that the cost of living, the living conditions of the
poor, and administrative corruption were not very grave problems, indicated an intention to vote for Luis Piñerúa by a large margin. Pessi-
mists supported Luis Herrera, although the gaps between the two
were not large. The similarity in the findings for the three issues

FIGURE 3–4
VOTING INTENTIONS AND MENTION OF WATER AS A PROBLEM, LARA AND MONAGAS, FALL 1978

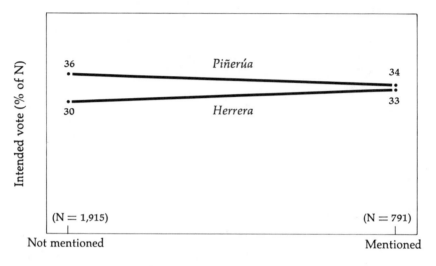

SOURCE: Mycon.

suggests that they may be subsumed under the overarching issue, satisfaction with the *adeco* administration of Carlos Andrés Pérez. Perhaps negative evaluations of change in one's own life, of inflation, and of poverty reflected dissatisfaction with the performance of the Pérez administration. If so, Piñerúa should have run very well among respondents with a high opinion of Pérez and very poorly among respondents with negative feelings toward him.

The correlation charted in Figure 3–5 suggests that holding Carlos Andrés Pérez in high esteem was tantamount to supporting Piñerúa and, conversely, that having no sympathy at all for the president meant rejecting Piñerúa. Among voters with high regard for Pérez, 76 percent expressed a preference for Piñerúa; among voters with low regard for Pérez, only a minuscule 3 percent said they were planning on voting for Piñerúa. Of the issues considered here, the electorate's evaluation of Carlos Andrés Pérez was that most capable of separating Herrera supporters from Piñerúa supporters.

This was good news for Piñerúa only to the extent that voters held Carlos Andrés Pérez in high esteem. Doing well among Pérez aficionados and poorly among other Venezuelans would win the election only if Pérez's supporters outnumbered his detractors. Fortunately for

FIGURE 3–5
Voting Intentions and Sympathy for Carlos Andres Perez, Lara and Monagas, Fall 1978

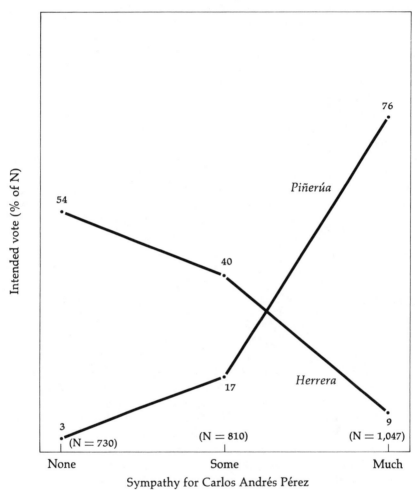

Source: Mycon.

Piñerúa, the largest category of voters, comprising 40 percent of the electorate, was that of Pérez supporters, while only 28 percent had no sympathy at all for the president. This distribution accounts for Piñerúa's lead, 54 percent to 46 percent, over Herrera in Mycon's two-party voting-intention surveys of September and October (see Table 3–6).

TABLE 3–5

COMPUTATION OF ADJUSTED TWO-PARTY VOTE, ESTIMATED FOR PINERUA

| | Sympathy for Carlos Andrés Pérez | | | Total Electorate |
	None	Some	Much	
A. Intended vote for Piñerúa, percentage of total	3	17	76	—
B. Intended vote for Piñerúa, percentage of two-party vote	5	30	90	—
C. Percentage of total electorate	28	31	40	100
D. Contribution to Piñerúa vote total	1.5	9.3	35.8	47

NOTE: Row D is row B multiplied by row C, to arrive at the contribution of each level of support for Pérez to the percentage of the total two-party vote attained by Piñerúa. Thus, 5 percent of the voters in the no-sympathy category intended to vote for Piñerúa. Since this category comprises 28 percent of the electorate, its contribution to Piñerúa's percentage of the total two-party vote is 1.5 percent.
SOURCE: Mycon.

Portents of defeat for Piñerúa, however, also lurk in the data graphed in Figure 3–5. Of the Pérez aficionados, 85 percent stated an intention to vote for either Herrera or Piñerúa. Only 15 percent of the voters in this category were supporting other candidates or were undecided. Since most voters in this category had made up their minds, there were few undecided votes for Piñerúa to pick up on election day. In contrast, in the two other categories, only 57 percent of the voters indicated intentions to vote for either of the two major party candidates; 43 percent were undecided or supporting other candidates. Thus, *the bulk of the undecided voters were in categories wherein the voters who had already made up their minds supported Luis Herrera by large margins.*

Table 3–5 presents the calculations by which the Mycon results were adjusted to take into account the probable choices of undecided voters. The assumption was that on election day the non-major-party and undecided voters in each category would divide their votes between the major-party candidates in the same proportions as the voters who reported definite intentions to vote for Piñerúa or Herrera. Thus, among voters with no sympathy at all for Carlos Andrés Pérez, 3 percent were for Piñerúa and 54 percent for Herrera. If all the votes had gone to only these two candidates, the results would have become 5 percent for Piñerúa and 95 percent for Herrera. In the middle category of respondents, those with some sympathy for Pérez,

30 percent were projected Piñerúa voters; and, in the category of Pérez aficionados, Piñerúa could expect to garner fully 90 percent of the vote. If the populace had been equally divided among the three categories, the average of Piñerúa's percentages in the three categories could be taken as an overall estimation of his vote. However, since the populace was not equally divided, Piñerúa's percentages, reported in row B, were multiplied by the percentages of the population in each category to produce a weighted average. These percentages, reported in row D, were summed to produce a new estimate of Piñerúa's proportion of the two-party vote.

Table 3–6 compares the results of the Mycon poll in Lara and Monagas with the actual results in the two states and in the nation as a whole. The straight Mycon findings, with third-party and undecided voters excluded, show Piñerúa the victor with 54 percent of the two-party vote. However, when third-party and undecided voters are taken into account, Piñerúa moves from winner to loser. The projected 47 percent of the two-party vote for Piñerúa is exactly his actual percentage of the two-party vote in Lara and Monagas and is close to the 48 percent of the two-party vote he garnered nationwide.

The findings of Figure 3–5 and Table 3–6 suggest four conclusions. First, they confirm the validity of Mycon's polling results. All of the major polling firms were consistent in showing Piñerúa slightly ahead.[23] When these findings were used to project a Piñerúa victory, the firms were in error not because their sampling frames were bad but because they probably assumed that undecided voters would vote more or less the same way as decided voters, taken overall. If the analysts had realized how strongly most undecided voters disapproved of Pérez and how closely such disapproval correlated with voting against Piñerúa, they probably would have realized that the *adeco* candidate was in trouble.

Second, when the results from Lara and Monagas are combined, the totals are very similar to the actual national totals. If Lara and Monagas had had preferences very different from those of Venezuela as a whole, the validity of much of the previous analysis, based primarily on Mycon data from Lara and Monagas, would be suspect. Instead, we can comfortably assert that the Lara/Monagas-based analyses are unlikely to differ substantially from what national survey analyses would have shown.

---

[23] Luis Baez Duarte, a top strategist of Acción Democrática, appeared on television shortly before the election with a survey of all the surveys. All of them showed Piñerúa the victor in a close race.

TABLE 3-6

Two-Party Voting Results and Survey Projections,
Lara and Monagas, 1978

(in percentages)

	Mycon Projections		Election Returns (two-party vote)	
	Lara and Monagas	Adjusted, Lara and Monagas	Lara and Monagas	Venezuela
Luis Piñerúa Ordaz	54	47	47	48
Luis Herrera Campíns	46	53	53	52
Total	100	100	100	100

Note: For method, see text and table 3-5.
Source: Author's calculations from Mycon data; official election returns.

Third, the Pérez-appreciation factor was very powerful as a predictor of the behavior of the Venezuelan electorate. Not only does it correlate with support for Herrera or Piñerúa more strongly than other issues, but for respondents not committed to either candidate it produces an accurate prediction of the election results: almost all of Pérez's supporters voted for Piñerúa and very few of his detractors favored the *adeco* candidate. Piñerúa did not establish a strong, separate identity capable of attracting voters disenchanted with Carlos Andrés Pérez. Limited mostly to Pérez supporters, Piñerúa lost to Herrera, who was able to forge a diverse coalition of COPEI and other voters united mostly by their desire to defeat the candidate of Acción Democrática, the party of Carlos Andrés Pérez.

Fourth, voters reported as undecided in the preelection polls cast their ballots decisively for Luis Herrera. Among voters who strongly supported either major party candidate, Piñerúa won a majority. If more of the less committed voters had either voted for Piñerúa or chosen minor party candidates, Herrera would have lost.

There is irony in these results. The reader might assume that Pérez was a very unpopular president and politician. Table 3–7 tells us, however, that Carlos Andrés Pérez was the most popular politician in Venezuela at the time of the Mycon surveys in Lara and Monagas. What this table also shows is that no politician commanded enthusiasm from a majority of Venezuelans. Carlos Andrés Pérez provided Piñerúa with a strong base of supporters, but not enough to win with-

TABLE 3–7

POPULAR SUPPORT FOR VENEZUELAN POLITICIANS, LARA AND
MONAGAS, FALL 1978

(in percentages)

	No Sympathy	Some Sympathy	Much Sympathy	Total (N)
Carlos Andrés Pérez (AD)	28	31	40	100 (2,591)
Luis Piñerúa Ordaz (AD)	41	22	37	100 (2,488)
Luis Herrera Campíns (COPEI)	46	24	31	100 (2,469)
Rómulo Betancourt (AD)	43	31	26	100 (2,420)
Rafael Caldera (COPEI)	35	32	33	100 (2,490)

NOTE: Figures may not add to totals because of rounding.
SOURCE: Mycon.

out support from other voters. Piñerúa's failure to expand this base
and Herrera's skill at attracting floating voters account for the latter's
victory.[24]

Herrera did not win because he was more popular as a candidate
than Piñerúa. Table 3–7 demonstrates, on the contrary, that the
voters seemed slightly more sympathetic to Piñerúa than to Herrera.
Table 3–8 presents citizens' responses to questions dealing with the
personal characteristics of the candidates. Although Herrera supporters often disagreed with Piñerúa supporters in their evaluations
of the candidates, the overall profiles of the candidates are very similar.
On only two characteristics, accelerating development and favoring
the rich, do differences in their ratings as large as five percentage points
emerge. In both of these instances Piñerúa was viewed more favorably
than Herrera. Herrera won because a majority of voters saw him as
the only viable alternative to continued *adeco* control, not because
they preferred him personally to Luis Piñerúa.

[24] Many of the Herrera advertisements referred to him as the "national candidate"
rather than the "COPEI candidate." In advertisements showing the candidates
side by side, the "national candidate" was contrasted to the "candidate of Acción
Democrática."

TABLE 3–8

ASSESSMENT OF CANDIDATES' PERSONAL QUALITIES, VOTERS
IN LARA AND MONAGAS, FALL 1978
(in percentages)

	Respondents Agreeing	
The Candidate Is:	Herrera	Piñerúa
Capable and intelligent	67	65
A man with high moral principles	67	66
A nationalist	65	67
A man who speaks for the people	62	66
A man who will accelerate development	55	61
Calm, level-headed	63	65
Ready to fight for social justice	58	61
Ready to guarantee personal security	57	61
Energetic	61	63
Able to defend the international interests of the country	59	63
Disposed to favor the rich	58	51
A man who thinks before acting	64	66
A good leader of the country	61	64
A man who will throw the thieves out of government	40	43

NOTE: N varies from 1,758 to 2,135. "Don't know" responses are excluded.
SOURCE: Mycon.

Table 3–9 illustrates the effect of party identification on voting intentions.[25] Both major-party candidates, but especially Herrera, were adept at keeping defections from their own party to a minimum. Eight-five percent of *adecos* had already decided to stick with Piñerúa, and 90 percent of COPEI identifiers were lined up behind Herrera. This table also shows the large numbers of voters who did not hold much sympathy for any party; fully 27 percent of the electorate fell into this category. Acción Democrática was indeed the largest party; 34 percent of the citizens expressed great sympathy for AD alone. However, 34 percent is not a majority of the electorate. COPEI, with

[25] To ascertain party identification interviewers asked respondents if they were party members or sympathizers and how much sympathy they had for each party. Respondents were coded as identifiers if they cited membership in a party or if they expressed a great deal of sympathy or much sympathy for a party. Those who expressed a great deal of sympathy or much sympathy for more than one party were coded as identifiers with more than one party.

TABLE 3–9

Voting Intentions and Party Identification, Lara and Monagas, Fall 1978

(in percentages)

Intended Vote	AD	COPEI	Left	AD and Left	AD and COPEI	COPEI and Left	Other, No Party
Luis Piñerúa	85	1	10	73	47	0	12
Luis Herrera	4	90	5	5	33	86	14
The left	0	0	66	8	5	9	4
Other	0	1	3	3	2	0	4
Undecided	11	8	16	13	14	6	67
Total	100	100	100	100	100	100	100
N	(928)	(641)	(204)	(40)	(66)	(91)	(736)

NOTE: To ascertain party identification interviewers asked respondents if they were party members or sympathizers and how much sympathy they had for each party. Respondents were coded as identifiers if they cited membership in a party or if they expressed a great deal of sympathy or much sympathy for a party. Those who expressed a great deal of sympathy for more than one party were coded as identifiers with more than one party. Columns may not add to totals because of rounding.
SOURCE: Mycon.

24 percent of the electorate, could combine with other non-*adeco* elements to forge such a majority. In 1978, the nonidentifiers who had not made up their minds at the time of the Mycon polls comprised 18 percent of the electorate. The majority of these voters, disenchanted with Carlos Andrés Pérez, probably voted for Herrera, enabling him to win the presidency.

A final bit of information on the candidates can be obtained through the use of "normal vote" analysis to determine if Piñerúa was running as well as an *adeco* candidate should have been expected to run and if Herrera was running ahead of or behind his expected COPEI vote.[26] This technique consists of computing expected voting percentages within categories of voters on the assumption that all of the major-party identifiers in the category will vote for their party's

---

[26] This technique was first used by Philip E. Converse, "The Concept of a Normal Vote," in Angus Campbell, Philip E. Converse, Warren E. Miller, and Donald E. Stokes, *Elections and the Political Order* (New York: Wiley, 1966), pp. 9-39. A later application, again in the context of presidential elections in the United States, is Richard W. Boyd, "Popular Control of Public Policy: A Normal Vote Analysis of the 1968 Election," *American Political Science Review*, vol. 66 (June 1972), pp. 429-49.

candidate. If the observed percentages, the voting intentions reported in the surveys, are lower in any category, the candidate has failed to draw his "normal" vote in the category. For example, Figure 3–6 relates the normal vote to sympathy for Carlos Andrés Pérez, the

FIGURE 3–6
RELATION BETWEEN "NORMAL" AND INTENDED VOTE AND SYMPATHY FOR CARLOS ANDRES PEREZ, LARA AND MONAGAS, FALL 1978

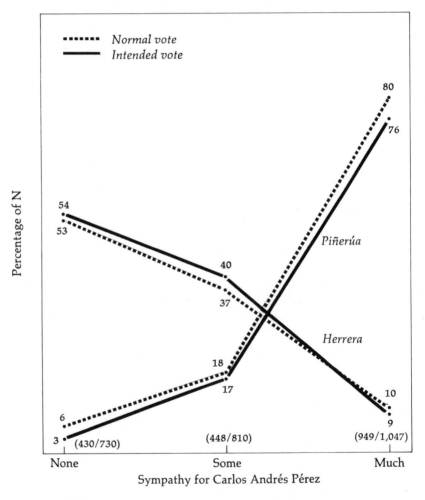

NOTE: For each sympathy category, the number of respondents is given in parentheses; the N on which the "normal" vote is based is listed first. For further explanation, see text.

SOURCE: Mycon.

issue most strongly dividing Herrera supporters from Piñerúa voters. The figure also shows the voting intentions reported in Figure 3–5. Eighty percent of the respondents with much sympathy for Pérez were *adecos*, so Piñerúa should have done very well indeed in this category. Conversely, only 10 percent of the voters very sympathetic to Pérez were COPEI identifiers, so Herrera's poor showing in this category comes as no surprise. A comparison of the normal vote with the intended vote for Piñerúa on this variable shows that Piñerúa was not losing *adeco* support because of the electorate's evaluation of Pérez. In no category is the difference between Piñerúa's expected vote and his observed vote even five percentage points. Similarly, the lines representing Herrera's expected vote and his observed vote are almost on top of one another. Herrera was not running ahead of the percentages one would expect any COPEI candidate to obtain.

Normal vote analysis was performed on every issue discussed in this section. In no instance did a difference of five percentage points or more between the intended vote and the normal vote appear for either Piñerúa or Herrera. Thus, the role of issues, including the Pérez-appreciation factor, was to produce changes in party identification. Few *adecos* disgruntled with their party continued to identify with Acción Democrática while supporting a non-*adeco* candidate or reporting themselves undecided in their voting intentions. Instead, disgruntled *adecos* left their party.[27] Similarly, most disgruntled COPEI identifiers, rather than keep their COPEI party identification while supporting other candidates, left the party either to join another or to identify with none. In the United States, major-party identifiers sometimes vote against their party's presidential candidate while still considering themselves good Democrats or good Republicans. This pattern was particularly common among Republicans who supported the Democrat Johnson in 1964 and among Democrats who supported the Republican Nixon in 1972. However, in Venezuela it is difficult to consider oneself a good *adeco* or a good *copeyano* while supporting the other party's presidential candidate. First, personalism is stronger in Venezuela. The parties are closely identified with their leaders. Second, the presidential nature of the Venezuelan political system ensures that the party which controls the presidency controls the nation. Venezuela's federalism is weak—the president appoints the governors of the states—and the executive branch of government dominates the other branches. There is at best a weak civil service.

---

[27] The Mycon survey found that 25 percent of the voters who reported supporting Pérez in 1973 did not intend to vote for Piñerúa and did not identify with Acción Democrática.

With all this power in the hands of the president, one cannot be a party allegiant while contributing to the party's loss of the presidency.

Why then is the Pérez-appreciation factor so significant? Clearly the answer is not that *adecos* dissatisfied with Pérez failed to vote for Piñerúa, because this simply is not the case. Only 6 percent of those with no sympathy at all for Pérez were *adecos*, and half of them still planned to vote for Piñerúa. The significance of the Pérez factor is that it polarized the electorate: generally speaking, voters were either Pérez supporters or Pérez detractors. The supporters, almost all of whom were *adecos*, voted for Piñerúa. The detractors voted for either Herrera or minor party candidates. With no minor party candidate mounting a serious challenge to AD and COPEI, voters who wanted to sweep the *adecos* out of power had no real option but to vote for Herrera. This explains why Herrera, a candidate with less personal popularity than Piñerúa and still less than Carlos Andrés Pérez, won the election.

The final issue of any campaign is the candidates. Luis Piñerúa's flaw was his inability to forge his own identity separate from that of Acción Democrática and Carlos Andrés Pérez. An old *adeco* warhorse, Piñerúa failed to engender enthusiasm in non-*adecos*, especially the young. Similarly, Luis Herrera failed to engender enthusiasm among voters who did not identify with COPEI, but he was able to garner many non-COPEI votes by presenting himself as the catchall candidate of opposition to AD. Many may not have liked Herrera any more than Piñerúa, but a vote for Herrera was a vote to replace the Government with new faces. For the instrumental voter, it was the only way of contributing to change.

Bases of Support

This description of the role of issues in the election has not involved a discussion of the socioeconomic bases of the candidates' support. Table 3–10 presents a breakdown of voting intentions within the economic strata discussed earlier in this chapter. The distribution of the sample is close to the DATOS population estimates reported earlier; the poorest group, Class E, is underrepresented and the richest group, Classes A and B, is overrepresented in the Mycon data, but these sampling divergences should not affect the validity of intergroup comparisons. Three findings appear noteworthy.

First, intergroup differences are not great. Both AD and COPEI claimed to represent the interests of all classes, of all Venezuelans, and each succeeded in attracting large segments of every group to its

TABLE 3–10

VOTING INTENTIONS AND ECONOMIC STRATUM, LARA AND
MONAGAS, FALL 1978

(in percentages)

Intended Vote	Economic Stratum			
	A and B Upper	C Middle	D Working	E Poor
Luis Herrera Campíns	25	33	30	28
Luis Piñerúa Ordaz	45	34	34	40
The left	8	8	6	3
Other	1	2	2	0
Undecided	21	24	27	28
Total	100	100	100	100
N	(177)	(789)	(1,256)	(413)

NOTE: These economic strata are those devised by DATOS except that the
upper class combines classes A and B. The DATOS class typology is discussed
in the first section of this chapter. Columns may not add to totals because of
rounding.
SOURCE: Mycon.

candidate: each economic stratum gave at least one-quarter of its
votes to each major party, and no group gave a majority to either AD
or COPEI. In 1978, class was simply not a powerful determinant of
voting intentions. The ability of class to account for voting intentions
seems positively puny by comparison with the Pérez-appreciation
factor. A researcher who wanted to know how a Venezuelan had
voted in 1978 without asking directly would not learn much by
inquiring into the fellow's class (or his education or religious beliefs,
as we shall see), but he would do very well to ask the fellow what he
thought of Carlos Andrés Pérez.

Second, a relation between major party voting and class does
exist, and it is curvilinear. Piñerúa did best among the poor (40 percent to 28 percent for Herrera) and the rich (45 percent to 25 percent).
The *adeco* candidate did worst, running evenly with Herrera, among
the middle and working classes. These figures would be adjusted
upward to Herrera's benefit if the votes of the largely anti-Pérez
undecided voters were projected into the major-party totals. Nevertheless, the finding would still hold that Piñerúa was (although the
differences are not huge) the candidate of the rich and of the poor.
This supposed anomaly may be explained in light of the history of
the parties in Venezuela. The poor are largely peasants or slum

81

dwellers relatively recently arrived from the countryside. As other authors in this volume have noted, Acción Democrática historically was the party of the peasants. Piñerúa continued to do disproportionately well with this group. In contrast, the rich are city people who in many cases became rich as a result of government support of private economic activities. Since for all but five of the years between 1958 and 1978 Venezuela had *adeco* leadership, rich Venezuelans would have little reason to risk a change. It is not surprising that people who became wealthy under *adeco* policies should disproportionately favor the *adeco* candidate.

The middle- and working-class groups were far enough from their roots often to forget their *campesino* and *adeco* origins yet close enough to the visible affluence of many Venezuelans to feel a sense of injustice: Carlos Andrés Pérez had not brought *them* affluence. Herrera combined support from members of COPEI, historically an upper- and middle-class party, with support from voters reacting against Pérez, to do well in Classes C and D.

Third, Table 3–10 provides interesting tidbits concerning support for parties of the left. These parties, whose platforms identify them as parties *for* the poor, are not parties *of* the poor in Venezuela. All of the parties—the Movement toward Socialism, the People's Electoral Movement, the Movement of the Revolutionary Left, and the Venezuelan Communist party—individually and collectively do worse among the poor, Class E, than among voters in the other groupings. It should not be inferred, however, that the left parties do well among the nonpoor; the left failed to pull 10 percent of the votes in any class.

At the same time, the extreme left parties' weak showing should not be interpreted as demonstrating that the far left has almost no support in Venezuela. Indeed, in the municipal elections of June 1979, left coalition candidates won 18 percent of the vote nationally. The difference between December and June is that the December election was held under a single-ballot, plurality system; so votes for third-party candidates for president were "wasted."[28] A voter who favored a left candidate such as José Vicente Rangel or Américo Martín and strongly opposed the *adecos* faced a dilemma: if this voter cast a ballot for Rangel, the vote would not help Herrera, the only candidate with a realistic chance of beating Piñerúa and driving the *adecos* from office. Yet, if this voter supported Herrera, the ballot would aid

---

[28] Electoral laws do have consequences for both voting behavior and party systems. See Douglas W. Rae, *The Political Consequences of Electoral Laws* (New Haven: Yale University Press, 1967).

TABLE 3–11

VOTING INTENTIONS AND EDUCATION, LARA AND MONAGAS, FALL 1978
(in percentages)

Intended Vote	Some Primary	Primary Completed	Some Secondary	Second- ary Com- pleted	Technical or Business School	University or Teachers College
Luis Herrera	29	37	30	27	32	25
Luis Piñerúa	37	35	34	34	38	32
The left	3	6	11	12	7	19
Other	1	1	3	5	1	1
Undecided	28	22	22	21	22	23
Total	100	100	100	100	100	100
N	(1,236)	(528)	(398)	(186)	(102)	(186)

NOTE: Columns may not add to totals because of rounding.
SOURCE: Mycon.

COPEI, not the left. Mycon data show that in this situation many left sympathizers voted for Herrera. Municipal council elections, on the other hand, are held under proportional representation, so in June no dilemma of "wasted" votes existed.

Since educational attainment is closely related to economic status, the relationship between education and voting intentions should parallel that between economic stratum and voting intentions. Table 3–11 demonstrates that this is indeed the case; there is a curvilinear relationship between Piñerúa's vote and the voters' level of education. By comparison with Herrera, Piñerúa did well among those with least education and with most. Among citizens who had not completed primary school, many of whom were illiterate, 37 percent were supporting Piñerúa and 29 percent intended to vote for Herrera. Among respondents with at least some university or teaching college experience, 32 percent were supporting Piñerúa and 25 percent favored Herrera. The middle groups, those with a primary school education, those with some high school training, and those with business or technical training, were Herrera's strongest categories, but only among the first of these groups was Herrera ahead of Piñerúa.

Also similar to the findings in regard to economic stratum is the weakness of the bivariate relationship. Herrera's vote in the six educational categories ranges from 25 percent to 37 percent; Piñerúa's vote has a range of 32 percent to 38 percent. Neither party can claim to be the party of a majority of the well-educated or of the educa-

TABLE 3–12

VOTING INTENTIONS AND AGE, LARA AND MONAGAS, FALL 1978

(in percentages)

Intended Vote	18–24	25–34	35–44	45–54	55–64	65+
Luis Herrera	31	30	35	28	27	25
Luis Piñerúa	31	32	39	38	42	35
The left	14	9	4	2	2	1
Other	3	2	1	1	2	1
Undecided	22	26	21	30	27	39
Total	100	100	100	100	100	100
N	(548)	(620)	(597)	(431)	(268)	(193)

NOTE: Columns may not add to totals because of rounding.
SOURCE: Mycon.

tionally deprived. That Piñerúa did better in some categories than in others should not obscure the reality that neither party did very poorly among voters at any level of education.

Table 3–11 also provides insights into the behavior of the well-educated. There is a noticeable difference between those with advanced work in technical or commercial colleges and those with university or teaching college experience. The difference does not lie in the distribution of the vote between the major parties; Piñerúa carried both groups by small margins. Instead, it lies in the incidence of support for nonmajor parties: 70 percent of those with technical education supported Herrera or Piñerúa, compared with only 57 percent of the other group. Nineteen percent of those with university experience intended to vote for a candidate of the left, in most instances José Vicente Rangel of the Movement toward Socialism. Studies have shown that technicians generally concentrate on their careers and accept the social structure, while university graduates sometimes become critics of those structures.[29] In light of the victories of many far-left candidates in campus elections in the 1970s, it is not surprising that far-left support is found disproportionately among the better educated. Even among this group, however, the level of support for the left was less than that given to either Herrera or Piñerúa.

Table 3–12 reports that Herrera did best vis-à-vis Piñerúa among voters under thirty-five years of age, who are the bulk of the Vene-

[29] Everett Carll Ladd, Jr., and Seymour Martin Lipset, *The Divided Academy* (New York: W. W. Norton, 1976).

zuelan electorate. But Mycon's undersampling of these younger voters (5 percent more of the sample should have been drawn from these younger categories) did not substantially distort the results since age is not a powerful determinant of the vote. In Herrera's worst grouping, those over sixty-five, he received the support of 25 percent; in his best grouping, the thirty-five- to forty-four-year-olds, the COPEI candidate pulled 35 percent. This small range, only ten percentage points, is only slightly smaller than Piñerúa's. The *adeco* candidate's worst group, the youngest voters, still gave him 31 percent of the vote; his best group, the fifty-five- to sixty-four-year-olds, gave him 42 percent of their vote. This range is only eleven percentage points.

Two other aspects of Table 3–12 deserve quick comment. With the idealistic romanticism of youth,[30] the young disproportionately supported candidates of the far left: 14 percent of the youngest voters indicated an intention to vote for left candidates and 9 percent of the voters twenty-five to thirty-four stated similar intentions. Fully 78 percent of the support for José Vicente Rangel, the candidate of the Movement toward Socialism, came from voters under thirty-five; similarly, Américo Martín, the candidate of the Movement of the Revolutionary Left, received 81 percent of his total vote from these younger voters, according to the Mycon surveys in Lara and Monagas. Although these far-left candidates did their best among the young, a majority of the young did support major party candidates; 62 percent of the young voters said they had made their minds up to vote for Herrera or Piñerúa.

Thirty-nine percent of the voters over sixty-four years of age told the Mycon interviewers that they had not yet decided which candidate would receive their votes or did not intend to vote. This figure is substantially higher than among other age groups. It may be, however, that older people were not more undecided than others but more reluctant to reveal their preferences to an interviewer. Most of these people's adult lives have been spent under undemocratic regimes— the dictatorship of Marcos Pérez Jiménez, various military juntas, and even the brutal dictatorship of Juan Vicente Gómez. Although procedural democracy has been in existence in Venezuela since 1958, many old people may question the stability of the regime. A coup

---

[30] Carlos Rangel argues that in Latin America revolutionaries are likely to be idealized as authentic descendants of those pure and noble savages who roamed the continent before the arrival of the corrupt Europeans. Rangel argues that this romanticization does not contribute to serious efforts at understanding and dealing with societal problems. See his *The Latin Americans: Their Love-Hate Relationship with the United States* (New York: Harcourt Brace Jovanovich, 1977).

TABLE 3–13

VOTING INTENTIONS AND SEX, LARA AND MONAGAS, FALL 1978

(in percentages)

Intended Vote	Males	Females
Luis Herrera	30	30
Luis Piñerúa	37	35
The left	9	5
Other	2	2
Undecided	23	27
Total	100	100
N	(1,271)	(1,413)

NOTE: Columns do not add to totals because of rounding.
SOURCE: Mycon.

would bring reprisals, and some voters may well have felt that revealing their political preferences would have been a foolish assumption of unnecessary risks.[31]

Table 3–13 shows that knowing a voter's sex provides little information about which candidate that voter is likely to choose. There is a tendency for Piñerúa to appeal more to male voters than to female voters, but it is slight. Sex is significant as a factor only in explaining the vote of left candidates, who ran almost twice as well among men as among women; José Vicente Rangel, the most popular of the left candidates, received 64 percent of his total vote from men although the electorate was almost equally divided between men and women. This finding reflects the higher incidence of fatalistic attitudes among women. Women were more likely than men to report that their life conditions had not changed in recent years and probably would not change in the future. People who expect little change, for better or for worse, are unlikely to support candidates who promise a drastic restructuring of society.[32]

In summary, demographic variables do not account for the voting intentions of the Venezuelan electorate. If one were to select at

[31] Another sign that some older Venezuelans are not entirely confident in the stability of the system is the crowding of supermarkets observed by the author immediately before the election. Many older Venezuelans stocked up on food in order to have sufficient quantities in case the election provoked disturbances bringing about disruptions in food delivery systems.
[32] Seymour Martin Lipset and Stein Rokkan, eds., *Party Systems and Voter Alignments: Cross-National Perspectives* (New York: Free Press, 1967), and footnote 21.

random 100 Herrera supporters and place them in a room, and then repeat this procedure with Piñerúa supporters, the two groups would look very similar. Careful scrutiny would reveal differences, but the similarities would predominate. The Herrera room would contain more middle-class and working-class people than the Piñerúa room, yet people of all economic strata would be found in both. The Piñerúa room would contain more illiterate peasants as well as more very well educated people and the Herrera room more Venezuelans with only a few years of schooling, but both would contain people at all levels of education. More younger voters and city people would be found i- the Herrera room than in the Piñerúa room, although the Piñerúa room would hold many from both groups. Every region of Venezuela would be well represented in both rooms although the Piñerúa room would hold more voters from the east and the Herrera room would contain more *copeyanos* from the west. On two factors, sex and religion, the groups would be virtually identical: equal numbers of men and women would be in both rooms, and over 90 percent would identify themselves as Catholics, with devout, practicing, and nominal adherents of the faith equally divided. Considering that Herrera was the Social Christian candidate, the finding that he did no better among the devout than Piñerúa is surprising.[33]

One hundred supporters of the left, selected at random and placed in a room, would not closely resemble the people in either the Herrera or the Piñerúa room. Two differences would be immediately evident to anyone comparing them: the left supporters would include many more males than females and more young Venezuelans than older ones. Sixty-one of the leftists would be males, a majority would be under thirty years of age, and almost none would be older Venezuelans. The left's dependence on youth would be even more pronounced if the supporters of Luis B. Prieto Figueroa were removed from the room. Prieto, the leader of the People's Electoral Movement since that party's formation by dissident *adecos* in 1968, ran better among women than among men and among older voters than among youth. The other left candidates, with their romantic, almost messianic appeals, found few friends over thirty.

In terms of other demographic variables, the left room would resemble the Piñerúa and Herrera rooms. Ironically, however, it would contain fewer poor Venezuelans and a few more university graduates or students than the others. Most of the left supporters would

---

[33] This finding comes from an analysis of the Mycon surveys in Lara and Monagas. Religiousness correlates positively with age. Since Piñerúa ran better among older Venezuelans than among younger voters, Herrera's failure to capture most of the votes of the devout may not be surprising after all.

fall into the middle and working classes, where most Herrera and Piñerúa supporters could also be found. Only in terms of maleness and youth were the left supporters different demographically from mainstream party supporters.

Conclusion

The Venezuelan electorate presented analysts with an enigma in 1978. Luis Piñerúa Ordaz was the candidate of Acción Democrática, the party that had won every election of the democratic era except 1968 when an internal split had ruined its chances. In 1978 all of the party's leaders, though admittedly with varying degrees of enthusiasm, rallied around the Piñerúa candidacy. Acción Democrática was in power; so the Government was able to spend large sums advertising its accomplishments and, by implication, suggesting that prosperity would reign under another AD administration. The current president, Carlos Andrés Pérez, was the most popular politician in Venezuela. With enormous sums in oil profits at its disposal, the Acción Democrática Government was able to embark on massive projects designed to produce a modern, industrialized economy. At the time of the 1978 election, Venezuela enjoyed the highest standard of living of any Latin American nation. Finally, Piñerúa's personal popularity was at least as high as Herrera's. The enigma is the question of how Piñerúa lost to the COPEI candidate in spite of all of these advantages.

The answer is found in the overriding importance of Carlos Andrés Pérez to the 1978 election. The fact that Pérez was the most popular politician in the country does not imply that a majority of Venezuelan voters liked him. Forty percent liked him a great deal, but 60 percent reacted negatively. Almost all of the 40 percent supported Piñerúa; very few of the 60 percent did. Luis Herrera, proclaiming himself the national candidate of opposition to Acción Democrática, received the votes of most anti-Pérez Venezuelans. Many of these voters apparently had little sympathy for COPEI or Herrera himself but wanted a change from Acción Democrática. Realizing that a vote for a far-left candidate or a spoiled vote would not help to put the party of Carlos Andrés Pérez out of office, they voted for Herrera. Herrera's success as a general opposition candidate contrasts sharply with Piñerúa's failure to broaden his support beyond staunch Pérez supporters, usually strong *adecos*. The weakness of the Piñerúa campaign and candidacy was its failure to attract voters except those strongly committed to Pérez. The absence of an independent appeal to any beyond staunch *adecos* cost Piñerúa the election.

The Herrera victory must be thought of more as a defeat for the *adecos* than as a triumph for Herrera or COPEI. Voters were reacting to Pérez and Acción Democrática, not expressing any great love for Herrera or COPEI. The electorate was not proclaiming its support for Social Christian ideology, nor was it providing a mandate for the programs Herrera had promised. Herrera's mandate was simply an endorsement of his slogan "Enough!"

The implications of this election for future ones are of the nature of opportunities rather than certainties. By winning, COPEI gained the opportunity to run the country for five years. If Herrera's performance is pleasing to a majority of Venezuelans, there is little to suggest that COPEI will not provide the winning candidate in 1983. If his performance is lacking, and/or if expectations are so high that any president must necessarily disappoint most Venezuelans, there is little to suggest that AD will not return to power. The 1978 election did not forge any Herrera coalition that might be expected to ensure COPEI victories in the future. The election did provide an opportunity for COPEI to demonstrate its governing abilities.

For Acción Democrática, defeat offers the opportunity, however unwanted, to provide an effective and constructive opposition to the COPEI Government. The defeat also forces the party to examine its structure, philosophy, and leadership. Depending upon the performance of the Herrera administration and the appeal of its own candidate, the party has an excellent chance of returning to power in 1984. The party must be particularly concerned wth strengthening its appeal to the young, the least *adeco* age group and an increasing percentage of the electorate. But, in spite of losing the presidency, AD leaders can take heart from the fact that there are still many more AD supporters than COPEI supporters.

Even the far left might discover an opportunity in its dismal showing. Many Herrera voters were left sympathizers who voted for Herrera to oust the *adecos* from office. These voters will probably become disenchanted with Herrera's moderate policies but are unlikely to support the hated *adecos* to oust COPEI.[34] If the left can unite behind an attractive candidate for the 1983 election, it may be able to approach the 18 percent it received in the June 1979 municipal elections. A better performance than this is unlikely since an over-

---

[34] In the 1960s *adeco* Governments fought against a guerrilla movement which modeled itself after Fidel Castro's effort in Cuba. With little popular support, most guerrillas were either killed or captured. Most of those who had been captured were freed as part of an amnesty of the COPEI Government of Rafael Caldera. Remembering the strong efforts of the *adeco* Governments against the guerrillas, the far left has great antipathy toward Acción Democrática.

whelming majority of voters reject far-left parties and candidates. However, if the country were to experience a severe economic decline, it is easy to imagine the far left gaining many adherents. Meanwhile, if the mainstream parties are successful in developing Venezuela, they may well reduce the far left to a handful of insignificant debating societies.

Perhaps the most important implication of the 1978 election stems from its mere existence. Every successful election develops the habits and expectations of procedural democracy. When the governing party loses an election and transfers power to a victorious opponent, procedural democracy itself is strengthened. The election strengthens the legitimacy of the government and makes other means of changing leaders unacceptable. In a region where violence usually accompanies changes of Government, the election of 1978 was a victory for the Venezuelan people regardless of which candidate won.

4

The Acción Democrática Campaign

David J. Myers

A mood of euphoria prevailed within Acción Democrática following the victory of Carlos Andrés Pérez over Lorenzo Fernández in the presidential election of December 9, 1973. In defeating the governing Social Christian party by a margin of 500,000 votes, Acción Democrática had won the sixth of seven elections held in Venezuela since the revolution of 1945, which toppled President Isaías Medina and opened the way for a mass-based, representative democracy.[1] COPEI's only victory had come in 1968, when Acción Democrática was divided between partisans of the party's rival presidential hopefuls, Gonzalo Barrios and Luis B. Prieto Figueroa.[2] Even under these conditions COPEI's margin of victory over Acción Democrática had been less than one percentage point.

In 1973 Acción Democrática's advantage over COPEI was twelve percentage points in the presidential balloting. This margin approached the difference between Rafael Caldera's vote in 1968 and the combined total for Barrios and Prieto. Also, Pérez's coattails reached into the congressional and municipal races. Acción Democrática gained control of the Senate, the Chamber of Deputies, and 70 percent of the

---

[1] The most complete account of the 1973 Venezuelan election campaign is John D. Martz and Enrique Baloyra, *Electoral Mobilization and Public Opinion: The Venezuelan Campaign of 1973* (Chapel Hill: University of North Carolina Press, 1976). Other useful works include Domingo Alberto Rangel, *El Gran Negocio* [The big deal] (Caracas: Vadell Hermanos, 1974) and Francisco Alvarez, Manuel Caballero, Américo Martín, Demetrio Boersner, Domingo Alberto Rangel, and Miguel Acosta Saignes, *La izquierda venezolana y las elecciones del 1973* [The Venezuelan left and the elections of 1973] (Caracas: Síntesis Dosmil, 1974).

[2] The most complete account of the 1968 election campaign is David J. Myers, *Democratic Campaigning in Venezuela: Caldera's Victory* (Caracas: Editorial Sucre, 1973).

municipal councils.[3] The day that Rafael Caldera passed the presidential sash to Carlos Andrés Pérez, there was reason to credit the widely heard slogan "Venezuela es un país adeco"—Venezuela is an AD country.

The first year of the Pérez administration seemed to confirm the most optimistic projections of growing Acción Democrática dominance. Dramatically rising petroleum prices more than tripled the central government's income. Expectations ran high as the new president announced a rash of innovative investments designed to raise standards of living and increase Venezuela's international influence.[4] Carlos Andrés Pérez's skill in presenting his innovative programs pushed his positive approval rating with the Venezuelan people to above 70 percent. Journalists, academics, and politicians began to speculate that Acción Democrática was on the threshold of achieving in Venezuela the kind of political dominance enjoyed by Mexico's Revolutionary Institutional party.[5]

In addition to restoring Acción Democrática to its accustomed role as Venezuela's dominant political party, the December 1973 elections strengthened the democratic system. For a second time since the 1958 revolution the popularly elected chief executive of one political party routinely passed presidential power to an elected successor from a rival political party. The 1973 elections also marked the first time that former guerrillas from the Movement of the Revolutionary Left had competed for votes with the less radical parties. Despite its defects, Venezuelan democracy seemed to have achieved widespread acceptance. Speculation centered not on its survival, but on whether it would evolve in the direction of single-party dominance or of two-party or multiparty competition.

At 1:25 A.M. on December 4, 1978, the Supreme Electoral Council released its first bulletin indicating a lead of roughly 1,000 votes for COPEI's Luis Herrera Campíns over Acción Democrática's Luis

---

[3] Martz and Baloyra, *Electoral Mobilization*, chap. 9.

[4] A useful discussion of the first half of the Pérez administration appears in the concluding chapter of John D. Martz and David J. Myers, eds., *Venezuela: The Democratic Experience* (New York: Praeger, 1977). See also Pedro Pablo Kuczynski, "The Economic Development of Venezuela: A Summary View as of 1975-1976," in Robert D. Bond, ed., *Contemporary Venezuela and Its Role in International Affairs* (New York: Council on Foreign Relations, 1977).

[5] Compare "Acción Democrática: la lucha interna por el poder" [Acción Democrática: the internal struggle for power], *Semana*, no. 324 (July 14, 1974), pp. 14-15; "Los 100 primeros días de Carlos Andrés: crecimiento de su figura y de la adhesión popular" [The first 100 days of Carlos Andrés: his growth in stature and his popularity], *Resumen*, no. 32 (June 16, 1974), pp. 16-17; and "La decadente proyección nacional del COPEI" [The declining national profile of COPEI], *Resumen*, no. 51 (October 27, 1974), p. 7.

Piñerúa Ordaz.[6] Other presidential candidates trailed far behind. The official tally, while representing less than 5 percent of the vote, was followed by an avalanche of informal returns indicating that Herrera would be the next chief executive. Shocked Acción Democrática leaders congratulated the victor and began discussing the kind of opposition they would conduct during the coming "constitutional period" (the five-year span between national elections). However, even Herrera supporters did not claim that COPEI was on the threshold of achieving single-party dominance. Herrera's narrow victory reflected a general Social Christian advance throughout the country. It was also facilitated by the votes of radical leftists who saw him as preferable to Piñerúa, an enemy of long standing.[7] The small-card vote, although to a lesser degree, confirmed the trend toward two-party dominance. For example, Acción Democrática and COPEI each elected twenty senators, while the Movement toward Socialism, which finished third, garnered only two. The December 3 balloting thus left Acción Democrática facing several minor parties but also one powerful opponent capable of challenging it in every region and state.

How can Acción Democrática's unexpected loss of presidential power be explained? What are the short- and medium-run implications for the party? This chapter will analyze these questions by looking at five basic features of Acción Democrática's 1978 election campaign: selection of the party's presidential candidate and its impact on the subsequent general election campaign; campaign organization; strategy and tactics; the party leaders' attempts to manipulate information during the campaign; and the shape of Piñerúa's narrow loss and what it portends for the party's future.

Selecting the Presidential Candidate

During the Caldera administration Carlos Andrés Pérez served as secretary general of Acción Democrática. Although the secretary general sits atop the party apparatus, Pérez shared power with Rómulo Betancourt and Gonzalo Barrios. Barrios, despite the disastrous intraparty division of 1967, missed retaining the presidency for Acción Democrática by only the narrowest of margins. He hoped for a second nomination. Former President Betancourt's deci-

---

[6] Personal observation by the author.

[7] Herrera received 383,000 more votes for president than COPEI received on the small card. Leftist presidential candidates, on the other hand, received many fewer votes than did their party's small-card slates. For example, Américo Martín (Movement of the Revolutionary Left) received 51,972 presidential votes and his party's legislative slate obtained 122,679.

sion to back the younger and more dynamic Pérez, however, closed the door to Barrios's presidential ambitions. Pérez's election victory in 1973 strengthened both his own standing and that of Rómulo Betancourt within Acción Democrática and confirmed Betancourt's impressive record for shrewd political judgments. Barrios, nevertheless, remained a respected and influential figure.

In office Carlos Andrés Pérez established himself as a dynamic and independent political leader. He promised rapid development based on resources made available to Venezuela by the sharp rise in petroleum prices that followed the 1973 Middle East war. Pérez also nudged Venezuela into a more dynamic role in international affairs. Domestically, the president chose to implement an economic policy that encouraged mixed enterprises. This involved cooperation between the Government and some of Venezuela's wealthiest and most influential families. It made many of Acción Democrática's committed socialists uncomfortable from the beginning. When allegations of illicit profits and charges of corruption began to circulate late in 1975, Acción Democrática became embroiled in a fratricidal struggle.[8] It was a key factor in the party's loss of the presidency in 1978.

Initially, the conflict within Acción Democrática appeared to be the anticipated expression of frustration by party loyalists who had not been asked to join the Government. Only gradually did the extent of President Pérez's estrangement from Betancourt make itself known. During the 1973 election campaign Betancourt once introduced Pérez as the "son I never had."[9] Eighteen months later the two men could hardly bring themselves to exchange pleasantries in public. On several occasions, only skillful mediation by Gonzalo Barrios prevented a public airing of the differences between Carlos Andrés Pérez and his one-time mentor.

As early as mid-1974 Rómulo Betancourt began maneuvering with Acción Democrática to ensure that his choice would receive the party's presidential nomination for 1978. The former president urged Octavio Lepage, the party's secretary general, to exchange places with Luis Piñerúa Ordaz, minister of interior relations. At that time Lepage was considered a potential presidential candidate. There was a great deal of speculation that party elders had decided to give him experience in the number two administrative job as preparation for running

---

[8] The most comprehensive account is Pedro Duno, Los doce apostoles [The twelve apostles] (Valencia: Vadell Hermanos, 1975). See also Sanin, Venezuela saudita [Venezuela arabianized] (Valencia: Vadell Hermanos, 1978).

[9] Rangel, El gran negocio, particularly chapter 3, touches on the Betancourt-Pérez relationship. Several members of Acción Democrática confirmed Betancourt's statement.

Venezuela during the next constitutional period. Luis Piñerúa, on the other hand, initially was seen as having weakened his presidential chances by leaving the cabinet.[10]

The decisive margin by which Piñerúa won election as Acción Democrática's secretary general in August 1975 suggested that his influence within the party organization ran deeper than anyone realized. From that moment on he had the inside track for his party's 1978 presidential nomination. Piñerúa's closing address to the 1975 party convention included an attack on President Pérez's policy of close collaboration with newly emerging entrepreneurial groups, the so-called Twelve Apostles.[11] This suggested that party-Government relations would at best be cool and correct during the remainder of Carlos Andrés Pérez's presidential term. The Betancourt-Pérez split was now reflected at the institutional level.

Carlos Andrés Pérez preferred that his close friend and collaborator David Morales Bello be the Acción Democrática presidential candidate.[12] However, no other major party leader so incited Rómulo Betancourt's wrath. The former president derided Morales Bello for having "abandoned" Luis Ruíz Pineda, the party's resistance leader inside Venezuela during much of the Pérez Jiménez regime. Morales Bello had been in an automobile with Ruíz Pineda when they were stopped by the Seguridad Nacional, Pérez Jiménez's dreaded secret police. Ruíz was killed but Morales escaped. The latter always claimed that given the situation each man had had to attempt a getaway as best he could. Nevertheless, while Rómulo Betancourt retained influence in the party, David Morales Bello had no chance of receiving its presidential nomination. The prospects of other leaders with some support within the party for a run at the presidency seemed almost as bleak.

Within Acción Democrática, the problem of political succession has never been resolved satisfactorily. In 1962, second-generation leaders loyal to Raúl Ramos Giménez split from Acción Democrática to form Acción Democrática-Oposición. Five years later, Acción Democrática lost the presidency when the party divided following a

---

[10] F. V. Izquierdo, "Piñerúa Ordaz: de primer ministro a hombre de partido" [From first man in the cabinet to man of the party], Resumen, no. 65 (February 2, 1975), p. 12.

[11] Rodolfo José Cárdenas, "El regreso de Betancourt" [The return of Betancourt], Resumen, no. 91 (August 3, 1975), p. 12.

[12] Carlos Dorante, "Voto directo y secreto para elecciones internas" [Direct, secret voting for the internal elections], Resumen, no. 172 (February 20, 1977), pp. 8-13. This was confirmed in conversations with various high party officials in 1977.

bloody battle for the presidential nomination between two leaders of the founding generation, Gonzalo Barrios and Luis B. Prieto Figueroa. Only frustrations associated with being in the opposition blunted challenges to the party elders' imposition of Carlos Andrés Pérez in 1972. The subsequent falling out between Pérez and Betancourt suggested that the struggle for Acción Democrática's 1978 presidential nomination would be pervasive, intense, and potentially debilitating.[13]

Rómulo Betancourt maintained that internal primary elections were the most equitable procedure for selecting and legitimating Acción Democrática's presidential nominee. This view was not universal within the party. Bitter and disputed primary elections had, after all, preceded the disastrous 1967 party division. Following the inauguration of Carlos Andrés Pérez and Lepage's departure for the Ministry of Interior Relations, however, Piñerúa and Betancourt controlled most Acción Democrática state organizations. This enabled them to impose their thinking at the 1976 annual party convention,[14] which scheduled primary elections for July 1977. Betancourt and Piñerúa were confident that they could win and that a primary election victory would strengthen the latter's appeal among both party members and independents.

Those who between 1974 and 1976 had been outmaneuvered by Piñerúa and Betancourt, including President Pérez, initially were undecided on what strategy to adopt toward the primary election. They knew that their minority status in most state organizations made a Piñerúa victory almost certain. They also calculated that some kind of challenge was necessary in order to maintain their influence within the party. Therefore, they chose to unite behind a single candidate, Jaime Lusinchi. Lusinchi's reputation was that of an affable and effective congressional leader. Never before had he been considered a serious presidential contender. Lusinchi, however, proved to be a popular and surprisingly effective campaigner.[15]

---

[13] "La tempestad" [The tempest], *Resumen*, no. 189 (June 19, 1977), pp. 4-13, analyzes the problems of Carlos Andrés Pérez and their implications for the 1978 elections. Another useful discussion appears in "La corrupción juega su carta: una candidatura independiente" [Corruption surfaces: an independent candidacy], *Zeta*, no. 185 (September 25, 1977).

[14] José Rodolfo Cárdenas, "Formulas para elegir candidatos presidenciales" [Procedures for electing presidential candidates], *Resumen*, no. 168 (January 3, 1977), p. 5.

[15] "Lo que juega en la elección de AD" [What is at stake in the AD election], *Resumen*, no. 193 (July 17, 1977), pp. 2-8. Compare Hector Stredel, "El CEN adeco" [The AD National Executive Committee], *Zeta*, no. 151 (January 30, 1977), p. 21.

During early 1976 supporters of Piñerúa and Lusinchi began trading accusations and attacking each other with vigor. Piñerúa stressed that he would be less partial toward new entrepreneurial groups when inviting participation in Venezuela's mixed corporations. He also attacked corruption and inefficiency in public services. Each of these themes widened the gap between himself and the Pérez administration. Lusinchi, on the other hand, attacked Piñerúa as lacking the leadership and educational qualifications necessary for a president. He also portrayed Piñerúa as highly sectarian and incapable of attracting independent voters. Overall, the force and skill of Lusinchi's attack severely detracted from Piñerúa's presidential image.

Luis Piñerúa Ordaz won 62 percent of the total vote in Acción Democrática's presidential primary. In so doing he clearly demonstrated his great appeal among party militants. Acción Democrática's widely publicized membership strength of 900,000, however, was not enough by itself to elect a president. Only 732,000 actually voted in the primary election. In this light, analysis by Teodoro Petkoff that Piñerúa represented the most "anticommunist," "sectarian," and "intolerant" elements of Acción Democrática foreshadowed a difficult uphill battle for the victor in his quest for needed independent votes.[16]

In accumulating 38 percent of the primary vote, Jaime Lusinchi lost every state but his native Anzoátegui and the Amazonas territory. Nevertheless, he did better than expected and established himself as a viable future presidential candidate. Analysis of the primary vote by Luis Fernando Chaves, a well-known Venezuelan social scientist, demonstrated that Lusinchi's appeal among swing voters and independents exceeded that of Piñerúa.[17] This supported a widely circulated initiative analysis by Teodoro Petkoff that Lusinchi was the Acción Democrática candidate with the greatest appeal among nonmilitants, and that Piñerúa would have considerable problems with the independents.

The primary election campaign hardened a cleavage within Acción Democrática that had appeared in the early years of the Pérez Government. In this situation, the wounds inflicted in the nomination struggle were slow to heal. Lusinchi did pledge to support Piñerúa in the general election campaign. However, he remained publicly cool during the final months of 1977. Relations between the Piñerúa and Pérez factions deteriorated further following the party's assembly in

---

[16] *El Nacional*, August 19, 1977, p. D-1.

[17] Luis Fernando Chaves, "Las elecciónes primerias de Acción Democrática" [Acción Democrática's primary elections], *Revista Geográfica*, vol. 15, nos. 1-2 (January-December 1978), University of the Andes, Mérida.

January 1978.[18] Former President Rómulo Betancourt selected this forum to repeat earlier charges of public immorality, crime, and deteriorating public services. In response, President Pérez reportedly threatened to withhold government support from the party's presidential campaign. Only nominally united, therefore, Acción Democrática approached the official opening of the 1978 general election campaign, on April 1, able to mobilize only a fraction of its considerable resources toward defeating Luis Herrera Campíns and the Social Christians.

Campaign Organization

Historically, Acción Democrática has enjoyed greater geographical and social penetration than any other Venezuelan political party. In 1978 the resources available to Luis Piñerúa because of Acción Democrática's incumbency and accompanying patronage ensured that his campaign would be highly structured in each municipality and in every consequential social and economic sector. Piñerúa's campaign, if anything, was over-organized on paper. However, the Acción Democrática leadership failed to establish clear channels of command and control among their many organizations. The party's presidential and legislative campaigns relied on permanent and intermittent organizations at both the national and regional levels.[19] (Permanent organizations are those that function during and between election campaigns; intermittent campaign organizations operate only during campaigns.) These organizations received funds from Caracas. Nevertheless, in large urban centers—Maracaibo, Valencia, and Barquisimeto—regional sources of financing acquired great significance. Finally, because Acción Democrática was in power during the 1978 election campaign, government bureaucracies became important elements in the party's electoral organizations.

National Campaign Organization. The National Executive Committee (CEN) normally is the "organ of maximum authority" within Acción Democrática. During the 1978 election campaign it had nineteen members.[20] They included secretaries of the party's bureaus dealing

---

[18] Personal observation by the author. See Howard Handelman, "The Making of a Venezuelan President 1978," *American Universities Field Staff Reports*, no. 45 (1978), p. 5; and "La breuhaha CAP-AD" [The CAP-AD brouhaha], *Auténtico*, no. 34 (January 31, 1978), pp. 14-15.

[19] These kinds of structure are defined in Myers, *Democratic Campaigning*, chap. 1. In most cases the regional organization controlled an area with the same geographic boundaries as the state.

[20] Interview with Luis Raúl Matos, December 4, 1978.

with unions, agriculture, professionals, educators, and youth, and notables like Rómulo Betancourt and Gonzalo Barrios. Political secretaries, the party's specially selected roving trouble-shooters, also sat on the CEN. The secretary of organization was one of the CEN's most influential members, but the party secretary general usually was first among equals. Acción Democrática's leader from the crucial state of Carabobo, Alejandro Izaguirre, served as the national secretary general after Piñerúa vacated the post prior to seeking his party's presidential nomination. Izaguirre did not attempt to dominate either the regular party or the election campaign organization. He played a different role. Personal friendships with both Carlos Andrés Pérez and Luis Piñerúa Ordaz allowed Izaguirre to act as a bridge between the party and the Government.

In times of election campaigning, the Organization Secretariat usually has been the most important element in Acción Democrática's organizational structure. The national secretary of organization has overall responsibility for the functioning of all organizations throughout the party hierarchy. During the 1973 campaign Luis Piñerúa was a highly successful and efficient national secretary of organization.[21] Luis Alfaro Ucero, the legendary political leader of the state of Monagas, served as secretary of organization during the 1978 campaign. He was assisted by Luis Raúl Matos, the national subsecretary of organization. Directly under Matos's supervision were the Divisions of Political Activism, Registration and Statistics, and Electoral Regularization. On the basis of the work of these divisions, Matos recommended policies to Alfaro, coordinated drives to attract new party members, and developed programs for turning out the vote, preventing electoral fraud, and speeding electoral returns from each state to party headquarters in Caracas. Finally, the national Organization Secretariat supervised each of the twenty-four regional secretaries of organization.[22]

Figure 4–1 outlines the complex and pervasive special campaign organization presided over by Reinaldo Leandro Mora and his Strategy Commission. Leandro Mora also held the office of first vice president within the party, a position that carried with it membership on the CEN. Initially the CEN envisioned that Leandro Mora would share power within the special campaign organization with Pedro Paris

---

[21] Martz and Baloyra, *Electoral Mobilization*, pp. 90-96.

[22] In most cases the regional organization encompassed a single state. The state of Sucre was an important exception. Because of rivalries between the state's eastern and western halves, Acción Democrática established a separate regional organization in each.

FIGURE 4–1

ACCION DEMOCRATICA'S NATIONAL ORGANIZATION, 1978 CAMPAIGN

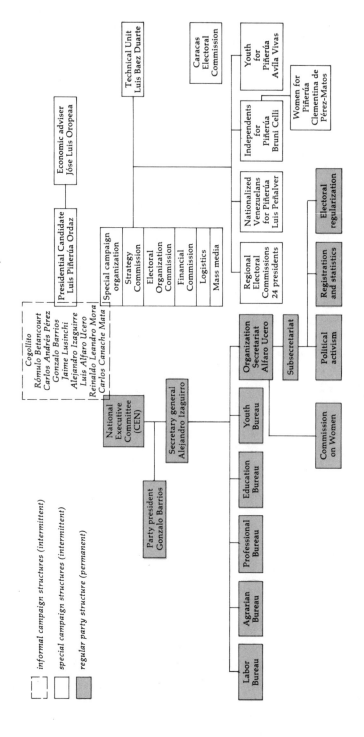

SOURCE: Author's observations.

Montesinos's Electoral Organization Commission, and to a lesser degree with the Commissions of Finance, Logistics, and Publicity. The Electoral Organization Commission never lived up to early expectations, and Paris Montesinos remained a secondary figure throughout the campaign. Gradually, Leandro Mora achieved a large measure of control over the special campaign organization's other commissions. The initial intention of the CEN regarding organizational parity within the special campaign apparatus, however, always cast doubt on the Strategy Commission's power to impose its authority.[23]

Leandro Mora enjoyed unambiguous authority over some elements of the special campaign organization. First in importance among these were the regional electoral commissions. Each regional Acción Democrática organization, usually with authority over an entire state, received its own electoral commission early in the campaign. In collaboration with the CEN, Leandro Mora named all electoral commission presidents. Within each state the electoral commission president spoke for the party on election matters. He also reported directly to Leandro Mora. Leandro Mora himself held the office of president of the Electoral Commission in Caracas, the location of one-fifth of the total national vote. Finally the chairman of the Strategy Commission directly controlled the technical unit headed by Luis Baez Duarte. All polling done for the campaign organization was sent directly to Baez Duarte. He discussed the strategic implications of findings about mass public opinion with Leandro Mora, and together they decided how to disseminate their interpretations to the special campaign and regular party organizations.[24]

The regular party organization, while recognizing the need for a special campaign organization, was never entirely comfortable with the idea of a second Acción Democrática infrastructure exercising overall authority in electoral matters. During 1973 most tensions emanating from this duality had been resolved by giving the party's secretary of organization, Luis Piñerúa, ultimate control. In 1978 Piñerúa believed he could exercise the same kind of control as the presidential candidate. A single individual, however, proved unable to perform well as coordinator of the regular and special campaign organizations and at the same time function effectively as the presidential candidate.

---

[23] Personal observation by the author, confirmed in discussions with Reinaldo Leandro Mora and Luis Alfaro Ucero.

[24] Interview with Luis Baez Duarte, November 29, 1978.

In the 1978 election campaign nobody did for Luis Piñerúa Ordaz what he had done in 1973 for Carlos Andrés Pérez. In 1973 Piñerúa had approved the scheduling of the candidate's campaign trips, helped design his newspaper advertisements, and overseen efforts to raise funds. He attempted to do these things again in 1978, and to carry the burdens of a presidential candidate. Piñerúa refused to delegate the authority of a chief of staff to either Alfaro Ucero or Leandro Mora. Disagreements between the regular and special campaign organizations on relatively minor matters were to be resolved by Piñerúa. But time did not permit the candidate to deal effectively with all such matters, and many were never decided or were resolved on the basis of cursory analysis.

The mechanism for coordinating the regular party organization and the campaign organization, at the national level, was an informal group of party notables popularly known as the *cogollito*.[25] The *cogollito* included former President Rómulo Betancourt, incumbent President Carlos Andrés Pérez, Acción Democrática President Gonzalo Barrios, defeated primary election candidate Jaime Lusinchi, party Secretary General Alejandro Izaguirre, party Secretary of Organization Luis Alfaro Ucero, Strategy Commission Chairman Reinaldo Leandro Mora, and Carlos Canache Mata. Luis Piñerúa also belonged to the *cogollito*. In matters of election campaigning and in the preparation of programs for his administration, Piñerúa spoke as the first among equals.

There were no scheduled weekly sessions of the *cogollito*, although most participants met at least once every ten days. President Carlos Andrés Pérez was the least regular attender, but as indicated earlier, Alejandro Izaguirre kept him informed. The *cogollito* itself proved inappropriate as a vehicle for planning offensive strategy or for overseeing the campaign on a day-to-day basis. It functioned more as a forum for analyzing how things were going and for developing replies to statements from other major political figures. It became a body that reacted to what others were doing, rather than a mechanism for strategic planning.

The planning and execution of Acción Democrática's campaign at the national level, as suggested earlier, centered around Luis Alfaro Ucero and Reinaldo Leandro Mora. These two competed for the presidential candidate's attention. Piñerúa lacked the time necessary

---

[25] Leopoldo Linares, "Gonzalo Barrios y las planchas" [Gonzalo Barrios and the party lists], *El Nacional*, August 8, 1978, discusses the operation of the *cogollito* at considerable length.

to resolve differences and coordinate Alfaro's regular party organizations and Leandro's special campaign organizations; so the two hierarchies' efforts were often redundant. Sometimes they even worked at cross purposes. Nationally, therefore, structural inefficiencies diluted the impact of many efforts on behalf of Acción Democrática and its presidential candidate.

Regional Campaign Organizations. Structurally, Acción Democrática's twenty-five regional campaign organizations strongly resembled each other (see Figure 4–2). The sectional or regional executive committee (CES) was the highest authority for the regular party organization within each state or territory.[26] Inside the CES, the regional party secretary general had the last word. He had overall responsibility for the regular party organization within the region, and he reported directly to the national secretary general. The regional secretary of organization, especially in electoral matters, was almost as influential as the secretary general. The regional secretary of organization implemented the policies of the national secretary of organization, as well as those of the regional secretary general. The regional secretary of organization also monitored the performance of each of the party's five regional bureaus and controlled its organization for women, the Women's Secretariat.

Venezuelan districts are geographic subdivisions of states or territories. Acción Democrática's subdivisions parallel those of the nation. Thus, there is an AD executive committee for each district. In the broadest sense, district executive committees are responsible to the regional or state secretary general. The regional secretary of organization, however, monitors daily performance at the district level. The district executive committee, in turn, supervises the municipal executive committees. District committees also communicate directly with "base" or neighborhood committees.

The base committees, in urban neighborhoods or rural hamlets, are the party's grass-roots organizations. They give ordinary members a place in the party hierarchy and, ideally, function as channels through which demands can be made upon the politicians and through which local politicians can appeal directly for electoral support. Party regulations stipulate that base committees are permanent. Between election campaigns, however, most base committees have generally ceased to exist. For example, when the party in Lara began in March 1978 to strengthen itself in anticipation of the December elections,

---

[26] The best discussion of Acción Democrática's structure is in John D. Martz, *Acción Democrática* (Princeton: Princeton University Press, 1966), pp. 161-67.

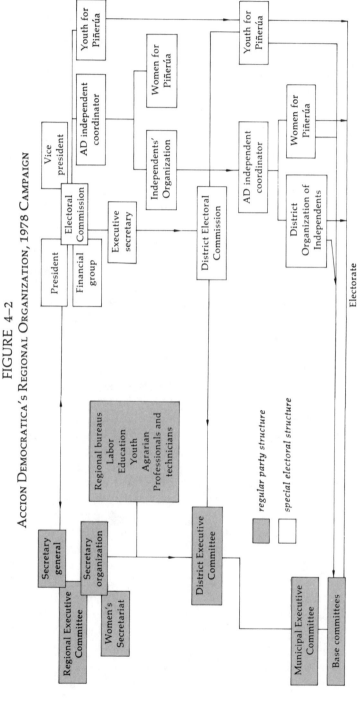

FIGURE 4-2

ACCION DEMOCRATICA'S REGIONAL ORGANIZATION, 1978 CAMPAIGN

NOTE: The Venezuelans use the word "regional," but in this context they mean "state." An organization of the kind outlined here existed in each state.

SOURCE: Author's observations in the states of Lara and Monagas.

it was discovered that three-fourths of the base committees had not met during the preceding three years.[27] In Barquisimeto, the capital and largest city in Lara, Acción Democrática was faced with the task of reactivating 3,500 of the 5,000 base committees that had functioned during the successful 1973 election campaign. The situation was only marginally better in Maturín, capital of the eastern state of Monagas. Monagas long had been considered the Venezuelan state with Acción Democrática's best regular party organization.

Central to Acción Democrática's special campaign organization in the state or region was an electoral commission. Its president, directly responsible to the national Strategy Commission, exercised supreme authority throughout the region or state on matters of election campaigning. Each president employed resources received from Caracas largely as he pleased. He also oversaw local fund-raising activities and decided upon the local interpretation of national strategies and tactics. In the more important regions, officers of the CEN and former members of President Pérez's cabinet served as electoral commission presidents. In only a few states, Monagas for example, was the electoral commission president confined to playing a secondary role in the election campaign. The reason for this in Monagas was that Acción Democrática's regular party organization seemed so strong that the additional benefits to be achieved by an electoral commission were considered marginal.

Coordination in each region between the regular party organization and the electoral commission depended heavily on the ability of the regional secretary general and the president of the regional electoral commission to work together. Secretaries general were often suspicious that electoral commission presidents intended to remain in the region or state as major figures after the campaign.[28] This challenged a regional secretary general's control over the regular party apparatus. On the other hand, electoral commission presidents often considered that the regular party organization had been negligent and had become inefficient. It was not uncommon for electoral commission presidents to act as if modernization of the region's regular party organization was an important part of their mission.

---

[27] Interview with Homero Parra, president of the Acción Democrática electoral commission in the state of Lara, March 17, 1978.

[28] For example, evidence of tensions between the president of the Lara election commission, Homero Parra, and Acción Democrática Secretary General Miguel Romero Antoni appeared in the local press and in party publications during August 1978. See Luis Mujica, "Es falso rumor de mi renuncia señala—el Doctor Homero Parra" [The rumor of my resignation is false—Dr. Homero Parra], Libertad (Barquisimeto), July 15, 1978, p. 3.

An electoral committee president who attempted to "update" the regular party organization, of course, did become a major political force within the region. This confirmed the worst fears of the secretaries general and their supporters on the regional executive committees that electoral commissions were major threats to their control over the party. Tensions between the regional executive committee and the regional electoral commissions varied directly in proportion to the intensity of such fears. In the worst cases, they produced a state of war between the regular party and special campaign organizations. The electoral commission president and the regional secretary general would then spend considerable time in Caracas attempting to build support among members of the CEN or the *cogollito*. Where this pattern was most pronounced—in the states of Carabobo, Lara, and Zulia—Acción Democrática and Luis Piñerúa made their poorest showing in the December 1978 elections.

Financing. Campaign financing remains one of the murkiest areas of Venezuelan politics. The lack of disclosure legislation makes it impossible to obtain a clear picture of the amount and sources of campaign contributions to political parties. This is also the case with information about how contributions are spent. It is obvious, however, that the costs of election campaigning in Venezuela are escalating rapidly. Martz and Baloyra estimated total expenditures for the 1973 election campaign at $104 million.[29] Domingo Alberto Rangel placed the cost of the 1978 campaign to Acción Democrática alone at $88 million.[30] This level of expenditure necessitated support from powerful interests, who expected some return in the form of favorable government policies. Since parties with little chance of winning are not likely to receive contributions from these interests, it has become increasingly difficult for any group other than the two dominant political parties to obtain sufficient funds to mount a competitive election campaign.

Acción Democrática received campaign contributions in 1978 from four basic sources: local entrepreneurs, multinational corporations, party militants, and government bureaucracies.[31] In 1973 Venezuela's private sector had favored Acción Democrática over COPEI. Five years later local businessmen, while contributing to

---

[29] Martz and Baloyra, *Electoral Mobilization*, pp. 201-3.

[30] Domingo Alberto Rangel, *La pipa rota* [The broken pipe] (Caracas: Vadell Hermanos, 1979), p. 65.

[31] This was the sense of many guarded conversations between the author and assorted party officials during 1978. It is shared by Rangel, *La pipa rota*, pp. 65-67.

both major political parties, again tended to prefer Acción Democrática. Party leaders, however, were sensitive to the charge that President Pérez had paid off campaign debts from 1973 with government
contracts to the businessmen popularly referred to as the Twelve
Apostles.[32] Former President Rómulo Betancourt repeatedly emphasized the need to shield the party from such charges in the future. At
the same time, Acción Democrática recognized the continuing importance of private sources of election campaign financing.

The sensitive job of raising funds for Acción Democrática's election campaign was given to Leopoldo Carnevali.[33] Carnevali had often
represented interests belonging to the Vollmers, one of the largest
and most powerful families in Venezuelan business. On several occasions the Vollmers had criticized the practices of Pérez's Twelve
Apostles. The Vollmers also enjoyed strong ties with influential
business circles in Western Europe and the United States. Carnevali's
connections, therefore, made him an ideal link between Acción Democrática, local entrepreneurs, and international capitalism. His activities
were among the most secret of the 1978 election campaign.

As a Social Democratic party, Acción Democrática never has
been comfortable depending on businessmen for election campaign
financing. When the Twelve Apostles first became an important
political issue, early in 1976, AD president Gonzalo Barrios directed
a task force to explore alternative methods of campaign financing.[34]
One solution was to recommend the creation of a party foundation
that would solicit and manage funds for the 1978 election campaign.
Acción Democrática's CEN subsequently authorized creation of the
foundation, empowering it to issue election bonds valued at 20 million
bolívares. Most bonds were sold to party members and friends. Also,
the five party bureaus—Education, Agriculture, Unions, Professionals,
and Youth—raised money directly from their members. These funds
went to Leopoldo Carnevali's Financial Commission.[35] The overall
amount raised by the bureaus is unknown, but conventional wisdom
held that it was far less than party revenues derived from private
sources.

The bureaucracy was the final major source of resources for the
Acción Democrática campaign. As in many countries, public officials

[32] "Esta vez AD no tendrá apostóles" [This time AD won't have apostles],
Resumen, no. 210 (November 13, 1977), p. 11.
[33] Rangel, *La pipa rota*, p. 66.
[34] "Esta vez AD no tendrá apostóles," p. 11.
[35] For example, see "Un millón de bolívares aportan los educadores para
financiar campaña electoral de Piñerúa" [Educators contribute 1 million bolívars
to Piñerúa's campaign], *El Impulso* (Barquisimeto), August 31, 1978.

owing their position to patronage appointments were expected to return a fixed percentage of their salaries to the appointing political party. Acción Democrática, which between 1974 and 1979 controlled all national and state bureaucracies, benefited greatly from this. Legally, the bureaucracies were expected to remain neutral in any election campaign. In practice, however, Venezuelan political parties have used government agencies under their control to strengthen their electoral prospects. Public administration-based assistance to Acción Democrática and Luis Piñerúa most often involved the discreet lending of personnel from national ministries and autonomous institutes to the national and regional campaign organizations. Also, the technical and public relations units of various state and national bureaucracies were expected to assist the government party. The value of these services is impossible to calculate. At a minimum, they saved tens of millions of dollars for Piñerúa and Acción Democrática.

The Administration of Carlos Andrés Pérez. Law and tradition prohibit the Venezuelan president or members of his cabinet from intervening overtly on behalf of candidates for office during election campaigns. Behind-the-scenes favoritism is another matter. In 1973 President Rafael Caldera did everything possible short of appearing publicly with Lorenzo Fernández to assist his presidential campaign. Earlier, Caldera had battled intensively within COPEI to ensure the nomination of Fernández. In 1977 Carlos Andrés Pérez, on the other hand, backed Luis Piñerúa's opponent in the Acción Democrática presidential primary. Piñerúa's attacks on the administration for corruption and inadequate delivery of public services reflected tensions between two factions of the governing party. As late as January 1978 President Pérez had threatened to withhold from Piñerúa the access to public resources normally enjoyed by the presidential candidate of the government party.

During February 1978 the COPEI candidate, Herrera Campíns, picked up and amplified Piñerúa's theme of administrative corruption and ineptitude.[36] Herrera's television commercial asked incessantly: "¿Dónde están los reales?"—where has all the money gone? This proved so effective that Acción Democrática strategists concluded that if they were to win in December they would have to abandon attacks on an administration controlled by their own party. Even the most severe critics of President Pérez within the party began to stress his positive accomplishments.

---

[36] Personal observation by the author during the first half of February 1978.

Carlos Andrés Pérez responded to the Social Christian attack with perhaps the most elaborate publicity campaign ever mounted in Venezuela. Organized by the well-known Venezuelan public relations firm CORPA, this campaign equaled the publicity efforts of the Piñerúa and Herrera organizations combined.[37] The CORPA campaign's first basic theme—that "step by step" the government was fulfilling its historic mission of modernizing Venezuela—was used on television, in major news magazines, and throughout the national and regional newspapers. In most advertisements the slogan was backed up with data showing rising agricultural production, photographs of new public works, and discussions of advances made in human resource development.

Tied in with the "step by step" theme was a second: "Digan lo que digan, hoy vivo mejor"—whatever they say, I am better off today. The purpose of this slogan was to convince the electorate that policies pursued by the Pérez administration already were beginning to show positive results. Each of the "whatever they say . . ." newspaper advertisements and television commercials featured an individual relating how his or her life had been improved by a program initiated under Pérez.

Beginning in June, Piñerúa strategists attempted to take advantage of the Government's intensive propaganda campaign. The party's publicity commission planned a campaign promising that Piñerúa would both carry on the important programs begun by Carlos Andrés Pérez and strike out in new directions of his own. Party Secretary General Alejandro Izaguirre hoped that this approach would close publicly the breach between Acción Democrática and the Pérez administration. The president of the Strategy Commission, Leandro Mora, argued in the CEN that if intraparty conflict could be suppressed, the way would be open to reassembling the electoral coalition that had propelled Carlos Andrés Pérez to the presidency in 1973.[38]

Conflict between the Government and the party proved difficult to suppress. Much of Luis Piñerúa's successful drive for the presidential nomination had been based on disenchantment with President Pérez. One of the slogans most identified with Piñerúa, "Correcto," implied that he was honorable and efficient—and that the incumbent administration was not. Not surprisingly, therefore, government officials often disliked and distrusted those controlling both the regular party apparatus and the special campaign organizations. With some justi-

---

[37] CORPA also handled the Acción Democrática campaign in 1973. Martz and Baloyra, *Electoral Mobilization*, p. 176.

[38] Interview with Reinaldo Leandro Mora, December 1, 1978.

fication, suspicion persisted within the party that Carlos Andrés Pérez was less than enthusiastic over the possibility of a Piñerúa presidency.

As election day approached, the Government seemed to become more genuinely supportive of Luis Piñerúa, but it was too late to implement a joint offensive strategy. The Pérez Government in its official propaganda only seemed interested in replying to whatever charge the Social Christians made—but it replied on such a massive scale as to overshadow Piñerúa and the Acción Democrática campaign.[39] Also, during October and November, President Pérez increasingly dominated the mass media. His charisma and strong public defense of his Government seemed to cast Piñerúa as a figure of secondary importance. Even Piñerúa's plans for governing appeared to pale in comparison with what Carlos Andrés Pérez already had accomplished. Consequently, massive as the Government's intervention in the campaign was, its impact on Piñerúa's candidacy and on Acción Democrática's congressional nominees was mixed.

Strategies of Mobilization

From 1946, the year of Venezuela's first free election based on universal suffrage, until 1978, Acción Democrática remained Venezuela's strongest and best organized political party. Who won and who lost general elections were determined by the ability of Acción Democrática leaders to hold together and mobilize the party's historic clientele. From a geographic perspective,[40] this involved rolling up majorities as high as 65 percent in the East, the Plains, and the West. The Andes were conceded to the Social Christians and the populous Center to any one of several third parties. In socioeconomic terms, Acción Democrática initially perceived itself as representing the workers, the peasants, and the small-town middle class. Also, the growth of a number of medium-sized cities in the interior of Venezuela after 1950 created a sizable urban proletariat that Acción Democrática counted as part of its clientele. Party mythology reflected this by portraying Acción Democrática as "el Partido del Pueblo"—the people's party.

---

[39] During the final weeks of the campaign, for example, almost half of the political advertising in prime time television was produced by CORPA and concerned the Pérez administration.

[40] This regional scheme is slightly different from that employed by David Blank in the chapter on regionalism. Here, the West includes the states of Falcón, Yaracuy, Lara, and Zulia. The East encompasses Anzoátegui, Sucre, Nueva Esparta, Bolívar, Monagas, the Amazon Territory, and the Amacuro Delta. This latter scheme has been widely used since I introduced it in *Democratic Campaigning in Venezuela.*

From time to time Rómulo Betancourt or Gonzalo Barrios would state that this signified that Acción Democrática represented all classes. Nevertheless, the party thought of itself as the defender of the have-nots.

Until Herrera Campíns's victory in December 1978, the only presidential election in which the historic Acción Democrática coalition had failed to win a plurality was 1968. That election followed the famous contested primary election between Gonzalo Barrios and Luis Beltran Prieto Figueroa. After Acción Democrática's CEN had refused to accept his apparent victory, Prieto left to form the People's Electoral Movement. Five years later, Carlos Andrés Pérez restored the presidency to Acción Democrática with one of the most resounding electoral triumphs in Venezuelan political history. Party leaders believed that Pérez had won in 1973 because he had succeeded in reassembling the historically dominant Acción Democrática coalition.[41]

Carlos Andrés Pérez brought together his party's historically dominant coalition, but he also added to it. Pérez came from the Andean state of Táchira. The entire Andean region, long a stronghold of the Social Christians, voted overwhelmingly in 1973 for its native son and for Acción Democrática. In 1958, 1963, and 1968 Venezuela's capital city gave a variety of third parties more votes than Acción Democrática. However, Carlos Andrés Pérez won Caracas by a substantial margin. In Caracas, and in cities of the interior, Pérez received important support from the emerging middle class. This sector traditionally had viewed Acción Democrática as a threatening alliance of peasants and the urban poor. In summary, previously hostile sectors voted unexpectedly for the Acción Democrática presidential candidate. By inflating the party's total vote, their support obscured substantial inroads that the Social Christians had made among groups once thought to be the exclusive preserve of Acción Democrática. These included urban workers, easterners, peasants, and the urban poor.

By the third year of the Pérez administration, the president's job approval rating was negative and getting worse. Herrera and Piñerúa, already seen by most observers as their respective parties' presidential nominees, were running neck and neck in the public opinion polls. An unusually large proportion of the electorate remained undecided. Consequently, by the end of 1976 the euphoria that once had led to speculation around party headquarters that Acción Democrática would be in power for the remainder of the century gave way to concern.

---

[41] Interviews with six members of the Acción Democrática CEN in June 1974.

The impetus to take a hard look at the party's standing with the electorate came from its Area Commissions.[42] These commissions, organized under prodding from Rómulo Betancourt and Gonzalo Barrios, were seen as the party's mechanism for monitoring and influencing government policy. Betancourt and Barrios envisioned periodic meetings between Pérez's cabinet ministers and their counterparts on the Area Commissions. The president, however, forbade his ministers to meet with Area Commission officials. He maintained that such an arrangement compromised unacceptably the separation between party and Government. Consequently, the Area Commissions were left hanging.

Rómulo Betancourt personally had persuaded Luis Alfaro Ucero, Acción Democrática's political leader in the eastern state of Monagas, to come to Caracas to oversee the Area Commissions. With little to do, the energetic Alfaro turned his attention to analyzing his party's prospects in the upcoming elections. He quickly concluded that its organization had deteriorated dangerously and that the leadership's assumptions about the sources of Acción Democrática strength were questionable. Alfaro's cogent analysis and his reputation as a master organizer convinced Betancourt, Barrios, and Piñerúa that he should be named national secretary of organization. Upon assuming this position, Luis Alfaro Ucero brought to the Organization Secretariat many of the talented professionals he had attracted to the Area Commissions.

The new secretary of organization anticipated that he would act as chief of staff for Piñerúa during the 1978 election campaign—the role that Piñerúa had played for Carlos Andrés Pérez in 1973. But Piñerúa never gave Alfaro the kind of authority over campaign chief Reinaldo Leandro Mora that Piñerúa had exercised over his counterpart five years earlier. This introduced inconsistencies and inefficiencies into Acción Democrática's 1978 campaign strategies. Nevertheless, on overall strategies Luis Alfaro Ucero and Reinaldo Leandro Mora were in agreement. These can be classified as strategies of consensus and strategies of conflict.

Strategies of consensus seek to maximize the vote of those employing them.[43] Alfaro Ucero and Leandro Mora agreed that to mobilize a winning coalition behind Luis Piñerúa they should both reinforce the party's traditional clientele and recruit independents

---

[42] In 1974 and 1975 the author consulted professionally with the firm of Pizzolante and Torres, which held contracts for developing the organizational structure for the Area Commissions.

[43] For a more detailed discussion see Martz and Baloyra, *Electoral Mobilization*, pp. xxvi-xxxvii.

and others who had made the 1973 triumph possible. Party leaders, as suggested earlier, saw their historic clientele both in terms of class and in terms of regionalism.

The party had good reason to believe that Piñerúa could count on strong support from the workers. More than half of the leadership positions in the Venezuelan Confederation of Labor were in the hands of Acción Democrática militants.[44] The Social Christians were very secondary within organized labor, and all parties of the left together were weaker still. José Vargas, the national president of the Venezuelan Confederation of Labor, strongly supported Acción Democrática and Luis Piñerúa. Party strategists planned to give Vargas high visibility throughout the election campaign.

Acción Democrática had dominated the National Peasant Federation since the 1945 revolution.[45] During the 1959–1964 coalition Government, however, the Social Christians began making significant inroads among the peasantry. These were especially striking in the states of Lara, Zulia, Barinas, and Portuguesa. In the East—the states of Monagas, Anzoátegui, Bolívar, Sucre, and Nueva Esparta—a minority of peasants historically supported the Democratic Republican Union. As the URD's strength declined nationally, much of its peasant clientele gravitated toward the Social Christians. Other eastern peasants who had split with Acción Democrática in 1967 were arduously courted by Social Christian organizers after the party returned to the opposition in 1974. Alfaro Ucero and Leandro Mora recognized that they would have a major problem in restoring the level of Acción Democrática dominance of an earlier decade among peasants.[46]

Except in Caracas, Acción Democrática had traditionally enjoyed support from the urban poor. In 1973 Carlos Andrés Pérez had carried the slums of Caracas. Luis Piñerúa hoped to repeat this feat in 1978. Acción Democrática, however, felt uneasy about the impact of rising prices on the political preferences of the least affluent. President Pérez had attempted to shield the urban poor against the worst effects of inflation through an elaborate program of subsidies for housing and

[44] The best discussion in English of the politics of Venezeulan unionism is Stuart I. Fagan, "Unionism and Democracy," in Martz and Myers, *Venezuela*, pp. 174-94.
[45] See John D. Powell, *Political Mobilization of the Venezuelan Peasant* (Cambridge: Harvard University Press, 1971).
[46] Interview with Luis Raúl Matos, subsecretary general of Acción Democrática for organization, July 12, 1977.

food.[47] During 1976 and 1977, however, disturbing reports were reaching Acción Democrática's Organization Secretariat that for the first time the Social Christians were making significant inroads among the lowest fifth of the population. Consequently, Acción Democrática strategists decided to stress the party's populist roots and resurrect the old charge that the Social Christians spoke only for the rich.

Another reinforcement strategy involved those who had supported the candidacy of Jaime Lusinchi in the 1977 primary election. Lusinchi believed that the harshness of Piñerúa's attack on him personally and on his supporters was unjustified in a party primary election. His support for Piñerúa initially appeared half-hearted. The same was true for many who had been associated with the Lusinchi candidacy. Piñerúa and Betancourt addressed this problem by incorporating Lusinchi into the *cogollito* and by reserving a significant number of places on the party's legislative lists for his supporters. These gestures suggest a strong sense within Acción Democrática's dominant wing of the need to restore and nourish the party's historic clientele.

The regional dimension of Acción Democrática's traditional coalition has become increasingly blurred since 1958.[48] Party strategists watched with disbelief and uneasiness as the Social Christians expanded out of their Andean stronghold in the elections of 1963 and 1968. In the latter election, they made significant gains in Caracas and became the strongest electoral force in the populous state of Zulia. In 1973, despite Carlos Andrés Pérez's resounding victory, the Social Christians garnered the largest vote in their history. With the exception of the Andes and the Center-West,[49] the Social Christians made impressive advances in all regions. Only in the East did Acción Democrática maintain anything like the two-to-one advantage over the Social Christians that it had once enjoyed outside of Caracas and the Andes.

Between 1974 and 1978 the Social Christians mounted successful organizing efforts in the Center-West, in the industrial states of Carabobo and Aragua, and in Zulia. Acción Democrática strategists

---

[47] This theme was elaborated in great detail by David Morales Bello in his speech to Congress on June 2, 1976. The speech is reprinted in Acción Democrática, *Defensa de la política económica del gobierno* [Defending the government's economic policy] (Caracas: Fracción Parlamentaria de Acción Democrática, 1976), pp. 41-58.

[48] David J. Myers, "Urban Voting, Structural Cleavage and Party System Evolution: The Case of Venezuela," *Comparative Politics*, vol. 8, no. 1 (October 1975), pp. 119-51.

[49] The Center-West includes the states of Falcón, Lara, and Yaracuy.

believed that Social Christian advances in these areas could be minimized or reversed by an intensive, year-long election campaign.[50] In any case, the party would use its historic majorities in the East, its newly developed strength in the Andes, and its growing popularity in metropolitan Caracas to win its fifth out of six presidential elections.

Acción Democrática also anticipated recruiting elements of the bourgeoisie and the emerging middle class. Relations between the party and the bourgeoisie had been characterized until the 1960s by mutual distrust and antagonism. Most businessmen had come from the Caracas oligarchy or the Andean political elite that governed during the first half of this century. Acción Democrática had seized power in 1945 by defeating the governing Caracas-Andes alliance. Once in power, the party had frightened the bourgeoisie with its public sector development programs and socialist rhetoric, and the business community's hostility toward Acción Democrática had been an important cause of the military coup in 1948. Ten years later, however, most businessmen had welcomed the overthrow of General Marcos Pérez Jiménez.[51]

The Betancourt administration (1959–1964) had pursued a policy of economic development through government-supervised capitalism that had reserved important sectors of the economy for private business activity. A continuation of this policy during the subsequent Leoni administration had convinced businessmen that they could live with Acción Democrática. Most AD leaders who opposed accommodation with the bourgeoisie had followed Luis Beltran Prieto Figueroa out of the party after the disputed 1967 primary election.

Businessmen in Venezuela seldom commit themselves entirely to one political party or administration.[52] Consequently, while profits were acceptable during the Betancourt and Leoni administrations, and very good during the Government of Carlos Andrés Pérez, Acción Democrática had to court business all over again to gain backing for Piñerúa. The decision by Leopoldo Carnevali to serve as president of the party's Financial Commission signaled that Piñerúa had made his peace with the private sector. Additional evidence of the party's strategy of courting businessmen was the presence of many prominent entrepreneurs on Acción Democrática's regional Committees of Independents.

---

[50] Interview with Luis Raúl Matos, July 12, 1977.

[51] This theme is analyzed in considerable detail by John Friedmann, *Venezuela: From Doctrine to Dialogue* (Syracuse: Syracuse University Press, 1965).

[52] José Antonio Gil, "Entrepreneurs and Regime Consolidation," in Martz and Myers, *Venezuela*, pp. 134-56.

The middle class was a second focus of recruitment. Conventional wisdom portrayed the middle class, especially in the large cities, as firmly committed to the Social Christians. In 1973, however, many middle-class voters had supported Carlos Andrés Pérez. Luis Alfaro Ucero and Reinaldo Leandro Mora both felt that Acción Democrática should arduously court the middle class in 1978. They believed that the most important political variable influencing middle-class voters was their extreme vulnerability to even the slightest vicissitudes of the Venezuelan economy. Therefore, middle-class voters would be highly vulnerable to appeals stressing the greater likelihood of stability and continued economic growth under a Piñerúa administration.[53]

Strategies of conflict aim at minimizing electoral support for one's opponents. Not surprisingly, the Social Christians were the focus of Acción Democrática's strategies of conflict. Alfaro Ucero and Leandro Mora attached the highest priority to generating antagonism between the Social Christians and the middle class and between the Social Christians and the peasants, who had been moving away from their Acción Democrática roots. The purpose of this strategy was to bring about a major realignment within the middle classes. COPEI was to be accused of having performed less capably than Acción Democrática in promoting economic development. At the same time, a parallel consensus strategy would appeal to the middle class, stressing that Piñerúa's administration would maintain or increase the rate of economic growth.

Acción Democrática also attempted to separate COPEI from the peasants by contrasting unfavorably the rural development programs of Rafael Caldera with those of Carlos Andrés Pérez. In addition, the government party believed initially that in some rural areas helping to maintain the People's Electoral Movement and the Democratic Republican Union as viable political parties would prevent their peasant supporters from gravitating to the Social Christians. As the campaign progressed, however, the Democratic Republican Union entered into a formal alliance with the Social Christians. The MEP's presidential candidate also indicated his preference for the Social Christians over Acción Democrática. This destroyed the utility of strategies aimed at strengthening these declining parties.[54]

---

[53] Confirmed in several conversations with Leandro Mora and Alfaro Ucero between March 15, 1978, and October 20, 1978.
[54] The URD-COPEI alliance is discussed at length in Don Herman's chapter on Herrera's campaign.

Acción Democrática strategists also developed several general themes for the attack on the Social Christians. The first was COPEI's dangerous unreliability. Here the intent was to fix in the electorate's consciousness the cleavage between Social Christian conservatives and the party's youthful advocates of community property. Contrasting the capitalist orientation of the one and the statist ideology of the other was seen as a means of discouraging support for Herrera among those who wanted stability. A second strategy was to label the Social Christians sure losers. Acción Democrática reasoned that if voters believed the Social Christian candidate could not win, leftists and other opponents would stick with their first choice on the presidential ballot, rather than vote for Herrera as a means of getting rid of Acción Democrática. Finally, the Social Christians were to be attacked as potentially soft on radical leftists who had attempted to overthrow the democratic system between 1960 and 1967. This final theme, like the stress on the danger to stability posed by internal contradictions within COPEI, aimed at convincing businessmen and the middle class that their interests were incompatible with voting for Luis Herrera Campíns.[55]

The process of selecting candidates for the party's legislative lists was used both to mobilize support and to recruit talent. The legislative offices to be filled by the December 3 election included senator, deputy, and state legislator, and the national party leaders had enormous leverage over the regional party organizations in drawing up the lists for each. For example, each state elected two senators, and each of the parties contesting the election presented two names in each state for the office of senator. Given the political realities of past voting patterns, the AD candidate listed first in each state was sure to be elected—and the AD candidate listed second had almost no chance. For any legislative office, location on the party list was all-important.

Within Acción Democrática the struggle to obtain secure positions on the party lists was consuming. The election campaign virtually stopped in early August 1978, when party leaders turned their attention to selecting legislative candidates and placing them on the party lists. Not until early September, when Secretary General Alejandro Izaguirre presented completed lists for each state to the Supreme Electoral Council, did campaigning again become the party's major concern.[56]

---

[55] *Resumen*, no. 539 (December 3, 1978), p. 10, contains a quick rundown of the Acción Democrática electoral strategy.

[56] *El Nacional*, August 13, 1978, contains a preliminary Acción Democrática

The candidate selection process began when each of Acción Democrática's regional Executive Committees (CES) selected its list of legislative candidates for the Senate, the Chamber of Deputies, and the state legislature. These choices were conveyed to the National Executive Committee (CEN). They took into account that national leaders with their political base in the submitting region would have choice spots on lists for the Senate or for the Chamber of Deputies. Discussions between the regional party officials and the CEN followed. When the CEN and the regional leaders finished analyzing who should be the party's candidates, regardless of whether they were in agreement, all lists were sent to the *cogollito* for final approval. For state legislators final approval was delegated to a sub-*cogollito* chaired by Arturo Hernández Grisanti, an influential member of the CEN.[57]

A variety of cross-cutting cleavages determined which hopefuls received coveted positions on the party lists and which did not. In the first place, positions were divided between those who had backed Piñerúa in the primary election and those who had favored Lusinchi. Roughly two-thirds of the list positions were reserved for the former. The proportion would have been even higher had not President Pérez intervened repeatedly on behalf of the Lusinchi faction. In this tense situation party President Gonzalo Barrios played an important mediating role.[58]

Many positions, as indicated above, were reserved for national party leaders. Thus, Gonzalo Barrios ran as the party's preferred senatorial candidate in the Federal District. Reinaldo Leandro Mora received this status in the state of Barinas. Other senatorial nominations went to the political leaders of major states like Eloy Parragua Villamarin in Zulia and Doris Parra de Orellana in Lara. Finally, some Senate seats were reserved for prestigious independents such as Admiral Wolfgang Larrazábal (Sucre) and Ramón J. Velásquez (Táchira).

These factors also influenced the selection of candidates for the Chamber of Deputies. In addition, the top people in the national

---

list for the national Congress. The same newspaper carried a feature article on August 20 entitled "AD y Copei dedicados a la elaboración de planchas" [AD and COPEI focus on drawing up their electoral lists]. *Semana* (Caracas), no. 530 (October 1, 1978), carried an after-the-fact account entitled "Las planchas: bombas 'solo-mata-gente' " [The electoral lists: bombs that only kill people].

[57] "Terminadas las listas al Congreso por el partido Acción Democrática" [AD's congressional lists are complete], *El Universal*, August 14, 1978.

[58] "El CEN y los CES de AD" [AD's CEN and CES], *Resumen*, no. 250 (August 20, 1978). See also Junio Pérez Blasini, "La rabatina por las planchas produce odios y amores desbordados [The scramble over the lists awakes extreme loves and hates], *Resumen*, no. 251 (August 27, 1978), pp. 6-7.

party bureaus received positions that assured them election to the Chamber. José Vargas, for example, was placed high on the list from Caracas. Vargas was the party's union leader and president of the national Venezuelan Confederation of Labor. Similarly, José Agreda, the national secretary of education, appeared third on the list from Carabobo, a populous industrial state. Three deputy positions also went to the Armas family. Controlling one of Venezuela's largest publishing chains, the Armas group enthusiastically backed Luis Piñerúa Ordaz.[59]

In addition to filling Acción Democrática's legislative leadership positions, decisions to place individuals on the party lists were one means of implementing strategy. Reserving positions for supporters of both Lusinchi and Piñerúa reinforced party unity by giving all factions a stake in the outcome of the election. The selection of independents like Velásquez signaled to the middle class that professionals who were not party members would be listened to by a Piñerúa administration. Larrazábal's placement on the lists was to reassure the urban poor, especially in Caracas, that Acción Democrática remained the "party of the people." It is to a more systematic discussion of how Acción Democrática implemented its mobilization strategy that we now turn.

Implementation and the Use of Information

During the late 1940s Acción Democrática could rely on an unmatched party organization to ensure it overwhelming electoral victories. In 1958, after the party emerged from a decade of underground activity, greater emphasis was placed on special campaign efforts. With the passing of another decade, Acción Democrática and the Social Christians both began to rely on public opinion polls as a means of discerning how they were doing as the election campaign progressed. In 1973, Carlos Andrés Pérez and Acción Democrática employed the well-known U.S. political consultant Joseph Napolitan. Napolitan's questionnaires probed for information about how parties and candidates could best make their case to the electorate. They were a major innovation in Venezuelan campaigning. Following the 1973 election, it was widely believed that Acción Democrática's unexpectedly decisive victory had been facilitated by Napolitan's transplanting of campaign management techniques from the United States,

---

[59] "El Candidato Luis Piñerúa podría introducir reajustes a listados aprobados por el CEN" [Piñerúa might modify the lists approved by the CEN], *El Nacional,* August 22, 1978.

and imported campaigning techniques and foreign political consultants were used to an unprecedented degree in the 1978 election campaign.[60]

Polling and Foreign Consultants. Throughout the 1974–1979 constitutional period Acción Democrática maintained loose contact with Joseph Napolitan, F. Clifton White, and George Gaither. All three had worked closely with Carlos Andrés Pérez in 1973. Therefore, when public opinion polls began to reflect growing dissatisfaction with the president and the governing party, it was natural for Acción Democrática to turn for advice to these same individuals. In late 1976 George Gaither was asked to undertake a comprehensive poll profiling the party's image, and Joseph Napolitan agreed to analyze the meaning of these findings for the upcoming 1978 elections. Meetings between Napolitan and Piñerúa, both before and after the primary election of July 1977, did not go smoothly. The two never established the kind of mutual trust that Napolitan and Carlos Andrés Pérez felt for each other.[61] Consequently, Napolitan withdrew as a major adviser.

Although Luis Piñerúa was skeptical about Napolitan's grasp of Venezuelan politics, he remained committed to public opinion polling as a major source of information in the planning of his election campaign. Piñerúa personally approved the contracting of George Gaither to undertake a series of monthly public opinion surveys between September 1977 and November 1978. The entire nation was to be polled. However, the Strategy Commission asked Gaither to design a sampling frame that would facilitate the identification of unique patterns of political party support in the following regions: Metropolitan Center, Center-West, Plains, Andes, Zulia, East, and Guayana. The cities of Caracas and Maracaibo also were to be separated from the overall national sample so they could be analyzed individually. The Analysis Unit of the Strategy Commission was entrusted with analyzing the electoral implications of Gaither's polls. It performed the same mission for several special polls the party contracted out to DATOS and Gallup. Luis Baez Duarte, a mathematician trained at the University of California, headed the closely guarded Analysis Unit located in the Alta Florida district of northeastern Caracas.[62]

Reinaldo Leandro Mora remained secretive throughout the campaign about the content and findings of all polling done for the party.

---

[60] See Martz and Baloyra, *Electoral Mobilization*, pp. 178-79.

[61] This was obvious to all of those (including the author) who served as political consultants to Acción Democrática in 1978. It was also confirmed in the December 4, 1978, interview with Luis Raúl Matos.

[62] The author discussed the findings of Acción Democrática's Gaither and Gallup polls with Baez Duarte on numerous occasions.

Upon receiving each Gaither poll, he asked Baez Durate to prepare a summary of its most important findings for the *cogollito*, the National Executive Committee, and selected members of the special campaign organization. The electoral implications of trends and patterns in public opinion were discussed in confidential meetings that sometimes included only Leandro Mora, Piñerúa, Betancourt, and Gonzalo Barrios. On more than one occasion Organization Secretary Luis Alfaro Ucero did not attend these meetings. Consequently, decisions within the Organization Secretariat affecting the electoral activity of the regular party organization were sometimes made without knowledge of any relevant information that had been uncovered in the public opinion surveys.

Several important regional party organizations received information from their own polling organizations and their own political consultants. In Caracas, for example, Leandro Mora hired the local polling firm of Merc-Analysis to take the political pulse of the capital city. The task of interpreting its findings was contracted to VOVICA, a subsidiary of the well-known public relations company CORPA. In Lara and Monagas a small North American consulting group, Mycon, undertook both strategic polling and analysis. Some local surveys were also done in Zulia. Otherwise, strategy was implemented at the regional level either on the basis of information sent out through the national Strategy Commission or on the basis of the local leaders' intuition.

The poll findings contained five basic messages: (1) that the election was close, (2) that the voters' perceptions of who could win influenced their choices, (3) that neither Herrera nor Piñerúa excited great passion, (4) that a range of services and conditions were not meeting popular expectations, and (5) that the overall impression of how things were going critically influenced the vote.[63] The findings set forth in Table 4–1 appeared in a Mycon report to the Electoral Commission in the state of Lara. They are typical of the information provided to Acción Democrática by pollsters and political consultants. The table profiles the degree of seriousness voters assigned to problems that newspaper reporters pointed out as indicating that things in general were going poorly or well.

Strategy Implementation and Issues. On the basis of the party's long history of electoral victories, the Strategy Commission gave highest

---

[63] These findings, with minor variations, were consistent throughout the country. The author had an opportunity to compare his findings in Lara and Monagas with those of Gallup, Gaither, and DATOS.

121

TABLE 4–1

VENEZUELA'S MOST SERIOUS PROBLEMS:
SURVEY OF VOTERS IN LARA, AUGUST 1978

(in percentages)

	"Very Serious" or "Exceptionally Serious" Rating among:		
Problem	Respondents supporting a presidential candidate (80%)	Undecided respondents who revealed 1973 vote (15%)	Undecided respondents who did not reveal 1973 vote (5%)
Cost of living	70	73	85
Housing	63	60	68
Scarcity of food	61	64	80
Crime	61	67	69
Corruption	60	50	67
Medical services	68	64	69
Unemployment	50	56	63
Education	42	43	47
Poverty	78	80	89
Lack of services	51	59	63
Illegal immigrants	40	37	46
Abandoned children	58	60	59
Transport	54	53	61

NOTE: N = 1,861. Residents were presented with a list of problems and asked to indicate how serious they were. The above percentages combine the "very serious" and "exceptionally serious" categories.
SOURCE: Mycon (see chapter 3, note to table 3-2).

priority to reuniting its traditional clientele. One group of implementing tactics appealed to historic party loyalties as a means of generating electoral support for Piñerúa. He was portrayed as the most recent in a long line of outstanding Acción Democrática leaders who had been elected to the presidency. Newspaper advertisements and party publications commonly displayed a sequence of photographs that began with Rómulo Gallegos, continued with Rómulo Betancourt, Raúl Leoni, and Carlos Andrés Pérez, and ended with Luis Piñerúa. A slick film chronicling Acción Democrática's thirty-seven years as a political party employed a modified version of this tactic. It was shown on national television and at party gatherings.[64]

A different tactic for reuniting the party's historic clientele was addressed to those who had supported Jaime Lusinchi in the primary election. During the closing months of the campaign Lusinchi and Piñerúa appeared together in public on numerous occasions. The party also circulated widely a photograph of Piñerúa and Lusinchi giving each other the typical Latin American embrace, the *abrazo*. Important Acción Democrática leaders such as Gonzalo Barrios and Carlos Canache Mata wrote numerous columns for the major Caracas newspapers aimed at selling Piñerúa's candidacy to sympathetic professionals and technicians.[65]

In addition to portraying Piñerúa as the legitimate heir of past Acción Democrática presidents, the Strategy Commission attempted to project an image of Piñerúa as a forceful leader in his own right. Leandro Mora gave basic responsibility for this to VOVICA, including the problems presented by Piñerúa's extremely short stature, his lack of formal education beyond the sixth grade, his generally dour appearance, and his inability to spark enthusiasm when speaking publicly.

On the positive side, Piñerúa was intelligent, and his administrative experience far overshadowed that of Luis Herrera. The Social Christian candidate was a creature of Congress; in contrast, Piñerúa had implemented President Betancourt's agrarian reform program and had served as President Leoni's governor in the state of Monagas and as President Pérez's minister of the interior. Piñerúa also boasted an impeccable record as an underground leader during the Pérez Jiménez dictatorship, a charming wife, and model children. Finally, he had secured his party's presidential nomination in a hotly contested primary election, which he had won by a margin of almost two-to-one.

VOVICA's approach was to ignore Piñerúa's negative personal attributes and stress the positive. His administrative experience and firm stand against corruption were the message of what became the

---

[64] These advertisements appeared throughout the regional and national press with increasing frequency after early September. The Acción Democrática film was copied on videotape and shown throughout the country.

[65] For an informative cross section of these columns see Carlos Canache Mata, "3 razones para triunfar" [Three reasons for winning], *El Nacional*, September 30, 1978; Gonzalo Barrios, "Lo que nos une" [What unites us], *El Nacional*, November 26, 1978; Pedro Paris Montesinos, "Piñerúa, autodidacto capaz" [Piñerúa, a capable, self-taught man], *El Informador* (Barquisimeto), September 1, 1978; and Alfredo Ramírez Torres, "La candidatura de Piñerúa" [Piñerúa's candidacy], *El Universal*, August 24, 1978.

dominant slogan of Piñerúa's campaign: "Capacidad y Firmeza para Gobernar"—the strength and competence to govern. Piñerúa's wife, Berenice, was given moderate prominence. She turned out to be an excellent campaigner, though the near death of her daughter from a ruptured appendix took her to Houston, Texas, during most of October and November. Also, during the final month of campaigning Piñerúa switched to a suit and tie. This contrasted with his earlier style of appearing in slacks and an open-necked shirt. The change was largely a reaction to Social Christian publicity that displayed Herrera in a dark suit and seated in a chair resembling the one used by Venezuela's president on ceremonial occasions.[66]

Acción Democrática also played on socioeconomic cleavages in courting its historic clientele. Piñerúa's platform, or program for governing, was subtitled "The Consolidation of Well-Being." This theme reflected the public opinion polls' finding that when individuals believed that things were going well and were likely to improve, they disproportionately favored Piñerúa and Acción Democrática. The first section of the program dealt with public services.[67] Party polling suggested that views about public services correlated strongly with perceptions of how things in general were going.

Acción Democrática's tactic for returning the rural poor to their political roots centered on promises to increase the availability of agricultural credits dramatically. Agricultural credits could be used to add farm animals, purchase seed, make other capital improvements, or improve housing. Piñerúa also promised to maintain price supports for agricultural products. These programs together were presented as a shield against inflation, a problem that peasants found intensely disturbing.

Inflation also bothered the urban poor, most acutely in the area of housing. President Pérez reorganized the housing bureaucracy in the middle of his presidential term, but the new arrangement never lived up to expectations. It became a major political liability for Acción Democrática. In several television commercials produced by VOVICA, Piñerúa walked through working-class neighborhoods and promised to make housing a major concern of his Government. However, Piñerúa again seemed to be responding to Herrera, who, in an

---

[66] This photograph of Herrera graced billboards throughout the country and appeared on the center of the green Social Christian card that was printed on the ballot.

[67] The party distributed the national government program for Piñerúa's administration in early November. Soon afterward similar programs appeared for each state. These documents were prepared by Leandro Mora's people in coordination with Piñerúa's office in Torre Maracaibo.

earlier television commercial, had charged Acción Democrática with having dealt ineffectively with housing problems.[68]

Recruitment strategies, as we have seen, focused primarily on independents, businessmen, and youth. Skyrocketing housing prices had affected middle-class independents as well as the poor, and Acción Democrática sought their support by promising that Piñerúa would channel new funds into the savings and loan associations. Down payments on houses and condominiums would be reduced, and mortgages would be spaced out over periods as long as forty years. Piñerúa also promised middle-class professionals and technicians that he would expand opportunities for their children to receive higher education and that he would develop new cultural facilities for medium-sized cities. Finally, party leaders reminded the large number of naturalized Venezuelans, most of whom were middle class, that Acción Democrática valued their economic and technical skills and that the party had sponsored legislation enabling foreigners with ten years' residence in the country to vote in the upcoming municipal elections.[69]

Acción Democrática did not appeal to businessmen in the mass media. Leopoldo Carnevali's acceptance of the chairmanship of Piñerúa's Financial Commission, however, was an important signal that his Government would continue the probusiness policies of other Acción Democrática administrations. If its courtship of business was low key, the Government party relied heavily on the media to attract new voters. Polling indicated that Piñerúa was doing poorly with the eighteen to twenty-three age group and that, given the closeness of the election, this could be decisive. Responsibility within the regular party organization for those coming of voting age rested with the Youth Bureau. Hector Alonzo López was the bureau's secretary. A persuasive and fiery speaker, Alonzo López acquitted himself well in a much publicized debate on national television with Donald Ramírez, his Social Christian counterpart. Piñerúa also used Alonzo López as a platform speaker at major party rallies. However, Alonzo López's oratorical skills far exceeded his abilities as an organizer. During his five years as national youth secretary the party's youth organization had deteriorated. Also, Alonzo López was close to

---

[68] For example, the Social Christians' controversial "Caucagüita" television commercial featured a young mother explaining how bad public services were in her neighborhood and how inattentive the Government had been to housing needs. Soon afterward Piñerúa began emphasizing that his administration would stress public services and housing.

[69] This theme was stressed at rallies for nationalized Venezuelans attended by the author in Monagas and Lara.

Carlos Andrés Pérez.[70] Piñerúa decided that the Youth Bureau would not be the fulcrum of his efforts to attract youth.

Virgilio Avila Vivas was selected to develop a special campaign organization to increase the appeal of Piñerúa and Acción Democrática among new voters. A former governor of the state of Nueva Esparta, the youthful Avila Vivas maintained good relations with all factions of the party. His success with youth in Nueva Esparta during the party's years in opposition demonstrated considerable ability to attract support from beyond Acción Democrática's historic clientele. Avila Vivas quickly assembled a team in Caracas that gave his Youth for Piñerúa movement high visibility. At the state level, however, the visibility and effectiveness of Youth for Piñerúa depended largely on the Electoral Commission president's willingness to fund the operation. In the state of Lara, Youth for Piñerúa played an important role. On the other hand, in the state of Monagas greater emphasis was placed on the party's regular youth organization.[71]

Youth for Piñerúa's contribution seemed positive throughout most of the campaign. Its introduction of a four-note plastic whistle that sounded the final bar of a popular Piñerúa jingle provided a moment of high camp and good fun. Unfortunately, during the final ten days of the campaign Avila Vivas himself became a political issue. His caricature graced the cover of the November 26 issue of the newsmagazine *Resumen,* and the lead article linked the former governor to official corruption that *Resumen's* editor, Jorge Olavarria, connected with the murder of Ramón Carmona, a well-known lawyer. *Resumen's* accusations were neither proved nor refuted prior to the balloting on December 3. After the article's appearance, however, Avila Vivas maintained a low profile and Youth for Piñerúa lost its customary exuberance.[72]

Acción Democrática's conflict strategy aimed at sowing discord between COPEI and four groups: businessmen, the middle class, peasants, and leftist voters who might be considering voting for Herrera. Here businessmen and the middle class were lumped together. The "community property" issue became the basic weapon for alienating businessmen and the middle class from Herrera and the

---

[70] Alonzo López's early ties with Carlos Andrés Pérez were confirmed in several informal conversations with John D. Martz.

[71] For an informative discussion of Youth for Piñerúa see Carlos Pérez Ariza, "Los nuevos adecos" [The new *adecos*], *Bohemia* (Caracas), no. 817 (November 20-26, 1978), pp. 32-33.

[72] *Resumen,* no. 264 (November 26, 1978).

Social Christians, and AD campaigners raised it whenever possible.[73] Social Christian youth had spoken of the means of production as community property since the early 1960s when they had begun seriously challenging the Communists in student politics at the Central University. The operational meaning of making all means of production community property remained unclear. However, the very words "community property" alarmed the private sector and many in the professional middle class. Social Christian strategists made a conscious decision to remain silent about community property throughout the campaign. Their Acción Democrática counterparts became increasingly frustrated because they could not draw any Social Christian into a public debate about community property. Leandro Mora finally decided to force the matter during the final weeks of the campaign. His decision resulted in the controversial watermelon advertisements. These advertisements, which appeared in all major newspapers, insinuated that the Social Christian party was like a watermelon—green on the outside and red on the inside. Green, of course, was the color associated with the Social Christians; red suggested communism. The message was unmistakable. It told entrepreneurs and the middle classes that if they voted for Herrera they would get a political party that at its core wanted to control all economic activity and abolish private property.

Housing and new agricultural credits were the cornerstones of Piñerúa's appeal to the rural poor. Regional radio stations discussed the meaning of these priorities for each region in early morning broadcasts tailored to peasant voters. These broadcasts also favorably compared the accomplishments of Carlos Andrés Pérez with those of his allegedly "do nothing" Social Christian predecessor. Never subtle, they were designed to convince peasants that their true interests did not lie with the Social Christians.

Implementing a conflict strategy that was intended to discourage lefist voters from supporting Luis Herrera Campíns involved clandestinely strengthening the presidential candidacies of José Vicente Rangel and Américo Martín. Acción Democrática surveys revealed that Piñerúa's support was "harder" than Herrera's.[74] Many leftists

---

[73] Community property was traced back to early Christianity when newly converted Christians were asked to turn over their worldly possessions to religious leaders for the use of all believers. For a brief discussion of the Social Christian view of property published in the mid-1960s see José Barbeito, *Introducción al pensamiento Socialcristiano* [Introduction to Social Christian thinking] (Caracas: COPEI, Secretaría de formación pública, n.d.), pp. 75-88.

[74] Mycon polls in Lara and Monagas. The "hardness" of the vote reflects the proportion of voters supporting the candidate who are not enthusiastic about any other candidate.

intended to vote for Herrera in hopes of denying Piñerúa the presidency. Given Piñerúa's close ties to Betancourt and his participation in the anticommunist policies of the 1960s, these leftists attached greater importance to keeping Piñerúa from assuming power than to expressing support for the candidate they really preferred, but who had no chance of winning. Acción Democrática strategists recognized immediately how potentially dangerous this attitude was given the closeness of the race. Consequently, they provided assistance to the Movement toward Socialism and the Movement of the Revolutionary Left in preparing last-minute television commercials.[75]

Another tactic designed to discourage the left from voting for Herrera was to convince voters that Piñerúa already had won. Acción Democrática strategists reasoned that if leftists believed Herrera had no chance of winning, they would vote for the candidate they really preferred: Rangel or Martín. Consequently, Leandro Mora put the chief of his Analysis Unit, Luis Baez Duarte, on national television. Baez Duarte presented findings from the October Gaither poll that gave Piñerúa a four-percentage-point advantage over Herrera. Fourteen percent remained undecided. Baez's presentation was intended to demonstrate that Piñerúa was a sure winner. The large number of MAS and MIR small-card voters who apparently marked their large card for Herrera, however, suggests that Baez may have convinced many leftists that the race was sufficiently close that voting for Herrera could deny Piñerúa the presidency.

Finally, in addition to implementing campaign strategies, Acción Democrática had to deal with two unexpected and potentially damaging issues: Luis Herrera's offer to debate Piñerúa on national television, and the infamous Carmona case. Herrera's challenge came in late August and provoked great anxiety within the *cogollito*. It was felt that Piñerúa's short stature, dourness, and lack of formal education would cost him votes in a face-to-face confrontation with Herrera. On the other hand, refusing the challenge would indicate weakness and a lack of confidence. The *cogollito* resolved this dilemma by agreeing to the debate but with the provision that it be held on November 30, the final day of the campaign. This was widely interpreted as an attempt to postpone the debate until the undecided voters had already made up their minds. And it suggested that Piñerúa feared the confrontation. The debate, in any case, never took place: the Supreme Electoral Council ruled that making it the final event of the campaign would discriminate against third-party candidates.[76]

---

[75] Interviews with several high-ranking CORPA executives, November 28, 1978.
[76] Luis Herrera's reply to Piñerúa's decision to debate, but not until Novem-

The second unanticipated issue, the murder of Caracas attorney Ramón Carmona, remained before the public during the closing months of the election campaign. Unknown assailants assassinated Carmona on the afternoon of July 28, 1978, while he waited at a traffic light on the Avenida Andrés Bello in Caracas. Carmona was involved at the time in a trial that threatened to uncover land speculation irregularities implicating major figures in the administration of President Pérez. The other attorney in the case was Mayra de Molina Gásperi, wife of the head of the respected national police force, the Policía Técnica Judicial (PTJ). Carmona's assassins initially were thought to be urban terrorists. Investigators, however, traced the killing to a special weapons squad that was attached to the office of the PTJ director, Manuel Molina Gásperi. The news caused a sensation. President Pérez immediately removed Molina and ordered a full investigation, which dragged on well past the election, and the Carmona case remained a major news story for the rest of the campaign.[77] No survey information exists on its electoral impact, but it probably played an important part in the last-minute movement of many undecided Caracas voters to Luis Herrera Campíns and the Social Christians.[78]

Outcome and Assessment

Piñerúa and his colleagues in the *cogollito* knew that the election would be close, but they expected to win. Acción Democrática, remembering that disputed votes had sealed the Caldera victory in 1968, initiated Operación Mosca, a program designed to train party activists to keep close watch on the electoral tables. The party also developed Operación Satélite, a kind of instant air mail service that relied on private planes to speed results from the local electoral juntas to the party's Analysis Unit in Caracas. Party technicians anticipated that the results would be known by 9:00 P.M. However, computer-related errors forced many voters on election day to scramble from the

---

ber 30, is discussed in *El Nacional* (October 12, 1978). Also see Keith Grant, "Debate Would Be No Dialogue of Mutes," *Daily Journal* (Caracas), October 18, 1978.

[77] See José Rodolfo Cárdenas, "Negocios ilícitos, chantages y el crimen de Carmona" [Illicit deals, blackmail, and the Carmona crime], *Resumen*, no. 264 (November 26, 1978), and "La teoría beta" [The beta theory], *Resumen*, no. 265 (December 3, 1978), pp. 14-17.

[78] The Merc-Analysis poll of Caracas voters in early November gave Piñerúa 29 percent, Herrera 26 percent, and 20 percent undecided. Before the Carmona scandal became a political issue, in August 1978, Piñerúa led Herrera 33 percent to 26 percent, and only 16 percent declared themselves undecided.

TABLE 4–2
Two-Party Presidential Vote, by Region, 1978
(in percentages)

Region	Region's Share of Total Valid Vote	Share of Regional Vote	
		Piñerúa	Herrera
Center	39.9	40.1	44.6
Plains	9.7	47.4	45.9
Zulia	11.3	40.0	51.1
Center-West	11.6	42.2	51.6
Andes	9.9	46.3	47.8
East	17.1	51.2	38.1
Venezuela	100.0	43.3	46.6

NOTE: Column does not add to total because of rounding.
SOURCE: Calculated from official bulletins of the Supreme Electoral Council.

polling place to which they thought they were assigned to the one where their names had been sent. With long lines waiting to vote as late as 6:30 P.M., the Supreme Electoral Council ordered that the polls remain open until 10:00 P.M. By 11:00 P.M., results from all over the country were pouring into the nerve center of Operación Satélite.[79] Within half an hour, Acción Democrática's leaders knew they would be going into the opposition.

Generally, Piñerúa did a bit worse than expected in every region (see Table 4–2). Close contests in the Andes and in the Plains deprived him of an expected 50,000-vote cushion, but substantial losses in the populous Center region, in Zulia, and in the Center-West proved his undoing. Acción Democrática's absolute majority in the East could not offset Herrera's strong showing in the other regions. Also, for the first time the Social Christians received more than a third of the total vote in each of the eastern states. Acción Democrática now faced a truly national opponent that was roughly its own size.

Though it lost the presidency, Acción Democrática did many things right. Candidates made themselves available to reporters and television journalists at strategically important moments.[80] The mass

---

[79] Operación Satélite functioned in 1978 much as it had in 1973. For a detailed discussion see Martz and Baloyra, *Electoral Mobilization*, pp. 95-96.
[80] Piñerúa, like Pérez, held weekly luncheons with reporters. Typical of the interviews AD leaders gave to the press is the one by Octavio Lepage that appeared in *El Universal*, September 1, 1978.

media and the business community were more favorably disposed toward the party than ever before. Piñerúa rallies were well attended, and his walk on the final day of the campaign through the working-class and middle-class areas of eastern Caracas was a huge success. Nationally, the party elected the same number of senators and members of the Chamber of Deputies as the Social Christians. Still, the question remains: Why did a political party that in 1973 had won a victory so overwhelming that pundits had speculated it would be in power for decades lose the presidency in 1978?

Three basic problems in the campaign contributed to Acción Democrática's defeat. First was the organizational and operational bottleneck in the party's campaign organization. Piñerúa, as indicated earlier, named no overall chief of staff. Leandro Mora and Alfaro Ucero operated the regular and special campaign organizations as personal fiefdoms. No comprehensive strategic plan seemed to exist. Thus, instead of the 7 commercials that Carlos Andrés Pérez had run over and over on television in 1973, Piñerúa's campaign produced 204.[81] These touched on so many themes that the electorate had difficulty knowing what the candidate's priorities were. Also, many of these commercials reacted to issues and charges leveled by the Social Christian candidate. With far fewer resources at his disposal, Herrera succeeded in placing Piñerúa on the defensive.

President Pérez's overshadowing of Luis Piñerúa also damaged Acción Democrática's electoral prospects. After Herrera attacked the Government by asking where all the money had gone, Carlos Andrés Pérez spared no expense in publicizing the accomplishments of his administration. His exposure on television and his swings through the countryside to inaugurate new public works made it appear that his accomplishments, and not Piñerúa's qualifications or programs, were the central issue.

The president's high visibility exacerbated the final basic factor working against Acción Democrática: Piñerúa's inability to generate excitement and enthusiasm. The contrast between Pérez's dynamism and Piñerúa's dourness was heightened when the activities of both were reported side by side on the nightly television news broadcasts. Piñerúa appeared uncomfortable with crowds, while the president was in his element when surrounded by adoring supporters. The impression grew that Piñerúa lacked confidence, and it was strengthened when he hedged his acceptance of Herrera's challenge for a nationwide television debate. In short, the interaction of organizational problems,

---

[81] Interview with Nicomedes Zuloaga, a major stockholder in CORPA, November 28, 1978.

Carlos Andrés Pérez's coolness toward Piñerúa and his unwillingness to allow the candidate to become the center of attention, and Piñerúa's lack of charisma tipped the balance in a very close election.

The future holds both dangers and opportunities for Acción Democrática. Its leaders must develop procedures for running the party and choosing presidential and legislative candidates that all factions will support. The Betancourt/Piñerúa and Pérez wings of the party will have to learn how to share power. Barely concealed conflict between the two in early 1979 consumed so much time and energy that Acción Democrática was unable to mount an effective campaign for the June municipal elections and sustained the worst electoral defeat in its history. The June elections also underscored the fact that —given the new situation, in which Acción Democrática is no longer clearly the country's first electoral force—the party must develop ideals, programs, and leaders that inspire loyalty among party members and attract independents. The alternative is to become a permanent minority.

5

The Christian Democratic Party

Donald L. Herman

Though dejected by defeat in 1973, the Christian Democratic (or Social Christian) party could not afford to spend long licking its wounds. Two matters required immediate attention: a new posture vis-à-vis Acción Democrática and the Pérez Government, and an effort to resolve intraparty differences. The party leaders concluded that it would be advantageous for COPEI to be slightly to the left of AD within the Venezuelan political spectrum. In this way they hoped to retain their broad support from the center and to continue to appeal to the peasants and the urban middle class.[1] As the major opposition party, COPEI would strive to be firm yet flexible, constructive, and nonsectarian; it decided not to define its role as clearly as it had done when opposing the Leoni Government.[2] During the first part of the AD administration, COPEI strongly criticized the Government on economic matters and foreign policy issues; then as the 1978 election approached, it focused on a broader range of issues.

Effective opposition required party unity. Those who had supported the candidacy of Luis Herrera Campíns and had seen their man lose the nomination to Lorenzo Fernández now worked very hard to regroup. They decided to work within COPEI in the hope that former President Rafael Caldera and the party were ready to support a more progressive candidate in the 1978 election. The party leaders decided to postpone the regional conventions until late 1974 and the national

---

[1] Interview with Hilarión Cardozo, March 27, 1974. Active for many years in the party, Cardozo was deputy secretary general of the party (1969-1971) and governor of Zulia (1971-1973). In 1979 he was Venezuelan ambassador to the OAS.

[2] Interview with Eduardo Fernández, March 26, 1974. Younger than Cardozo, Fernández was deputy secretary general of the party (1974-1976) and director of COPEI's parliamentary group (1974-1979).

convention until late 1975. As a result, Pedro Pablo Aguilar would remain secretary general and the struggle over his position would be deferred. This, Caldera believed, would allow the former president time to reassert himself within the party.

Mounting the Campaign

Choosing the Presidential Candidate. Throughout 1974 and 1975, groups within the party negotiated and campaigned to get their men selected for secretary general of the party and presidential candidate.[3] As in the past, party politics dictated a close connection between the struggle for the two positions. Herrera was in a difficult situation. He knew that Caldera did not want him to be the presidential candidate, and he also knew that if he were to have any chance for the nomination, he had to have the support of the secretary general. He would either have to receive the nod from Aguilar—himself a Caldera supporter—or back someone to replace him as secretary general.

Sometime in 1975 Caldera made a crucial decision. He let it be known that he did not like the way in which Aguilar had handled the 1973 election (he probably was looking for a scapegoat) and that he wanted him replaced as secretary general. His candidate for the position was the former minister of public works, José Curiel. Aguilar had a choice: he could bow to the wishes of Caldera or he could align himself with one of the forces within the party to defeat Caldera's candidate. Aguilar and Herrera reached an agreement to support each other. If they were successful, Aguilar would be reelected secretary general and Herrera would become the party's presidential candidate.[4] At the party's Fourteenth National Convention in December 1975, Aguilar defeated Curiel, by 810 votes to 332.

By early 1976, the Herrera-Aguilar forces had triumphed in nearly all of the state conventions and in the party's "functional organizations" (concerned with peasants, labor, youth, women, teachers, professionals, and technicians). Realizing his supporters would lose out in the next national convention, Caldera reportedly reached an understanding with Herrera in January 1976. The party's National Committee was almost evenly divided between their respective supporters, and Caldera agreed to support Herrera as the party's presi-

---

[3] The following discussion is based on information in Donald L. Herman, *Christian Democracy in Venezuela* (Chapel Hill: University of North Carolina Press, 1980).

[4] Much of this information is based on correspondence with COPEI leaders and members and discussions with colleagues.

dential candidate. They also agreed that well-known Caldera supporters would play an active role during the campaign. At the party's Fifteenth National Convention, in August 1977, Herrera was unanimously proclaimed the presidential candidate. Arístides Beaujon, a former secretary general, who was supported by only 300 of the 4,200 delegates, had withdrawn from the race.[5]

Choosing the Legislative Candidates. In the summer of 1978, the party formed a commission under Aguilar, consisting of Caldera and Herrera supporters, to choose candidates for Congress, the state assemblies, and the principal municipal councils.[6] The commission received two lists of potential candidates: one for Congress and one for the state assemblies and municipal councils. The lists originated in the districts, were passed up through the regions, and eventually reached the commission. The commission was allowed to make changes on a maximum of 30 percent of the names and on the order in which they were listed. In addition, it decided that 33 percent of the places on the lists would be reserved for officers of the party, independents, and members of political groups other than COPEI that supported Herrera.

According to one observer, Caldera and Herrera each privately submitted his own list as well.[7] The selection process was very tense, and the COPEI campaign stopped for a few weeks in August until the matter was settled. The commission held frequent meetings with Caldera and Herrera, during which the ex-president and the presidential candidate revised their respective lists and argued for them before the commission.[8] During the deliberations, the commission also discussed the lists with some of the party's regional directors.

In early September, the commission completed its task and presented one integrated list to the party's National Committee. Besides including supporters of Herrera and Caldera, the commission allotted good slots on the legislative list to a number of other political parties and groups who were supporting Herrera's candidacy: it gave the URD one candidate for senator and four for deputy; OPINA,

---

[5] See the discussion in *Resumen*, August 14, 1977.

[6] Interview with Pedro Méndez Mora, December 14, 1978. Méndez works with COPEI's national secretary of [ideological] formation. He teaches party activists to understand better the ideological components of Christian Democracy. Also see the discussion in *El Universal*, July 1, 1978.

[7] Interview, December 12, 1978. He asked to remain anonymous.

[8] See *El Nacional*, August 19, 22, and 23, 1978; *El Universal*, August 15, 27, and 28, 1978; *Informador*, August 22, 1978; *Ultimas noticias*, August 29 and 30, 1978.

one for deputy; FDP, one for municipal councilor in the Federal District; and independents, five or six for deputy. In the end, the party agreed upon an integrated legislative list and united behind Herrera's candidacy. However, the complexity of the selection process as it now stands could lead to serious problems in future elections, weakening internal party support for the presidential candidate.

Organizing the Campaign. COPEI organized its campaign around two bodies: the National Committee, which is a permanent ruling body of the party, and an electoral committee, the National Electoral Command, responsible only for election campaigns (see Figure 5–1). Some National Committee members also served on the electoral committee. The two groups met every Thursday to coordinate campaign strategy and tactics, and every Wednesday they met with the presidential candidate. During the last twenty days prior to the election, they met with Herrera every day.[9] As the campaign intensified, the party formed other groups, such as the Strategy Commission, which included Caldera and Herrera. Numerous other committees were formed on the national and local levels: a committee of independents, a committee of athletes, a committee of immigrants voting in their first election, and so on.

The Strategy Commission was very important. Besides Caldera and Herrera, its members included Godofredo González, Pedro Pablo Aguilar, Eduardo Fernández, Juan José Rachadell, Abdón Vivas Terán, Oswaldo Alvarez Paz, Luis Enrique Oberto, and other members of the National Electoral Command. Because of the makeup of its membership—especially the presence of Caldera, Herrera, and Aguilar—its decisions took precedence over those of other organizations.

Although the COPEI campaign structure was clearly defined, it was also flexible enough to incorporate key individuals as the need arose. For example, more than 100 national and regional directors met a few months before the election and decided, among other things, to involve Lorenzo Fernández and Arístides Beaujon in certain party programs. They wanted the active participation of an ex–presidential candidate and an ex–secretary general to strengthen the campaign and reinforce party unity.

The four principal coordinators of the campaign were Rafael Montes de Oca (campaign director), José Curiel (the functional orga-

[9] Interview with Hilarión Cardozo, December 15, 1978. During the campaign, Cardozo represented COPEI on the Supreme Electoral Council and was the party's coordinator of political analysis and national strategy. In the election, he won a seat in the Senate from the state of Zulia.

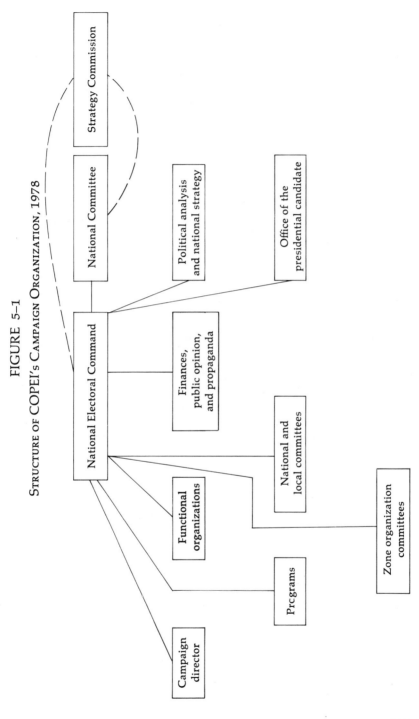

FIGURE 5–1

STRUCTURE OF COPEI's CAMPAIGN ORGANIZATION, 1978

nizations), Enrique Pérez Olivares (finances, public opinion, and propaganda), and Hilarión Cardozo (political analysis and national strategy). The close cooperation between Caldera and Herrera supporters during the campaign is reflected in the fact that Montes de Oca was a strong supporter of Herrera and the others had been closely identified with Caldera.

To channel the campaign effort in specific areas, the party organized various programs, each with its own director.[10] Some of these were directed toward specific segments of the electorate—city people, labor, peasants, women, youth. Others organized the work of the campaign: there was a program for political activists and one for general coordination and oversight, another on finances, and one concerned with public opinion and propaganda that handled the media and worked with the states to develop ways of dealing with local issues. The party did not organize in districts and municipalities, as it had done in 1968 and 1973. Instead, it divided states into socio-economic subdivisions under Zone Organization Committees.

Finances. The statutes list financial sources for the party. National congressmen and members of other national bodies are expected to pay to the party a percentage of their salaries fixed by resolution or by the national convention. State legislators and members of municipal and district bodies contribute a percentage fixed by the national or regional conventions. Contributions are also made by regional committees and individual party members. Some of these funds, along with special contributions, may be diverted to electoral campaigns. As in previous elections, COPEI members and independents on the legislative lists contributed to the 1978 campaign. The party also received funds from domestic industrialists and foreign sources as in the past. The "Twelve Apostles" contributed to COPEI as did the West German Christian Democratic party.

Strategy and tactics. COPEI hired the American campaign consultant David Garth—a veteran of the successful campaign of Governor Hugh Carey of New York and Mayor Edward Koch of New York City—to advise it on its use of the media. Garth spent seventy-five days in Venezuela and worked with Pérez Olivares in matters dealing with public opinion and propaganda.[11] Garth suggested that

---

[10] Interview with Pedro Méndez Mora, December 14, 1978.

[11] Garth's role in the campaign is based on a variety of sources: a postelectoral interview by National Public Broadcasting, "All Things Considered"; interviews with several Christian Democrats; *Latin America Political Report*, May 26, 1978; *El Universal*, December 11, 1978; *Daily Journal*, December 13, 1978.

COPEI orient its campaign around the issues. The candidate should go to the people, particularly in the *barrios;* one of the party's very effective slogans—"Pa'mi Luis"—was in working-class slang. Songs and jingles might have been used in previous campaigns, but this time, according to Garth, COPEI should speak out honestly and not try to paint a pretty picture. He also advised that Herrera should appear personally in most of the television ads because the people identified with him. Garth based his advice on opinion polls he had taken in Venezuela, as well as on experience in other campaigns.

The party commissioned monthly polls in each state, by district, which provided the basis for the reports on political analysis and national strategy written by Hilarión Cardozo and others.[12] It also made an in-depth analysis of electoral patterns, focusing on several areas: (1) votes COPEI could capture, including those of 1973 voters who were not firmly committed to any party and of new voters in 1978; (2) indicators of effectiveness, identifying states and districts where party work and political propaganda would be most effective; (3) indicators of AD weakness, especially a high incidence of people who had voted for AD in 1973 but who were not committed and had a tendency toward mobility; and (4) indicators of mobility, either vote switching from 1968 to 1973 or voting for the first time in 1973.

In one of his reports, Cardozo listed four strategic objectives. First, the party must optimize the efficiency of its partisan work. The electoral command must be unified yet flexible, allowing for local initiatives. Every activity must have a purpose within the overall plan, and the party's message must be presented clearly so that the electorate would not be confused. Second, Herrera should use the reality of two-party polarization to his advantage. In focusing upon national problems, the voters must understand that only Herrera was capable of realizing change. They should be told not to waste

---

[12] Among the reports were "Análisis de movilidad electoral para 1978" [Analysis of electoral mobility for 1978]; Hilarión Cardozo, "Informe del coordinador nacional de estrategía del partido Socialcristiano COPEI" [Report of the national coordinator of strategy of the Social Christian party COPEI], December 1977; National Campaign Command, Strategy Coordination, "Nuevos lineamientos estratégicos para la campaña aprobados por el Comando de Campaña" [New strategic lines for the campaign approved by the Campaign Command], January 31, 1978; Hilarión Cardozo, "Carrera presidencial" [Presidential course], July 1978; Hilarión Cardozo, "Intervención del coordinador de estrategía en la reunión del día . . . de septiembre de 1978, con los secretarios generales y los secretarios de organización" [Speech by the coordinator of strategy at the meeting of . . . September 1978, with the secretaries general and the secretaries of organization], September 1978; Boris Bunimov Parra and others, "Recomendaciones—Informe no. 2" [Recommendations—report no. 2], 1978.

their vote on any other presidential candidate. Third, the party must identify the Government, Piñerúa, and AD as one and the same. Piñerúa must be made to represent the defense and continuation of what existed. Fourth, Herrera must be presented as the candidate of the entire country, a Christian Democrat but one representing all Venezuelans' hope for a better life. The campaign must be personalized, and all groups must be encouraged to identify with the image of the candidate.

Another report discussed the lines of strategy that had been approved by the electoral command. On the basis of poll results—indicating, for example, that people were disturbed by the Government's unfulfilled promises—the party was urged to compare the record of the Caldera Government with that of President Pérez and to place greater emphasis on the problem of inflation.

The COPEI strategists sometimes made sophisticated use of data. Thus, they suggested that the campaign should emphasize the positive image of the candidate in those districts where electoral mobility was greatest, that is, in areas where the population was mobile and politically uncommitted. On the other hand, the party should be emphasized in districts that had traditionally voted for COPEI candidates. The report added that the party should always place slightly less emphasis on itself than on the presidential candidate.

The Christian Democrats were disturbed by the polls indicating that most of the voters believed Piñerúa would win. Even most Herrera supporters believed this to be so. Consequently, the party made a major effort to convince the voters that Herrera could and would win. They concentrated on the young and on such leaders of public opinion as professionals, industrialists, and trade union officials. Several reports spelled out how COPEI should attack the Pérez administration, Piñerúa, and Acción Democrática, but they advised against attacking candidates from the smaller parties on the grounds that this would only make them appear more important and divert attention from the real political adversary, AD.

As the campaign came to an end, COPEI supporters were reminded to emphasize the phrases that the voters themselves had used in responding to opinion polls, repeating them whenever possible, reinforcing the belief that dissatisfaction was widespread: The AD was "indifferent to the problems of the people," its leaders thought "only of enriching themselves," its style was one of "fraud and corruption"; the government was "incapable" and "corrupt," "offered much and delivered little"; President Pérez "lied," was "inflexible," did not have "the stature of a president." Party workers were urged to create a highly emotional atmosphere that would bring COPEI and its candidate to victory.

They also tried to demonstrate the party's unity and solidarity—in contrast to the other parties' disarray. This was one of the purposes of Operación Cumbre (operation summit), which brought the highest national leaders of the party together with Herrera in various states for meetings, press conferences, and other activities with regional leaders. Several issues were sidestepped in order to avoid conflicts during the campaign.[13] The party decided not to take a position, for example, on the Venezuelan-Colombian dispute over the demarcation of the Gulf of Venezuela and on certain strikes that had taken place in 1978. When AD accused Herrera of holding communist views because of his statements on the communitarian society, Herrera denied the charge but did not become engaged in any great controversy. Thus, COPEI managed to take a position vis-à-vis AD, without precipitating unnecessary disagreements among its own militants.

The Phases of the Campaign

The COPEI campaign passed through three phases. During the first, various party leaders including the presidential candidate attacked Acción Democrática, the Pérez administration, and Piñerúa. This proved to be so effective that it was carried over into the next two phases. The second phase began around the middle of October and presented the alternative to what phase one had criticized. Finally, the third phase, beginning fifteen to twenty days before the election, emphasized Herrera's personal attributes.[14]

COPEI on the Offensive. In a sense, the business of denouncing AD began when COPEI became the principal opposition after the 1973 election. But during the 1978 electoral campaign, the attack on the Government became very harsh. In addition to Herrera, Godofredo González, Eduardo Fernández, Caldera, Montes de Oca, and others took the AD Government to task. Other political leaders who supported Herrera, like Jóvito Villalba of the URD and Jorge Dáger of the FDP, also made speeches attacking the *adecos*.

COPEI focused its attack on several national problems: inflation, lack of public order, personal insecurity, the need for better

---

[13] Interview with Hilarión Cardozo, December 15, 1978.

[14] Interview with Asdrubal Aguiar Aranguren, December 13, 1978. Aguiar Aranguren is a lawyer and a professor of international law at the Catholic University in Caracas. During the campaign, he worked with COPEI's electoral committee as the deputy director of the Office of the Presidential Candidate.

housing, urban development, and public services, the problems of the very poor (the *marginados*, those on the margin of society), the shortcomings of agriculture and education, and administrative corruption. The Christian Democrats maintained that serious problems persisted because President Pérez had been too concerned with world problems to fulfill his electoral promises. According to Eduardo Fernández, "We need a president who, instead of being preoccupied with being the leader of the Third World, is occupied with this Venezuelan world." [15]

COPEI denounced administrative corruption throughout the campaign. (One party document listed over eighty cases of administrative corruption from 1974 to 1978.) In part, this involved the misuse of funds by public corporations.[16] The director of the sanitation corporation was criticized by the Controlaría, which monitors government spending, and serious accusations were made against CADAFE, the electricity corporation, and the state-owned petrochemical industry. Doubt was also cast on the propriety of the commissions paid by Boeing for the contract of the presidential airplane. "Where has all the money gone?" asked COPEI's ads. The implication was that the Pérez Government, despite the billions at its disposal as a result of the rise in petroleum prices, had failed to alleviate the human misery that plagued the country. As a prominent magazine pointed out, the slogan pressed the Government to explain how it had spent the additional petroleum income; it created doubt about AD's capacity to administer the country and forced Piñerúa to defend its record.[17]

There had been individual cases of corruption under Caldera, but none as far-reaching as those that emerged under the Pérez administration, in particular the Carmona case. This began when Ramón Carmona Vásquez, a Caracas attorney who had been investigating corruption and the misuse of public funds, was assassinated on July 28, 1978. The director of the police force was implicated, and he was removed for obstructing justice. Subsequently, an examining magistrate ordered the arrest of five police officers, members of an anti-terrorist squad, in connection with the murder. The magazine *Resumen* linked the murder with land deals on the Venezuelan island of Margarita. The case received considerable television and press coverage. Although various Christian Democrats hammered away at

---

[15] *El Universal*, October 17, 1978.

[16] Interview with Alejandro Alfonzo, December 16, 1978. Alfonzo is the director of Conciencia 21, a private institute of social research.

[17] *Resumen*, May 28, 1978.

the administrative corruption issue throughout the campaign, Herrera saved his criticism of the handling of the Carmona case until the end, when it could do most damage to AD. At his last press conference, on November 22, he asked a series of questions about this and other scandals, underlining the general charge of government corruption and inefficiency.[18]

Former President Caldera played an important role in the campaign, especially in this first phase. Returning from abroad, he became active during the three months before the election, particularly the last six weeks. This was part of an overall plan: Herrera wanted his own image as a presidential candidate to be strong before Caldera took an active part. In contrast to Piñerúa, who many believed was Betancourt's chosen candidate, Herrera wanted the voters to know that he was his own man.[19] Once this was established, Caldera traveled throughout the country, giving television interviews and press conferences and attending rallies with Herrera and other COPEI leaders. In all of these activities his major theme was to denounce the Pérez administration. He also repeated a COPEI slogan from 1968 warning against "Mexicanization."

Eduardo Fernández, in his capacity as leader of the COPEI parliamentary group, spoke in the Chamber of Deputies; Rafael Caldera (who, as a former president, automatically became a senator) spoke in the Senate. On one occasion, Caldera responded to a message to the Congress from President Pérez, denouncing the Government for not pursuing projects launched under previous administrations, notably, university improvements, the expansion of the steel industry, and the development of the southern part of the country along the Brazilian border.[20] Several of the projects he mentioned had been abandoned indefinitely. "Where has all the money gone?" Caldera asked, for education, health, housing, agriculture, the water supply for Caracas. Caldera also denounced the size of the public debt and unproductive public investment.

Herrera also criticized the Pérez administration and focused upon these issues. But whereas Caldera directed his attacks against President Pérez, Herrera concentrated on the AD candidate.[21] He accused Piñerúa of repeating the promises President Pérez had made during the 1973 electoral campaign and never kept. And in attacking the

---

[18] *El Universal*, November 23, 1978.

[19] Interview with Jesús Angel Paz Galarraga of MEP, December 11, 1978.

[20] *Resumen*, April 23, 1978.

[21] See *El Universal*, February 19, 1978, and August 10 and 17, 1978; *El Nacional*, August 20, 1978.

Government's programs, Herrera frequently reminded his listeners that Piñerúa had been a member of that Government and therefore shared responsibility for its shortcomings. Time and again the COPEI candidate denounced his AD opponent for proposing unoriginal solutions to the country's problems, including transportation, mail and telephones, and the water supply.

In September, Herrera challenged Piñerúa to a television debate. At first Piñerúa refused, but he then said that he would debate his opponent on the last day of the campaign. The Supreme Electoral Council stated that any debate would have to take place at least forty-eight hours before the beginning of the vote; the minor parties also objected to a television debate between the two major candidates. Piñerúa in effect had declined to debate Herrera, and the Christian Democrats used the incident against him. In one television ad Herrera rolled up his sleeves and asked why Piñerúa had refused to face him.

The COPEI Alternative. Ideas and options for the second phase were actually developed a few years before the 1978 electoral campaign got under way. As early as 1972 the party had initiated studies of major problems by specialists,[22] and in 1975 it began to develop a program of government under the directorship of Enrique Oberto. Discussions were held throughout the country over a two- to three-year period. However, once Herrera was nominated, he was allowed to modify the program.

Herrera's ideas can be taken from a variety of sources.[23] He concentrated on domestic concerns and directed relatively little attention toward foreign policy. For the purposes of analysis, we can group his ideas into four major categories: education, participatory democracy, the "promoter state," and specific issues (agriculture, housing, administrative corruption). Herrera's first priority was education; during the campaign he stated that he would be the "president of education," which he regarded as a means of creating the conditions under which could be initiated a process that would raise the economic, social, and cultural level of the poor. He also said:

---

[22] Ramón Adolfo Illarramendy, "Hacia la democracia de participación" [Toward participatory democracy], Nueva política, January-March 1972.

[23] Herrera has published books, pamphlets, and articles too numerous to list here. For his ideas pertaining specifically to the election campaign, see Partido Socialcristiano COPEI, "Mi compromiso con Venezuela" [My commitment to Venezuela], Programa de gobierno para el período 1979-1983 [Government program for the period 1979-1983]; Alfredo Peña, Conversaciones con Luis Herrera Campíns [Conversations with Luis Herrera Campíns] (Caracas: Editorial Ateneo, 1978).

A change of outlook and the creation of a true consciousness . . . are crucial elements in permitting people to rise
above marginality and . . . progress toward the material and
cultural benefits in work, housing, education, health, transportation, and recreation necessary to humanize the environment and make life less harsh.[24]

Herrera wanted more than better schools, skilled manpower, voca-
tional and professional centers in every region, and "eight areas of
higher education." He wanted to instill in the people a social consciousness and a sense of social responsibility. Education would be
the vehicle for raising the masses from the depths of despair.

As people became better educated, they would be able to participate meaningfully in the democratic process, for there was too
much paternalism in the country with the *adeco* Government and
party all-powerful. It would be necessary to replace the paternalistic
mentality in order to prepare people for participatory democracy.[25]

In a sense, the idea of participatory democracy reinforces the
Christian Democratic belief in a pluralistic society, in which various
organizations—trade unions, youth groups, labor, peasants—influence
decision making so that power is dispersed rather than centralized,
shared rather than concentrated in the government. Through participatory democracy, the people would create their own civic organizations—economic, cultural, recreational—so that they would not
be isolated. These organizations would be involved in local planning
and would send representatives to the regional and national meetings. In some cases the state would assign tasks to the organizations
for the execution of plans for housing, medical services, education,
and recreation. Through such efforts the people would raise their own
social consciousness and perfect democracy.

During the campaign, Herrera insisted that the people were not
valued; the all-powerful state was insensitive to their needs. He called

---

[24] Luis Herrera, "La educación es primero: síntesis del programa de gobierno
del candidato de COPEI [Education is first: synthesis of the COPEI candidate's
program], *COPEI 78* (Maracay, 1978), p. 2.

[25] For additional sources on participatory democracy, see COPEI Strategy
Commission, "Síntesis de las bases del programa de gobierno del candidato
presidencial de COPEI" [Synthesis of the bases of the program of government
of the COPEI presidential candidate] (Carabobo), 1977; Eduardo Fernández, "La
democracia participativa" [Participatory democracy], published by the COPEI
parliamentary group (Caracas), 1978; Conciencia 21, "Conceptos emitidos por
el Dr. Luis Herrera Campíns durante su campaña electoral período enero-junio"
[Ideas expressed by Dr. Luis Herrera Campíns during his campaign, January-
June] (Caracas), 1978; *SIC*, no. 409, November 1978.

for a "promoter state," whose power would be creative, stimulating societal initiative for the people's benefit:

> I offer the Venezuelan people a promoter state: not the liberal state that observes without taking action, not the interventionist state of fascist totalitarianism or of Marxist-communist totalitarianism. I offer [the people] a promoter state because the state is becoming more and more powerful in our country—most recently with the nationalization of iron and petroleum—and I want it to be converted into a promoter state that will stimulate the activity of persons, of associations, . . . that will think and imagine, create and perfect, that will facilitate and rationalize its activity, and that, in addition, will require the Government to define its priorities and will encourage participation, that among its fundamental tasks will take on the immense and profound challenge of raising people above social marginality.[26]

In that they sought to maximize the development of the human person, Herrera's priorities were consistent with Christian Democratic doctrine. Education, participatory democracy, and the promoter state were to be linked in a great human effort whose goal was the defeat of misery and the realization of human potentiality.

Herrera offered specific proposals for solving the country's problems.[27] The agriculture problem, for example, he said could be solved by following three basic policies: (1) give the peasants idle land held by the government, (2) increase productivity through careful management of loan and investment programs, and (3) improve the quality of rural life through more effective public services, better housing, and improved health care. He stated he would give better attention to zoning and natural disaster prevention than they had received in the past, and if it became necessary, he would establish a national irrigation institute.

Herrera promised that 600,000 housing units would be erected during his administration. He also called for a concerted effort in the public and private sectors to increase housing construction to 150,000 units per year after 1984.

---

[26] From Herrera's acceptance speech to COPEI's nominating convention, quoted by Ramón Guillermo Avelado, "Sobre el estado promotor" [On the promoter state], published by the COPEI parliamentary group (Caracas), 1978.

[27] For some of Herrera's proposals, see Peña, *Conversaciones*, p. 63; *Daily Journal*, November 11, 1978; Partido Socialcristiano COPEI, "Repuestas del Senador Luis Herrera Campíns sobre temas de interés nacional e internacional" [Answers of Senator Luis Herrera Campíns on themes of national and international interest].

Herrera suggested that administrative corruption was intimately tied to the civic and moral development of the citizen and that people were more interested in how much a person had than in who he was. It was the duty of government to institute ethical values and uphold them in society. The government must appoint only honest people to jobs, for example. It must keep an eye on the life style of government officials, since this could indicate whether they were enriching themselves illegally. The discretionary power of officials (especially to approve or delay contracts and thus charge fees) must be carefully regulated so that they could be held accountable for their actions. The government should also control "permitology," the practice of requiring numerous permits for any regulated activity, each from a different government office, and thereby increasing the opportunities for bribery. In general, Herrera took the position that he would do fewer things better. He also made it clear that he would concentrate on domestic affairs rather than on foreign policy.

The Home Stretch. The last two weeks before the election were characterized by Herrera's strong attacks on Piñerúa designed to erode his credibility and to place his abilities in doubt. At the same time, Herrera's personal image was played up. As they had throughout the campaign, speakers both from COPEI and from the smaller parties that supported Herrera referred to his sensitivity to the problems of the *marginados*. They described him as a tranquil, simple person, yet strong in the face of problems. He was the Venezuelan best equipped intellectually, politically, and morally to direct the destiny of the country.[28] During this phase of the campaign COPEI's use of marches, fiestas, and songs increased.

Special Focuses of the Campaign

The Industrial Corridor. The Christian Democrats concentrated their campaign effort on the heavily populated industrial corridor along the north-central coast and the northwest part of the country, running from Caracas to Zulia and south to Mérida.[29] Approximately 55 percent of the electorate lives there. Particular party leaders spent a great deal of time in certain cities and states—Eduardo Fernández in Caracas, Valmore Acevedo in Táchira, and Hilarión Cardozo in Zulia.

[28] See *El Nacional*, November 26 and 27, 1978.
[29] Interview with Pedro Pablo Aguilar, December 15, 1978.

Cardozo's campaigning in Zulia illustrates the Christian Democrats' concerted efforts in particular areas.[30] The secretary general of COPEI in the state, Guanipo Matos, had died, and the August COPEI poll showed Piñerúa leading Herrera 39 percent to 35 percent. Cardozo, who is from Zulia and had been governor of the state, went there in August and remained for three months. He met frequently with various groups, and Caldera made several trips to the state (once for two weeks) to help him. He utilized the media—newspapers, television, and radio—and changed his advertisements every two days. Radio was the most important medium since 90 percent of the people did not have television. Cardozo concentrated on door-to-door contacts, especially in the rural areas where AD was strong.

His message was simple: The Caldera Government was once very active in the state. Are you satisfied now? If you are not satisfied, bring back Caldera's party; vote for Luis Herrera Campíns and for change. You know me—I kept my promises to you as governor. Support me now for the Senate and Herrera for president. By November, the tide had turned in Zulia. A new party poll showed that Herrera had moved ahead with 52 percent of the vote.

The Marginados. The *marginados* constitute approximately 30 percent of the population. Since voting is obligatory in Venezuela, the *marginados* vote in large numbers and are an important bloc of voting strength. Using regional and national leaders, COPEI concentrated on door-to-door contact. In addition, it made very effective use of short TV films. Beginning with one made in the *barrio* of Caucagüita, these featured real poor people, rather than actors, speaking about their problems. These television and radio spots, known as *caucagüitas,* were often repetitive, but even if the middle class tuned out, the poor would continue to watch and listen to other poor people talk about the "national shame of Venezuela."

Historically, AD had been identified with democracy and the poor. One could always meet an *adeco* political leader in the *barrios* where it was very difficult to find a COPEI leader.[31] But COPEI and Herrera sought to change this, questioning the quality of democracy under AD, denouncing presidentialism and the weak Congress, the concentration of economic and political power in the state, paternal-

---

[30] Interview with Hilarión Cardozo, December 15, 1978.

[31] Interviews with Arturo Fremont and Freddy Valera, December 14, 1978. Both are political directors of MAS. Fremont is a director of the metallurgical trade union and a member of the MAS National Directorate. Valera is the former director of the Student Federation of University Centers and a regional director of MAS in Carabobo.

ism, and the overwhelming power of the *adeco* party and Government. Gearing its campaign to the poor, COPEI asked whether the people actually were any better off.

The Youth. Party organizations were given specific responsibilities under the overall electoral plan, but they were allowed to mold them according to their particular areas of expertise. The party's youth group, the JRC, was in charge of winning the youth vote for COPEI. This was a significant task in a year when the eighteen- to twenty-three-year-olds, voting in their first election, made up approximately 24 percent of the electorate. In addition to concentrating on the universities and schools, the JRC made a special effort to win the independent voters among the youth. Many of them supported Herrera without aligning themselves with COPEI.

The JRC participated in six separately organized campaign efforts: (1) a recruitment program under the slogan "Contact 78," emphasizing one-to-one contacts with new voters; (2) some twenty weekend outings to important cities that mobilized forty or fifty young people each, making house-to-house visits, especially to *marginados;* (3) forty or so higher-level conferences to discuss the country's problems; (4) a recruitment program during the last month of the campaign, which attempted to identify prospective COPEI supporters by having them fill out information sheets, as well as publicizing the party and its candidate; (5) a series of programs on local problems during the first phase of the campaign which sent JRC speakers out to address interested groups; and (6) a congress of athletes and an appearance by the best local athlete at a COPEI rally in each state.[32]

The Undecided and the Left. Many of the undecided considered themselves independents; this group comprised 20 to 25 percent of the electorate. What appealed to them about Herrera was that he was the candidate not only of COPEI but of all sectors of society. He had the support of URD, FDP, and OPINA; then, almost on the eve of the election, a new political group, Nuevo Orden (NOR), declared its support for Herrera.[33] These groups were not important numerically, but they allowed Herrera to present himself as the national candidate. It was to the undecided that Herrera directed his final appeal, attacking the myth of AD invincibility.

---

[32] Interview with Abelardo Vásquez, December 18, 1978. Vásquez is a member of the National Directorate of the JRC. He is an economist and a professor in the School of Economics of the Central University of Venezuela.

[33] *El Mundo,* November 29, 1978.

The voters on the left normally support MAS, MIR, MEP, the Communist party, and a few smaller groups. Herrera addressed a message to them and to the supporters of other smaller political parties: Your candidate for president has no chance of winning; if you want to change the Government, vote for me because I am the only viable alternative to a continuation of the AD status quo.

Evaluation

Dimensions of the COPEI Victory. Herrera won in the states that mattered most—those in the heavily populated northwest—and he did better than previous COPEI candidates in the east, in the west, and in Caracas. In fact, he improved on the 1973 COPEI vote in every state, district, and territory—overall by more than 50 percent.

For the first time in the party's history, the difference between COPEI's vote in the presidential and legislative races was very narrow, and COPEI's vote on the small card matched AD's. This indicated broad COPEI support throughout the country, prompting one party leader to remark that for the first time COPEI was indeed a national party. Many people, including many supporters of the small left-wing parties, voted for Herrera on the large card and for other parties on the small card, for a variety of reasons. Some young Christian Democrats, for example, supported Herrera for president but voted for MAS and MIR in the legislative election. They perhaps wanted to see a better balance in the Congress; others wanted to keep the president and the two major parties on their toes.

Reasons for the Victory. The Christian Democrats believed that there were five principal reasons for their victory: increasing polarization, the candidates, the anti-Government vote, the *marginados*, and the strength of the party's campaign efforts throughout the country.[34]

Increasing polarization, particularly Herrera's use of it, was probably the main factor in the COPEI victory. The two major parties dominated the media, creating an either-or psychology among the people.[35] In accordance with the party's strategy, Herrera exploited this, presenting himself as the only real alternative to AD, and most of the undecided voters responded. A significant percentage of the leftist voters, mainly those from MEP and MIR, also supported

---

[34] Interviews with various Christian Democrats, including Pedro Pablo Aguilar and Hilarión Cardozo, December 15, 1978.

[35] See the study by Conciencia 21, "Análisis de medios de comunicación social" [Analysis of methods of social communication], September 4-October 1, 1978.

Herrera on the large card. (Although some *adecos* maintained there was a leftist-COPEI agreement, this was not the case.) In a sense, Herrera's leftist support was further evidence that he was indeed the only viable candidate opposing AD; in part it was a protest vote against the *adeco* party, candidate, and Government. Villalba used his own appeal to change the minds of many eastern voters and to convince them that Herrera was a truly national candidate and the only one worthy of their support. Because of the closeness of the election, Villalba's role was a significant element in Herrera's campaign plan.

The difference between the candidates was another major factor. Learning from its experience in 1973, the party deliberately projected a more positive image of the candidate—someone who was strong, firm, and in control. In addition, Herrera was unassuming, displayed a good sense of humor, and made a better impression in the television interviews than Piñerúa. And it was a serious tactical mistake for Piñerúa to reject Herrera's challenge to a television debate.

In a developing country, to a greater degree than in developed countries, there is social dissatisfaction and a tendency to blame the Government for most ills. In elections, this phenomenon favors the opposition. The anti-Government vote—compounded by the high incidence of crime, inflation, inadequate public services, and particularly extensive administrative corruption—turned a significant number of voters to Herrera and COPEI. Thus, the party's strategy of denunciation proved to be particularly effective. In a sense, COPEI was the center of the campaign. Piñerúa had to defend the Government, and the campaign revolved around COPEI's actions and positions on the issues.

The party decided to make a greater effort than in 1973 to direct the campaign toward the *marginados*. Much of the program of government it drew up and many of Herrera's speeches referred to the plight of the poor and the need to raise the level of the lowest class. The support of the *marginados* proved to be crucial for COPEI: for the first time in the party's history, a high percentage of the darker-skinned, poorer people voted in large numbers for the party and its presidential candidate.

And finally, the party leaders admitted that poor coordination between the party and the electoral committee had been a serious problem during the 1973 election campaign. To avoid this problem they created one apparatus; the National Committee and the electoral committee functioned as a unit, analyzing together the reports by members of the electoral committee and the monthly polls commissioned by the party. The party was more unified than AD, the Calderistas and Herreristas worked together, and the party machinery operated more efficiently on all levels throughout the country—in the *barrios*, in the districts, and in the states.

COPEI's Future. Compared with the leaders of the other political parties, who face serious internal problems, the COPEI leaders are optimistic about the party. They do not believe there is any significant ideological, generational, or strategic split; the right, left, and center find support in all the generations.[36] Nevertheless, problems have arisen since Herrera's election.

When a party is out of power, the rank and file are united against the governing party. But when the party itself wins power, party-Government tensions arise because there are not enough jobs to offer all the party faithful. This occurred during the Caldera Government, and President Herrera faced the problem in Zulia shortly after assuming office. Other Christian Democrats have criticized the president for appointing too many nonparty ministers to his cabinet.[37]

A more serious question concerns the comparative power and influence of Caldera and Herrera within COPEI. Herrera said he accepted the fact that Caldera was the supreme leader of COPEI—but added that as president *he* would be the leader of all Venezuelans.[38] Now that Herrera has been elected, it remains to be seen who will determine the strategic and tactical line of COPEI in the future. This will depend in part upon who controls the party machinery on the national and state levels. We have seen that Herrera's nomination gave the combined Herrera-Aguilar forces a predominant position. It will also depend upon which force, Caldera or Herrera-Aguilar, is the major influence in the lists for Congress, state assemblies, and municipal councils. But regardless of these factors, Caldera will continue to have a great deal of prestige within the party and the country.

Three days after the election, Caldera and Betancourt met in the latter's home.[39] They agreed that AD would not unduly obstruct the Herrera Government's program in Congress, and the COPEI Government would not unduly harass Acción Democrática. The

---

[36] Interview with Pedro Pablo Aguilar, December 15, 1978.

[37] *Latin America Political Report*, April 6, 1979.

[38] Peña, *Conversaciones*, pp. 25-27.

[39] Reported in *Resumen*, December 24, 1978.

meeting (not the first between the two ex-presidents) had two important implications. First, Caldera continues to be a major factor in the political life of the country, as he has been for over forty years; he probably did not ask for Herrera's permission to hold the meeting. Second, Caldera will be able to run for president again in 1983. According to the constitution, a president must wait for two terms before he can run again, and Caldera could be the first person in the country's history to try it. Thus during the five years of Herrera's term of office, the country and COPEI may witness an interesting phenomenon: a COPEI ex-president and president vying to increase their influence within the party and addressing themselves to the major national and international issues.

In November 1979, COPEI held a national convention to choose a secretary general and National Committee. Eduardo Fernández, a strong Caldera supporter, narrowly defeated Pedro Aguilar, 801 votes against 714.[40] The National Committee's makeup also reflects the renewed strength of the Caldera forces. Although the Caldera group appears to be on the ascendant within the party at this writing, no one person or force seems likely to dominate COPEI for an extended period of time.

---

[40] See *Latin America Weekly Report*, November 16, 1979.

6

The Minor Parties

John D. Martz

The multiparty system that had evolved in Venezuela after 1958 was suddenly in a shambles following the 1973 elections. The AD-COPEI polarization had decimated the other parties; presidential candidates Paz, Rangel, and Villalba had totaled but 12.4 percent of the vote, while another seven nominees had won less than 1 percent each. The congressional returns were equally devastating (see Table 6–1). In accordance with Article 26 of the Law of Parties, a host of organizations receiving less than 1 percent of the vote lost their legal status: OPINA, PNI, MD, IP, FUN, MAN, PSD, FND, MPJ, MDI, PRN, FE, Alcina, ARPA, and FIPO.[1] Even Jóvito Villalba's URD stood on the brink of extinction, and the *perezjimenistas* dropped precipitously. Only on the left, owing largely to the emergence of the MAS, was there a semblance of representation from parties other than those of "El Status."

During the presidency of Carlos Andrés Pérez, the left was the sole minor-party sector in a position to articulate a clear congressional record. The MAS in particular attempted to establish an identity of its own, although its leaders differed over their proper congressional role vis-à-vis the Government. As a consequence the party sometimes supported Pérez's programs, then turned around and attacked the Government with vehemence. The rivalry within the left was omnipresent, as the MAS resisted the blandishments of the MEP, the MIR, and the PCV in their call for a united front. In the meantime,

---

[1] Most of these "micro-parties," as Venezuelans call them, had little meaningful political orientation and were simply identified with tiny groups of leaders; this was true of OPINA, MAN, PSD, FE, Alcina, ARPA, FIPO, and IP. Those of a *perezjimenista* orientation included PNI, FUN, and MPJ. The FND was the remnant of the mid-1960s organization of Arturo Uslar Pietri and, like the MD, adopted a probusiness stance.

154

TABLE 6–1

DISTRIBUTION OF SEATS IN THE SENATE AND CHAMBER OF DEPUTIES,
1969 AND 1974

	Senate		Chamber of Deputies	
Party	1969	1974	1969	1974
AD	19	28	63	102
COPEI	16	13	59	64
MEP	5	2	25	8
CCN	4	1	21	7
URD	3	1	20	5
FDP	2	—	10	—
FND	1	—	4	—
PCV (UPA)	1	—	5	2
PRIN (PRN)	1	—	4	—
MAN	—	—	1	—
PSD	—	—	1	—
MAS	—	2	—	9
MIR	—	—	—	1
PNI	—	—	—	1
OPINA	—	—	—	1
Total	52	49[a]	213	200

[a] Includes the two lifetime seats of former Presidents Betancourt and Caldera.
SOURCE: Supreme Electoral Council.

the other lesser parties took the steps necessary to reregister with the Supreme Electoral Council. And the possibility remained that new electoral forces, basing their appeal upon denunciations of the prevailing party system, would emerge to challenge Acción Democrática and COPEI. For clarity's sake, the array of minor parties and candidates that ultimately contested the 1978 elections have been clustered here in three groups: the left, the antiparty candidates, and other groups.[2]

Candidate Selection

The Left. Throughout the Pérez years, the basic issue for the left was the possibility of a Marxist coalition headed by a unity candidate. The Movement toward Socialism, despite occasional gestures toward

[2] Because it supported Luis Herrera Campíns in 1978, the URD is discussed in the chapter on the COPEI campaign.

its rivals, staunchly insisted upon standing apart. MAS strategy, devised in earlier years by Secretary General Pompeyo Márquez, envisioned a scenario in which the party would establish its primacy on the left through elections and ultimately absorb or eliminate the competition. At the same time, however, the MAS was plagued by the conflicting presidential ambitions of Márquez and of its young ideological spokesman, Teodoro Petkoff. Both were pointing toward personal hegemony within the party in order to secure the nomination for 1983. In the meantime José Vicente Rangel, who was not a member of any party, sought to run for president for the second time.

The Márquez-Petkoff struggle was resolved in favor of the former by November 1976, with his supporters entrenched in the organization and Rangel unofficially selected as the nominee. Petkoff, after considering resigning from the MAS to launch his own candidacy, chose instead to continue the fight within the party. "If my [potential] candidacy has served the MAS's revolutionary affirmation, I will continue it. . . . We feel the need to strengthen the search for the original and specific values underlying MAS's socialism, from their theoretical dimension to their implications for the militant and for a coherent leadership structure."[3] On July 20, 1977, Rangel was formally designated the MAS candidate, but his campaign failed to generate much interest, and Petkoff continued to snipe at him from time to time. Meanwhile, the efforts of the other leftist parties to form a common front were beginning to fade.

The situation for the People's Electoral Movement was particularly difficult. Although still retaining some strength in organized labor, the party had declined precipitously since 1968. Collaboration with Acción Democrática was totally unacceptable, but some MEP members seriously contemplated an alliance with COPEI. Neither Luis B. Prieto Figueroa, founder of the MEP, nor Jesús Angel Paz Galarraga viewed this as a viable option, however. In the absence of the broad-based leftist coalition the MEP had already advocated in 1973, the only choice was another candidacy of the septuagenarian Prieto, in hopes that his charisma might attract the votes necessary to ensure survival. On September 24, 1977, the "Maestro" was nominated by the MEP. Later approaches were made to the MAS, all of which, predictably, were rebuffed.

The Movement of the Revolutionary Left also sought a union with other Marxist groups, although with less sense of desperation than the MEP. Endowed with the mystique of their years as guerrillas fighting for a transformed Venezuela, MIR militants were active after

---

[3] *SIC* (Caracas), vol. 40, no. 391 (January 1977), pp. 38-89.

1973 in both student and workers' organizations. The party competed successfully against the MAS in the steelworkers' union and in several elections of student representatives to a wide array of university bodies. Capitalizing in part on the internal difficulties of MAS, the MIR believed itself capable of mounting a major challenge for control of the Venezuelan Marxist movement. The MEP, it was felt, would disappear with the passing of Prieto from the political scene. MIR leaders, viewing Rangel as the best-known political figure on the left, initially hoped to support him, whether or not in formal alliance with the MAS. On March 31, 1976, the party officially announced its intention of running Rangel once again. In July, however, Rangel publicly refused the MIR's support.

Any remaining prospect of leftist unity disappeared in November 1977 following the MIR's victory over the MAS in elections at the Central University by some 7,000 to 5,600 votes. A week later the MIR decisively defeated the MAS at both the University of the Andes and the University of Carabobo. This produced a new wave of debate and infighting within the MAS, with Petkoff and his supporters blaming the debacle on Rangel's ineffectiveness as a candidate. While the decision was not reversed, the MAS emerged with a determination to press even more vigorously its quest for hegemony on the left. The MIR, feeling itself on the upswing, moved to launch the candidacy of its own Américo Martín, a former guerrilla fighter and a worthy rival to Petkoff for the ideological and generational leadership of young Venezuelan leftists. Projecting himself as a more truly leftist and revolutionary leader than José Vicente Rangel, Martín moved ahead with his own campaign.

All of this activity relegated the aging founders of Venezuelan Marxism to a minor role. Eduardo Machado's breakaway from his brother Gustavo to create the Vanguardia Comunista was, in the light of the PCV's debility, ludicrous in the extreme. With the patriarchal Gustavo unable to run because of age and health, the PCV nominated its most attractive younger leader, Héctor Mújica. Among the few Communists of his generation who had not gone with the MAS following the division of the PCV in 1968, he undertook to rid the party of its pro-Moscow "Bolshevik" image without renouncing Marxist–Leninist orthodoxy. Though he expected little more than 3 percent of the vote, Mújica brought to the PCV its first breath of air in years, along with the promise of besting the MAS and MIR within a few years. "Reality has shown that the scientific bases of Marxism-Leninism are those which will permit the development of a classless society and the inauguration of a true socialist experience,"

Mújica proclaimed.[4] None of the other self-styled Marxist candidates, he maintained, had a correct ideological understanding of the Venezuelan experience.

By the close of 1977, then, the left had chosen four competing candidates. It was even more grievously divided than in 1973 as it entered the election year. The MAS, its internal differences papered over, approached the campaign without the enthusiasm it had lent Rangel five years earlier. Distancing itself from other Marxists, the party, through Petkoff, increasingly termed itself "Eurocommunist" rather than Marxist in the traditional sense. The MIR continued its efforts among iron and steel workers while counting on Américo Martín to be a more convincing revolutionary than Rangel. The Communists hoped that Mújica's winning personality would revive their sagging fortunes. In the MEP, the prominence of the venerable but still vigorous Prieto was the only basis for survival. With the 1978 campaign picking up in intensity, the left not only was seriously fragmented once again, but also was further challenged by the possible candidacies of two potential antiparty non-Marxists, the television personality Renny Ottolina and a former governor of Caracas, Diego Arria.

The Antiparty Candidates. Reinaldo Ottolina Pinto, known by all as Renny, was Venezuela's most popular and brilliant showman. Interviewer, master of ceremonies, entertainment entrepreneur, and salesman par excellence, he had conquered all worlds but the political. Rumors of his candidacy in early 1977 were initially treated as a joke, but by midyear his hat had sailed into the ring with the declaration that Venezuelans no longer believed in political parties. In a short time the publicity and media master had launched an expensive campaign centered on regular broadcasts over a network of some thirty stations. While his political views were unknown—in 1973 he had endorsed Carlos Andrés Pérez—Renny represented an alternative to COPEI and Acción Democrática which was presumably in the mainstream. His candidacy, while highly unlikely to be successful, was nonetheless an unknown that threatened several other contenders.

On the left, the MAS's hope of attracting votes from non-Marxists disillusioned with the Government was dimmed by Renny's candidacy. Similarly, COPEI's quest for anti-Pérez voters was endangered. The only party likely to benefit seemed to be Acción Democrática, which envisioned a victory based on the votes of party

---

[4] "Héctor Mújica avanza en la izquierda" [Héctor Mújica advances on the left], *Auténtico* (Caracas), no. 55 (June 26, 1978), p. 23.

loyalists sufficiently numerous to outpoll a divided opposition. It was further noted that Ottolina's generous financial backers included businessmen previously identified with Betancourt, leading some to conclude that the candidacy was itself a shrewd political maneuver by the veteran *adeco*. Of particular importance was the congressional delegation that Renny might carry into office for, should he poll some 10 percent of the vote, such a bloc might well hold the balance of power between the AD and COPEI. So it was that the famed showman introduced a new and unexpected ingredient into the electoral brew, one that might have major consequences for the system.

The formation of Ottolina's Movimiento de Integridad Nacional (MIN) and the initiation of its campaign were also directly prejudicial to the aspirations of another would-be independent candidate, Diego Arria Salicetti. A bright and photogenic public figure well versed in the use of the media, Arria had seen a meteoric rise to prominence. It had created deep resentment in both COPEI and Acción Democrática. After having served as President Caldera's director of national tourism, he had dramatically resigned in early 1973 to found Causa Común and, shortly thereafter, to endorse the Pérez candidacy. He soon established a close friendship with the AD nominee, advising him on image building and manipulation of the media. This led to his joint appointment as governor of the Federal District and president of the Centro Simón Bolívar, a massively funded public corporation responsible for major construction and urban expansion in the capital. Thus he achieved both political authority and control over a huge budget, one not subject to review by the comptroller's office.

Arria swiftly became Caracas's most visible and popular governor. Relying deftly on the media to sharpen his image, he pursued a host of popular if sometimes cosmetic policies: the creation of public parks in the city, the closing of the old center of town to vehicular traffic, the removal of sidewalk peddlers and vendors, and other populistic initiatives. In the process he virtually ignored the city council and turned a deaf ear to *adeco* politicians seeking to influence policies and to benefit from the patronage available to a governor. Within a short time Arria was anathema to the AD leadership, especially Rómulo Betancourt. Yet he remained protected through his ties to Pérez. After nearly three years as governor, he moved to the new Ministry of Information and Tourism in February 1977, which placed him even closer to the president.

For a time it appeared that he might be considering a rapprochement with Acción Democrática, and at one point his wife formally joined the party, but his bridges to a number of important party regulars were already burned, and Arria began to contemplate an independent presidential candidacy. Buoyed by polls showing him to be the most popular public official in Caracas, Arria reasoned that the two dominant parties would poll little more than half the vote, with MAS falling short of 15 percent. Thus the time appeared propitious for an independent candidate. A strong showing in 1978 might well pave the way for a successful bid in 1983. This reasoning, whatever its validity, was clearly inoperable, however, if Arria were forced to split the non-Marxist independent vote with Renny. Not until March 1978, a few days after Ottolina's death in a plane crash, did Arria initiate his own personal antiparty campaign.

Other Groups. The presidential bug had already bitten other prospective candidates, several of whom once again sought the imprimatur of Marcos Pérez Jiménez. Hoping to serve as his surrogate in 1978, such rightists as Alejandro Gómez Silva and Pablo Salas Castillo entered the fray. Gómez, who had backed Arturo Uslar Pietri and the FND in 1963, had later tried to swing that party behind Pérez Jiménez. Failing in the effort, he had then created the Frente Unido Nacionalista (FUN). Withdrawing Gómez's candidacy from the 1973 presidential race after being rebuffed by the former dictator, FUN ran thirteenth in the congressional elections with 0.4 percent of the vote. By 1977, however, the reconstituted FUN again sought to represent the right.

Much the same was true of Salas Castillo, who had been a close adviser of Pérez Jiménez during the dictatorship. He had been the organizational director of the Cruzada Cívica Nacionalista for the 1968 election, when *perezjimenismo* had enjoyed a resurgence in the congressional balloting, but he was subsequently unable to hold together its diverse membership. During the 1973 campaign he went so far as to propose that the dictator's wife run for president and one of his daughters for deputy from Caracas. Ultimately he too was unable to secure the general's blessing, however, and he suspended his candidacy in November 1973. The CCN ran fifth with 4.3 percent of the congressional vote, which allowed Salas Castillo to claim that his party was the leading *perezjimenista* grouping. Becoming the leader of the CCN delegation, he again undertook to organize a united rightist campaign in 1978 under the banner of the exiled general.

One additional figure also entered the race—Leonardo Montiel Ortega. A voluble political gadfly who had emerged as leader of the second generation in the URD, by 1973 he stood second only to the ineffable Villalba. He served as Villalba's campaign chief and for a time appeared likely to inherit the mantle of URD leadership. With the party's debacle that year, however, he was deprived of a seat in Congress. Not long thereafter he was forced out of the URD by Villalba, ever jealous of potential successors. Remaining in the public eye by various means (including a minor part in a television soap opera), Montiel Ortega announced his candidacy and undertook a quixotic bid for the presidency in 1978 under the banner of the Movimiento Renovador Nacional, known as MORENA.

The Campaign

The Rival Marxist Campaigns. The political ambitions which produced four rival candidacies on the left had internal as well as inter-party ramifications. The MAS, though it had purportedly resolved the problems of dissension, was plagued by internecine strife throughout 1978. Teodoro Petkoff regrouped his followers while becoming increasingly vocal in his espousal of Eurocommunism as the wave of the future for Venezuela. José Vicente Rangel found attention drawn away from his own campaigning; Petkoff and Márquez tacitly joined forces against him preparatory to their own struggle for the 1983 nomination. While the party hoped Rangel would finish third, its strategy extended well beyond the 1978 competition. The fundamental concerns were two: establishing clear primacy over other parties of the left, and gaining enough congressional seats to offer visible opposition to the victor, whether he were AD's candidate or COPEI's.

The MAS campaign was less an attack on the parties of "El Status"—although they were strongly criticized—than an effort to promote the party's doctrine. Coupled with this were attacks on the other parties of the left as ideologically confused (MIR), bourgeois reformist (MEP), or Stalinist and dependent on the Soviet Union (PCV). In further developing its own doctrinal position, the MAS spoke warmly of both the Italian and the Spanish Communists, and Petkoff made a well-publicized European trek to confer with Euro-communist leaders. Rangel himself put forth the same message, while stressing on the campaign trail that the MAS approach was democratic and representative. He also attempted, as he had in 1973, to convey the image of a grave and self-abnegating leader. Although a better-known figure than he had been in his first race, Rangel had at the same time lost the freshness of his earlier candidacy. His relative weakness within the MAS organization itself was hardly a secret. Moreover, the party's aspirations in 1978 were clearly endangered by the candidacies of Renny and Arria.

161

The campaign placed particular emphasis on attracting the youth vote; among the most familiar slogans was "La patria joven"—the young country. Numerous groups of pro-Rangel independents were formed as a means of playing upon antagonisms toward COPEI and AD. The future of Venezuela, the voters were told, could be changed by a vote for the MAS, a new national force; it was not necessary to continue suffering the failures of the two dominant parties. As the party manifesto said, "The true alternative to the process of frustration and national dissolution is the construction of a socialist democracy that sincerely and effectively guarantees political, economic, social, and human liberties." With regard to the political left it said, "By supporting Rangel's candidacy we are deliberately encouraging all sectors of the socialist camp to join in a great movement that will make the triumph of socialism a certainty in Venezuela."[5]

In its final months the MAS campaign failed to build up genuine momentum. Several of the most widely heralded rallies in Caracas drew disappointing and less than festive crowds. Rangel's rating in the polls generally ran at 10 percent or less; clearly he might finish no better than fourth. Party tacticians found it difficult to convince disenchanted voters that MAS was a serious option; not only did COPEI offer a more realistic choice, but it was difficult to assess the impact of the antiparty personalistic campaigns. The chance that the unusually large proportion of undecided voters might swell the MAS totals was a slender reed on which to base hopes for a strong showing. But at the least, there seemed some basis for thinking that the party might outpoll the other leftist parties, which had run very weak campaigns.

For the MIR, initially buoyed by its victories over the MAS in student and labor elections, Américo Martín was seen as a bright and attractive young candidate with potentially greater appeal than the austere Rangel. Yet it was only with reluctance that the party finally accepted the impossibility of a united left. As late as August 9, 1978, the MIR officially proposed a six-point plan for union, including the call for the creation of a single parliamentary bloc in the next Congress. Martín himself proved less effective as an orator and public figure than he was as an ideologue. Moreover, it was difficult to present a doctrinal message standing in clear contradistinction to that of the MAS. With MIR's resources even more limited than those of the MAS, it proved impossible to knit together a well-organized campaign. Such MIR slogans as "Manos limpias"—clean hands— were of limited appeal.

---

[5] "Manifiesto al país" [Manifesto to the nation], *El Nacional* (Caracas), August 20, 1978, p. D-20.

The MEP campaign was better designed, although heavily reliant upon the popularity and warmth people still felt for Luis B. Prieto. Surrounding himself with the few advisers who had not returned to Acción Democrática or withdrawn from politics, the "Maestro" developed a strategy of concentrating on areas of relative strength— most notably Zulia and portions of the East—while attempting to mobilize those of his supporters remaining within the labor movement. Heavy emphasis was placed upon Prieto's personal appearances, which still drew respectable and generally enthusiastic crowds. The campaign platform was less explicitly ideological than that of Paz Galarraga in 1973. No longer encumbered by an alliance with the Communists, the MEP placed greater emphasis on populistic appeals, stressing the integrity of Prieto and his half-century struggle on behalf of the impoverished and dispossessed.

On August 23, Prieto and the party leadership signed a widely heralded notarized document setting forth their campaign promises. This "commitment to the people," released simultaneously at meetings throughout the country, pledged a Government based on the "tripod of urban, educational, and true agrarian reform." Thus the MEP and its candidate were publicly committed to achieving an honest and "authentic" democracy. "Authentic democracy is as good, honest, and efficient as the good, honest, and efficient men who have the sacred responsibility of directing it," the party proclaimed.[6] The MEP's position was broadly reminiscent of its position in 1968 following its departure from Acción Democrática: it largely eschewed the socialist message that had been developed for 1973. It was perhaps less than coincidental that the architect of the earlier MEP swing to the left, Secretary General Paz, was little in evidence during the 1978 campaign.[7]

The Communist party of Venezuela, with young leaders finally emerging to help direct its fortunes, demonstrated more imagination and energy than it had in recent years. Héctor Mújica himself was effective in personal appearances, more so than either Rangel or Martín. The party's campaign strategy was to stress his personality and soft-pedal party identification. Great emphasis was given to groups of independent supporters, who were repeatedly brought to meetings with "Héctor." The PCV also developed a list of what would be Mújica's first twenty decrees as president. While these included such basic changes as massive nationalization, expropriation

[6] "Compromiso" [Commitment], *Panorama* (Maracaibo), August 27, 1978, p. 19.

[7] Among the best expressions of Prieto's orientation was the interview "Prieto candidato [Prieto candidate], *Semana* (Caracas), vol. 10, no. 482 (October 9, 1977), pp. 10-14.

of large landholdings, and strict limits on the profits of big business, greater stress was placed on populistic commitments to better wages, a massive urban housing program, severe penalties for perpetrators of official corruption, and efforts to improve life in the *barrios*. The PCV played down ideology, resorting only sporadically to Marxist slogans that might unsettle the electorate.

On the eve of elections, the prospects of the left were mixed at best. The polls continued to indicate that only Rangel would draw more than 1 or 2 percent of the vote. Most of the parties appeared likely to win one or two seats in Congress at best. Such mini-groups as Eduardo Machado's Vanguardia Comunista (VUC) and the Liga Socialista, both of which supported Rangel, had little prospect of surviving as legally registered parties. Barring an unanticipated vote for Prieto, the MEP appeared on the brink of extinction. But some interest centered on the respective showings of the MAS, the MIR, and the PCV, with a view to the possible organizational consolidation of the left during the 1979–1984 term. And many were particularly curious to see how Diego Arria would fare.

The Arria Campaign. When 1978 dawned, Renny Ottolina was the sole centrist challenger to COPEI and Acción Democrática, and Arria's intentions remained uncertain. Renny's media-based appeals were reaching large numbers of voters with great frequency, although a series of his broadcast "commentaries" were restricted as actually constituting partisan electoral activity. Substantial financial support had been generated, and Renny began touring the country in the traditional fashion. The limitations placed on his radio and television blitz were effectively offset by the extensive coverage his campaign received in the daily press and in news weeklies. His message was unfailingly the same: the country no longer believed in political parties; it had tested them for twenty years and found them wanting.[8] Ottolina's MIN was attracting growing numbers of young if politically inexperienced enthusiasts, and he was holding steady at some 10–12 percent in the polls, consistently ahead of Rangel, when his candidacy was ended by his death in the crash of his private plane on March 16, 1978.

The MIN remained in the race but refused to endorse any other presidential nominee. The tragic conclusion of Ottolina's campaign greatly enhanced Diego Arria's prospects, however, and one day later he announced his resignation as minister of information and

---

[8] For a revealing interview, see "¿Qué es el 'fenómeno Renny'?" [What is the Renny phenomenon?], *Resumen*, vol. 17, no. 210 (November 13, 1977), pp. 3-8.

tourism. With any possibility of joining Acción Democrática foreclosed by his consistent defiance of the party under the Pérez administration, Arria issued a ringing statement of praise for Pérez and veiled denunciation of Betancourt. Reviving his virtually defunct Causa Común as an organizational vehicle, he negotiated substantial financial backing and undertook a campaign heavily reliant upon the media, designed to make the most of his telegenic image. He also sought and to some extent secured sympathetic treatment from the De Armas communication empire and from both the news weekly *Auténtico* and the conservative Caracas daily *El Universal*.

Announcing his candidacy on television on May 21, 1978, Arria immediately became a complicating factor for both COPEI and Acción Democrática. Ottolina's appeal had been greatest with pro-Pérez voters disappointed in the Government; Arria appeared more likely to attract disenchanted *barrio* voters who would otherwise have leaned toward COPEI. Yet this was all speculative. After an unsuccessful effort to hire David Garth as his campaign adviser, Arria turned to U.S. pollster Patrick Caddell. Calling his candidacy the only meaningful democratic option for voters opposed to the failings of the existing parties, he conducted a campaign long on image building and short on an integrated program. His campaign propaganda featured pictures of the smiling young candidate reaching out and saying "Dale tu mano"—give me your hand. His personal appeal was enhanced by the ever-present cane he required as the result of a serious automobile accident years earlier and by the presence of Tiqui, his beautiful second wife.

While making the customary public appearances throughout Venezuela, Arria centered his resources on the media campaign. Television viewers were inundated with pictures of the candidate, often accompanied by Tiqui, strolling through city slums while the voice-over promised that such conditions would be remedied. By September he had risen to some 10 percent in the polls. Like Ottolina earlier, he had outdistanced all the other minor candidates on the basis of an antiparty personalistic appeal. It was unclear, however, whether his support was hurting Herrera or Piñerúa, and Arria's strength was strongly centered in the metropolitan Caracas area; in other parts of the country where he traveled later in the campaign there was little evidence that Arria was attracting voters away from the two major parties.

Arria's long-range goal was to hold the balance of power between more or less equal COPEI and Acción Democrática groups in Congress, a position from which another presidential bid might be mounted in 1983. In seeking to translate into votes his past visibility in the Pérez Government and his youthful magnetism, Arria invariably placed highest priority on communications and the media. His chief enemy in the media was magazine publisher Jorge Olavarria, whose widely read *Resumen* relentlessly attacked Arria for corruption, mismanagement, and a cavalier attitude toward civil liberties. In addition, his image suffered a blow in November when his chauffeur, while off duty, shot and killed in broad daylight the driver of a car with which his had just collided. This incident probably dissipated any last-minute momentum Arria's campaign might have acquired. Yet it remained possible that Arria would win the desired position in the new Congress, and the damage his candidacy might do to either COPEI or Acción Democrática, especially in Caracas, awaited the verdict of the voters. In the meantime, the sporadic efforts of the other secondary candidates seemed unlikely to affect the outcome significantly.

Montiel and the Perezjimenista Campaigns. Leonardo Montiel Ortega was never a serious contender; he even had difficulty finding people to run on his MORENA ticket. His attacks on the two dominant parties were interspersed with vehement denunciations of Arria and Causa Común that were more personal than political. Of the *perezjimenista* campaigns, that of Pablo Salas Castillo was marginally the most active. His platform was essentially innocuous, and he devoted his efforts largely to establishing his credentials as a surrogate for Pérez Jiménez. The familiar red symbol and Indian heads identified with the Cruzada Cívica Nacionalista were exploited to suggest the support of the former dictator, though in fact Pérez Jiménez never endorsed anyone. Gómez Silva used the same tactic, displaying a picture of himself shaking hands with Pérez Jiménez and slogans like "de no ser Pérez Jiménez, Gómez Silva presidente"—if not Pérez Jiménez, then Gómez Silva for president. His United Nationalist Front billed itself as the authentic *perezjimenista* party, with its limited electoral propaganda generally citing the personal merits of the candidate rather than expounding a program of action.

The Elections and the Aftermath

A Slight Decline for the Left. The Movement toward Socialism outdistanced its competitors on the left but fell short of its aspirations, while COPEI and Acción Democrática's joint share of the vote was greater than ever. José Vicente Rangel ran third with 272,595 votes,

TABLE 6–2

Performance of the Left, Presidential and Legislative Elections, 1978

	Vote	Percentage
Presidential Candidates (large card)		
Rangel (MAS, VUC)	272,595	5.1
Prieto (MEP)	58,723	1.1
Martín (MIR)	51,972	1.0
Mújica (PCV)	28,835	0.5
Total	412,125	7.7
Party Lists (small card)		
MAS	319,730	6.1
VUC	46,063	0.9
Socialist League	30,251	0.6
MEP	115,944	2.2
MIR	122,672	2.3
PCV	55,068	1.0
Total	689,728	13.1

Source: Venezuela, Supreme Electoral Council, *Escrutinio de la votación de diciembre de 1978* [Returns of the December 1978 election] (Caracas: Imprenta Nacional, 1979).

or 5.1 percent of the total. Placing fifth through seventh were Prieto (1.1 percent), Martín (1.0 percent), and Mújica (0.5 percent). Their combined vote totaled slightly more than half that of Rangel. Overall, the four leftist nominees polled 7.7 percent of the vote, a drop of some two points from 1973. The pattern was similar on the small-card voting, although the totals were perceptibly higher than in the presidential race. As in 1973 but to a greater extent, voters with leftist preferences had been swayed by the economy-of-the-vote argument. Many voted their hearts in the legislative election while choosing the lesser evil between the two Luises running for president. Where 7.7 percent supported leftist presidential nominees, 13.1 percent selected a Marxist party's small card (see Table 6–2).

As for the MAS, in 1973 it had finished in a virtual tie with the MEP; now it could claim an advantage over its rivals on the left and the largest delegation in both the Senate and the Chamber of Deputies of any leftist party. There were only two leftist senators, both MAS candidates chosen by application of the electoral quotient. Twenty-one leftist deputies were elected, twelve through the quotient. Eleven

TABLE 6–3

CONGRESSIONAL REPRESENTATION OF THE LEFT, 1974–1984

(in seats)

	1974–1979		1979–1984	
Party	Senate	Chamber	Senate	Chamber
MAS	2	9	2	11
MEP	2	8	0	3
MIR	0	1	0	4
PCV	0	2	0	1
VUC and Socialist League	0	0	0	2
Total	4	20	2	21

SOURCE: Supreme Electoral Council.

came from the MAS, four from the MIR, three from the MEP, and one each from the PCV, the Communist Vanguard, and the Socialist League (see Table 6–3). Among the more prominent figures to enter the new Congress were Pompeyo Márquez in the Senate and, in the lower chamber, Rangel, Martín, Teodoro Petkoff, and Gustavo Machado.

In the wake of the elections, negotiations were undertaken to form a united congressional delegation of the left and to consider running a single list of candidates in the June 1979 municipal elections. It seemed likely that at least the MAS would be selective in its dealings with the new administration. This was the experience during the Pérez years. Whatever the attitudes toward President Herrera, however, internal struggles promised to be brutal. The rivalry between Márquez and Petkoff for control of the MAS was not susceptible of compromise. The latter spent much of the campaign working for sympathetic congressional candidates and fully intended to be the candidate in 1983. Márquez, in contrast, remained a superb party tactician and would undoubtedly benefit from whatever remaining prestige Rangel could bring to bear. At the same time, the MAS could not assume the definitive demise of the other parties.

The major challenge on the left might come from Américo Martín and the MIR. Despite their disappointment over the 1978 returns, the MIR still had small but militant pockets of strength among the iron and steel workers. More important, it constituted a major force in the universities, where Petkoff's own strength was concentrated. He and Martín, rivals since their university days, appeared evenly matched in the fight for domination of the student movement. To the extent that Martín was successful, the MAS would be damaged, its internal conflict exacerbated. For the Communists, the emergence of Héctor Mújica would further complicate efforts to achieve a united left. The MEP would continue its decline of recent years; its single remaining asset, Luis B. Prieto, would be eighty before the next elections, and, as 1978 proved, his personal prestige was no longer sufficient to sustain the party.

Defeat for Arria and the Small Groups. The Arria campaign culminated in resounding electoral defeat. The erstwhile antiparty candidate finished fourth with 90,379 votes, a scant 1.7 percent of the total. In the light of his hopes for a third-place finish with at least 10 percent, this showing could only be characterized as an unmitigated disaster. Causa Común placed but one candidate in the lower house, and that through the quotient. Thus Arria was also deprived of any bargaining role in the new Congress. Barely forty and a skillful practitioner of media politics, Arria nonetheless faced dim prospects in the immediate future and remained anathema to many COPEI as well as AD supporters.

Within the larger political context, Arria's failure revealed several important characteristics of Venezuela's political system. First, a lavishly financed media campaign making use of the most sophisticated techniques is insufficient in itself to produce success at the polls. The Venezuelan electorate has had extensive exposure to the modern technology of electioneering, and it demands substance as well as style. Second, the era for antiparty electoral phenomena has passed. Unlike Uslar Pietri in 1963 or Burelli Rivas in 1968, a presidential aspirant in the late 1970s could not compete effectively on the basis of personality, style, and denunciations of the party system. Third, the monopolization of the vote by COPEI and the AD, which have coopted the broad political center, is more deeply embedded than ever before. Superior organization, hundreds of thousands of party members, unity of action, and broad doctrinal bases for campaign platforms ensure the continuation and extension of what has become fundamentally a two-party system.

As for the remaining minor candidates, their showings speak for themselves. Montiel Ortega received 13,754 votes, or 0.2 percent, and MORENA narrowly failed to win a congressional seat through the quotient. The *perezjimenistas* also failed to win any seats; Gómez Silva and Salas Castillo polled 0.2 and 0.1 percent of the vote respectively. If there is a place for rightist candidates in the Venezuelan scheme, recent elections do not show it. Neither do they provide

evidence that conservative sectors of society view parties and candidates with enthusiasm. For economic and commercial leaders dis-
tressed by what they see as Venezuela's exaggerated statism, the
answer has been an effort to exert pressure within COPEI and Acción
Democrática. A truly conservative party is no longer considered a
viable option.

In summary, the 1978 elections reinforced the 1973 experience
and confirmed the domination of the two major parties. The leftist
electoral sector remains small and, in the absence of meaningful
unification, has little chance of mounting a challenge to COPEI and
the AD. It does provide a salubrious outlet for antisystem views and
to a limited degree may help keep the two giants sensitive to popular
demands that might otherwise be ignored. The small parties are therefore not without their value to the contemporary system. However,
barring major governmental failures or economic disaster, the fate of
public policy remains the responsibility of COPEI and Acción Democrática. For all other parties, the term "minor" appears eminently
suited.

7

The Media and the Campaign

Robert E. O'Connor

Analyzing the Venezuelan election of 1973 Martz and Baloyra wrote: "No other political campaign in Latin America has been as richly endowed with political communications, use of media, and intensive public relations activities."[1] That campaign showed that the party out of power could win if it combined an effective use of the media with a strong candidate. Both *adecos* and Social Christians entered the 1978 race determined not to be outcampaigned, and their efforts matched—perhaps surpassed—in intensity the campaign of 1973.

The Print Media

Newspapers. Venezuela's newspapers can be characterized as Caracas dominated, mostly nonpartisan, and generally free of government censorship.[2] Each of these three characteristics requires elaboration.

David Blank, John Martz, and especially David J. Myers helped me by commenting extensively on an early version of this chapter. Dean Thomas Magner of the College of Liberal Arts of The Pennsylvania State University helped by providing financial assistance. None of these individuals is responsible for errors or weaknesses which remain.

[1] John D. Martz and Enrique A. Baloyra, *Electoral Mobilization and Public Opinion: The Venezuelan Campaign of 1973* (Chapel Hill: University of North Carolina Press, 1976), p. 167.

[2] Efforts to communicate political messages through the printed word have a long history in Venezuela. Early issues of the *Gaceta de Caracas*, first published in 1808, contain lengthy discussions of both political ideologies and political controversies in Venezuela. For a history of the press during the colonial period and the first republic, see Pedro Grases, *Historia de la imprenta en Venezuela hasta el fin de la primera república (1812)* [History of the press in Venezuela until the end of the first republic (1812)], Ediciones de la Presidencia de la República (Caracas: Editorial Arte, 1967).

Howard I. Blutstein writes, "In 1976 the preeminence and national influence of the Caracas press was virtually unchallenged."[3] This remained true in 1978, although the papers based in rapidly growing provincial cities continued to expand and to improve in quality. Over forty papers appear daily in Venezuela, but the bulk of the circulation comes from those printed in Caracas and distributed by air throughout the nation. The Venezuelan press includes both prestige newspapers and less staid, higher circulation newspapers. *El Nacional* and *El Universal* are prestige newspapers with circulations over 100,000 and wide readership among elites throughout the country. *Panorama*, an exception to the dominance of the Caracas press, is a prestige newspaper printed in Maracaibo and distributed throughout the nearby states. *Ultimas Noticias* is the most popular tabloid, and *2001* and *Meridiano*, which emphasize sports and garish color photographs, often of beach scenes, have the widest circulation. All of these newspapers except *Panorama* are published in Caracas and all are privately owned, as is every newspaper in Venezuela.

Venezuelan newspapers are generally nonpartisan—which is not to say that their reporting is totally objective or fair to all parties at all times. Like papers in the United States, they tend to slant toward a major party (rarely toward a party of the far left), but without closely following a particular party line. They also tend to present a wide range of opinion. Along with their own supposedly objective campaign coverage, most of which merely reports politicians' speeches or statements to the press, Venezuelan newspapers provide many opportunities for the parties themselves to express their opinions. Indeed, "Of the two basic media functions of informing and of providing a forum for debate," writes Robert Pierce, "most Latin Americans traditionally have valued the latter more highly. They have seen it as natural that 'the winds of doctrine' should be 'let loose to play upon the earth,' in Milton's words."[4] In 1978, all of the newspapers accepted advertisements from parties, major and minor, and most turned over their editorial columns to guest writers, usually politicians, who extolled the virtues of various candidates.[5] A few newspapers also ran editorials of their own. As a result, a single edition of a newspaper might contain signed editorials by the head of Youth for Piñerúa, the director of Independents for Herrera, and

---

[3] Howard I. Blutstein et al., *Area Handbook for Venezuela* (Washington, D.C., 1977), p. 101.

[4] Robert N. Pierce, *Keeping the Flame: Media and Government in Latin America* (New York: Hastings House, 1979), p. 148.

[5] As a substitute for an editorial, some newspapers run a daily *mancheta*, a one-sentence epigram offering a wry comment on political matters.

the campaign manager of José Vicente Rangel, the candidate of the Movement toward Socialism. Regardless of its own orientation, each paper gave its readers the opportunity to learn what the various parties thought of each other and of the candidates, and exposed them to a wide range of opinion.[6]

The term "nonpartisan" is not intended to imply that strict standards of journalistic ethics are always upheld or that the newspapers have always been evenhanded. In 1968 Miguel Angel Capriles, the owner of *El Universal* and several other newspapers and magazines, promised Rafael Caldera, the COPEI candidate, to praise him effusively in print in return for a place on the COPEI slate and other favors. *El Nacional,* the other prestige newspaper, responded by closing its editorial pages to COPEI.[7] Although no newspapers refused to accept advertisements from parties in 1978, a somewhat comparable agreement between a party and a publishing mogul came to light, this time involving Acción Democrática, which agreed to slate members of the De Armas family in return for favorable coverage in the family's newspapers, primarily *Meridiano* and *2001.* Since these newspapers did not mount consistent or libelous attacks upon Herrera and did accept advertisements and editorials from COPEI, however, this arrangement was received with less rancor than the agreement between Caldera and Capriles in 1968.

Other common departures from strict journalistic ethics include the doctoring of pictures, usually to increase the size of crowds at mass meetings, and the taking of bribes in return for favorable coverage of local party leaders in provincial papers. The notion that reporters should never accept favors from politicians whose activities they are reporting has not permeated all elements of the Venezuelan press corps.

The newspapers maintain their nonpartisan stance not by hiring nonpartisan reporters, but by hiring partisan reporters of differing persuasions: few journalists claim to be nonpartisan. Their union, to which almost all reporters belong, contains factions identified with various parties, including a particularly strong group committed to the Movement toward Socialism. An owner can maintain a balance among conflicting partisans by hiring reporters supporting different parties and by mandating that adequate space be allotted to cover the platforms and campaigns of the major candidates.

---

[6] Blutstein, *Area Handbook,* p. 102.

[7] This incident is discussed at length in David J. Myers, *Democratic Campaigning in Venezuela: Caldera's Victory* (Caracas: Fundación La Salle, 1973), and briefly in Martz and Baloyra, *Electoral Mobilization,* p. 26.

Venezuelan newspapers can be characterized as relatively free of censorship, especially by comparison with most in the Third World. As noted above, all papers accepted advertisements and opened their editorial pages to all parties, including all minor parties. Nevertheless, reporters and editors operate in an atmosphere not entirely free from government censorship.

The government has three means of influencing the press. First, it has the statutory authority to limit what it feels are excesses by the press. Article 56 of the Venezuelan constitution permits the government to confiscate any material that "incites disobedience of the laws." The Law of Journalism requires journalists, although not editorial writers, to obtain a license, and this may be revoked for deliberate misinformation, efforts to harm individuals, refusal to correct errors, and similar lapses of journalistic integrity.[8] Also, various libel laws, including one specifically dealing with defamation of character of the president of the republic, provide additional authority for attacks upon the independence of the press. In recent years, these laws have rarely been invoked, but their existence may dampen a newspaper's willingness to tackle controversial subjects.

During the campaign, the Government, through the Supreme Electoral Council, has the authority to regulate the amount of newspaper space the parties can purchase and to ban deceptive advertisements. Although the newspapers seemed dominated by political advertisements during the campaign, AD and COPEI would have purchased even more space had the Supreme Electoral Council not intervened. One of the few advertisements blocked by the council in 1978 was a color picture of Diego Arria in front of a backdrop in the colors of the Venezuelan flag. Arria argued that he was not trying to identify his campaign with Venezuelan patriotism in a cheap effort to garner votes, but the council thought otherwise.

Second, the government has at times invoked measures censoring the press. There is not a long tradition of an uncensored press. Under the dictatorship of Marcos Pérez Jiménez, overthrown in 1958, the Ministry of the Interior exercised prior censorship. Then, in the early years of the democracy, Article 56 was often invoked to quash articles sympathetic to the Communist guerrillas attempting to replace the young regime. In recent years a series of incidents, generally involving magazines rather than newspapers, have demonstrated that freedom of the press is not an absolute right. In 1976 after the kidnapping of

---

[8] This Law of Journalism was signed August 4, 1972. The licensing requirement is not intended to imply that the government closely controls the School of Journalism at the Central University. In fact, at one time, Héctor Mújica, the Communist party candidate for president in 1978, was its director.

William F. Niehous, an American businessman working in Caracas, for example, the Government put pressure on the media not to carry the manifestoes the kidnappers sought to publicize. Agents of the national police went so far as to enter the offices of several newspapers, including *El Nacional,* to discourage publication of the kidnappers' demands. Although the Government later apologized for the over-reaction of the national police, the incident served notice to the newspapers that strong-arm actions by the government were not unthinkable.[9]

Third, newspapers are at least partially dependent for their revenues on government advertising, particularly in the provinces, where private advertisers are few.[10] Pierce argues, "Although the use of advertising as a weapon in the hands of government is not well documented in Venezuela, it is accepted as a way of life among media leaders."[11] One incident reported by Pierce involved the Pérez Government's dissatisfaction with the support the newspaper *2001* was giving to the major opposition party. After a government official made a phone call to the owner of *2001* threatening the loss of government advertising if the paper did not present more balanced reporting, the owner replaced several reporters with new ones more sympathetic to the government.[12]

These three restraints on the freedom of newspapers to publish what they wanted during the campaign of 1978 should not overshadow the genuine availability of differing points of view in the press. The newspapers did allow the parties to make their positions and their candidates widely known throughout the campaign.

Newsmagazines. Besides newspapers, the print media in Venezuela include a wide range of magazines—notably, for our purposes, six weekly newsmagazines with wide circulations. Like Venezuela's newspapers, they are Caracas dominated; all six are published in Caracas and focus heavily on events in the capital. This is not surprising in light of the centralization of government in Venezuela and the status of Caracas as financial and cultural, as well as political, capital. Not only the magazines' news pages but also their advertisements, for medical personnel or theaters or restaurants, are oriented toward Caracas. Newsmagazines published outside the capital bear a closer

---

[9] Pierce, *Keeping the Flame,* pp. 173-74.
[10] Blutstein, *Area Handbook,* p. 102.
[11] Pierce, *Keeping the Flame,* p. 176.
[12] Ibid.

resemblance to chamber of commerce puffery than they do to publications concerned with the serious analysis of national events.[13]

Although "political partisanship is generally more pronounced than with the newspapers,"[14] the six major newsmagazines are not party organs.[15] Instead, each tends to reflect the views and even the personality of its editor. During the 1978 campaign, for example, *Resumen*, founded in 1973 and still edited by its founder, Jorge Olavarria, was highly critical of President Carlos Andrés Pérez without endorsing the opposition. Some issues of *Resumen* devoted over half of their pages to making and documenting serious charges against the president.[16] Yet Olavarria's enmity was not directed at Acción Democrática. One issue charging the administration with extreme corruption also featured an article headed "Piñerúa against Corruption" and made no mention of Herrera's position on the issue.[17] Highly opinionated, the magazine reflected the views not of AD or COPEI but of Jorge Olavarria.

Of the other five major newsmagazines, *Zeta* was one of the two favorable toward the candidacy of Luis Piñerúa. Edited by Rafael Poleo, *Zeta* tended to favor the Government. An article like "In Miranda the Objectives of Government Are Being Accomplished"[18] would never have been found in *Resumen*. Nevertheless, *Zeta* did not refrain from running material favorable to Herrera. Two articles it ran shortly before the election detailing *adeco* problems in the state of Carabobo and showing Betty de Herrera to be a warm campaigner could not have pleased Acción Democrática.[19]

Of the 1973 election coverage, Martz and Baloyra wrote, "With the newsmagazines, pro-COPEI and anti-AD sentiment was dominant, in most cases strongly biasing alleged 'news' stories."[20] This held true in 1978 for *Auténtico* and *Semana*. The former, modeled on the British *Economist*, often used the interview format, and Social Christians were interviewed much more frequently than *adecos*. On the other hand, it employed the Gallup organization and reported its findings honestly. *Semana* emphasized the Herrera candidacy and the

---

[13] Magazines such as *Barquisimeto* do exist, but they are much lower in quality than the magazines published in Caracas.

[14] Martz and Baloyra, *Electoral Mobilization*, p. 304.

[15] The minor parties published their own magazines such as the MAS's *Punto*, but these publications had low circulations and usually appeared irregularly.

[16] See, for example, *Resumen*, no. 264 (November 26, 1978).

[17] Ibid., p. 26.

[18] *Zeta*, no. 246 (November 26, 1978), pp. 46-47.

[19] Ibid., pp. 12-14.

[20] Martz and Baloyra, *Electoral Mobilization*, p. 305.

problems of the Pérez Government much more often than it wrote positively of Piñerúa, though in its campaign coverage *Semana* resembled *Time* or *Newsweek* more than a clearly ideological publication.

Finally, *Bohemia* and *Elite*, both with wide readerships, are only marginally newsmagazines. In layout and contents they suggest a combination of *People*, *Life*, and the *National Enquirer*. Most of the explicitly political material they carry comes in the form of interviews or editorials, including editorials signed by politicians. A typical campaign issue of *Bohemia* ran an interview with minor-party candidate Leonardo Montiel Ortega and an editorial by José Vicente Rangel, candidate of the Movement toward Socialism. The issue also included "The Master Stroke of Onassis or How Jackie Lost Two Hundred Million Dollars," "The Boy Who Defeated Leukemia," "Hispanics in the United States: The Minority That Is Already a Majority," "Be Careful with Detergents and Solvents," "The Overthrow of Gallegos Traumatized the Youth of '48," and a pictorial feature entitled "Sun Bath."[21]

Elite, though it devoted even fewer pages to the campaign than *Bohemia*, was the most obviously partisan of the newsmagazines. Published by the Capriles family, which at one time had been strongly identified with COPEI, *Elite* carried many pieces favorable to the Government. One campaign issue ran a cover story extolling Piñerúa as the champion of the free press; inside, another article praised the state-run power company's efforts to meet the energy problem—and Herrera was nowhere mentioned.[22] The loyalties of the Capriles family had shifted.

Though the parties themselves did not advertise in the newsmagazines, taken together these six provided a thorough analysis of the candidates and the campaign. Like the newspapers, however, they did so in an atmosphere not entirely free from government censorship. The same laws that give the government the authority to limit excesses in newspapers apply to newsmagazines, and the knowledge that the government has the authority to confiscate materials and arrest editors who "incite disobedience of the laws" or libel the president is likely to make an editor think twice before printing information critical of the Government. Moreover, these laws have been invoked. They are not merely relics of an earlier era no responsible editor need fear. One instance of confiscation occurred in 1976. Salóm Mesa Espinosa, a member of Congress from the People's Electoral Movement, was accused of participating in the kidnapping of

---

[21] *Bohemia*, no. 817 (November 20, 1978).
[22] *Elite*, no. 2,765 (September 22, 1978).

William F. Niehous. Since some of the kidnappers had worn military uniforms, the crime was viewed as falling under the jurisdiction of the military courts, and Salóm Mesa's parliamentary immunity was denied. While in jail, Salóm Mesa wrote a letter in which he proclaimed his innocence and claimed that Carlos Andrés Pérez had accepted money from the Central Intelligence Agency. The left-wing weekly *Punto* published the letter, only to have all copies of the issue seized by the military.[23]

Another instance of confiscation occurred during the 1978 campaign. In the edition of *Resumen* which was to reach the streets immediately before the election, Jorge Olavarria presented evidence connecting President Pérez with the murder of Ramón Carmona, a well-known Caracas attorney, by members of the national police. Though Olavarria was permitted to leave the country rather than face trial for defamation of the president, the entire issue of *Resumen* was impounded.

Government advertising is an important source of revenue for the newsmagazines. Each issue of *Zeta, Bohemia, Auténtico, Semana,* and *Elite* during the campaign contained between four and six pages of government advertisements. *Resumen* had fewer government advertisements, and as Olavarria's attacks on Carlos Andrés Pérez increased, the advertisements disappeared entirely. The government's advertisements came either from the Ministry of Information (the "I am better off today" and "Step by step, we are doing the government's work" campaigns) or from government corporations such as the telephone company and the electric company. As Olavarria discovered, the government would only accept certain sorts of criticism before it withdrew its advertisements.

Despite these elements of censorship, the newsmagazines did function to provide campaign analyses from differing points of view. Especially when one includes the smaller circulation publications, the Venezuelan newsmagazines provided a myriad of views representing varied points on the ideological spectrum. The diversity of views available becomes even more impressive when one remembers that Venezuelan consumers of newsmagazines are the same people who read newspapers. Together, the newspapers and magazines provided a thorough description and interpretation of the 1978 campaign.

---

[23] See *Punto* (September 8, 1976), p. 5. The *New York Times* (February 22, 1977) also claimed that Pérez had accepted money from the Central Intelligence Agency, but at an earlier time than Salóm Mesa had charged. Though still in prison, Salóm Mesa ran again for his seat in the 1978 election; he won and was freed to resume his career in Congress. William Niehous gained his freedom as the result of a police assault on the kidnappers' hideaway.

It can be argued that not all of these publications are mass media, but all of them contribute to the formation of public opinion.[24] Some do so directly by reaching mass readerships, others indirectly by influencing opinion leaders who influence less interested citizens, the two-step flow of communications.[25] *Auténtico* is not a best seller compared with *Ultimas Noticias* or *Bohemia*, but it is read by at least several thousand self-selected citizens who are concerned with the political matters it discusses. The significance of a publication is measured not just by its numbers of readers, but by who those readers are. Particularly in a developing country with a capital-city-centered elite filling undifferentiated leadership roles, knowing which publications that elite reads is crucial for understanding the role of the media.

A third print medium, however, appeals directly to the masses, and it is free, uncensored by government, and intensely partisan. The political posters and paintings found throughout the country during the campaign fall within the definition of mass communication.

Either printed or stenciled with spray paint, campaign messages appeared not only on billboards but also on trees, pavements, the sides of automobiles, the exterior walls of churches, private houses, and buildings of all sorts. Only the statue of Simón Bolívar in the central square of almost every town was off-limits to political messages. Walking around one block of the business district of Barquisimeto, the capital of the state of Lara, two days before the election, the author counted 111 separate posters or painted political messages. This included only those signs along the side on which the author was walking and only those large enough to be clearly visible to a passing motorist—among them a painted wall at least twelve feet by twelve feet. Completing a similar stroll around a typical middle-class residential block, the author counted 32 messages.[26] During the campaign, Venezuelans did not have to buy newspapers or newsmagazines to read political messages—they could not escape them.

---

[24] Charles R. Wright defines a mass medium as one that provides mass communication "directed toward relatively large, heterogeneous, and anonymous audiences; messages are transmitted publicly, oftentimes to reach most audience members simultaneously, and are transient in character; the communicator tends to be, or to operate within, a complex organization that may involve great expense." *Mass Communication: A Sociological Perspective* (New York: Random House, 1959), pp. 13, 15 .

[25] The two-step flow idea originated in Paul F. Lazarsfeld et al., *The People's Choice*, 2d ed. (New York: Columbia University Press, 1948), pp. 152-56.

[26] The architecture of Venezuelan middle-class housing is conducive to this form of communication. Typically, houses are surrounded by walls which extend to the sidewalk. Signs are attached to or painted on these walls, not the actual walls of the houses.

179

The preparation and distribution of these printed or painted messages was well organized by the parties, and few of the painted messages looked like conventional graffiti scrawled by individual enthusiasts. Instead, most were the work of teams using cardboard stencils so that the images would be clear and the lettering even. Another indication that these communications were part of the organized campaign is that the slogans on the walls changed in step with those in the newspaper advertisements. For example, the Herrera messages in the spring of 1978 proclaimed, "Luis Herrera will set this right." Then in the summer they argued, "Luis Herrera is going to win." The final theme was, "Venezuela has the wealth, Luis Herrera has the will." This was deliberate mass communication emanating from a complex organization, the Social Christian party.

Besides supplementing other forms of party advertising, signs were significant in the opportunity they gave the minor parties. Lacking funds to purchase time on the broadcast media or much space in the newspapers, the minor parties had enough committed party loyalists to make extensive use of posters and paintings, reminding the electorate that there were alternatives to AD and COPEI. This was an ideal use of their resources. The enormous popularity of political signs is significant also for what it indicates about Venezuelan democracy. Many of these signs are posted on private property without the owners' permission; yet the owners do not rush out to remove them. Thousands are attached to utility polls and other publicly owned surfaces; yet they are not quickly removed by the authorities. In the United States, where campaigning tends to be viewed as a necessary and somewhat unpleasant aspect of the political system, such displays would be viewed as an unacceptable intrusion of politics into the lives of private individuals.[27] In Venezuela, they are viewed as indicative of the vitality of the campaign process and the democratic system.[28] While North Americans prize the individual's right not to be molested by campaign communications, Venezuelans focus on the rights of campaigners and the importance of campaigning as the centerpiece of the democratic political system.

---

[27] On the public's view of appropriate political activities in the United States, see H. Mark Roelofs, *Ideology and Myth in American Politics* (Boston: Little, Brown, 1976).

[28] Immediately after the election most newspapers published numerous opinion columns expressing pride in the campaign and the election. The author could not find a single article criticizing the signs as an unnecessary or excessive aspect of the election.

The Broadcast Media

Television. Political broadcasting has a shorter history than political communication through the printed word. The transmission of oral and visual images, however, is a significant aspect of political campaigns, quite possibly the most important in determining the outcome of an election.[29] As in other countries, in Venezuela the role of television has grown enormously in recent years. Figures on the number of television sets in Venezuela and the viewing habits of the audience are not exact, but it is clear that most Venezuelans have access to television and watch it. Martz and Baloyra write, "By the decade of the 1970s, 90 percent of the population lived in areas reached by television, with an estimated 50 percent of households owning televisions."[30] Both of these percentages rose steadily throughout the decade. Blutstein estimates that "in 1976, there were close to one million television receivers in the country."[31]

During the 1978 election campaign the sophistication and variety of televised political communication were truly remarkable. Anyone watching Venevisión, one of the two national commercial networks, on November 26, 1978—a typical evening late in the campaign—was exposed to forty-one political advertisements between 8:00 P.M. and 11:15 P.M. (see Table 7–1). Each of the eleven advertising breaks or "sets" also included an announcement from the Supreme Electoral Council with instructions on the mechanics of voting. The forty-one political advertisements, each lasting between fifteen seconds and five minutes, and the eleven Supreme Electoral Council messages were interspersed among the many advertisements for commercial products. In addition, the news and interview shows with political guests conveyed political messages. Even the casual viewer of Venezuelan television during the campaign could not have avoided encountering hundreds of political messages.

This conclusion is confirmed by the public opinion polls. According to a Mycon survey administered in the state of Monagas during February 1979, half of the electorate reported that television had been an important source of information in the forming of their judgments on how to vote. This figure is especially impressive in light of the comparatively traditional economy and way of life of Monagas, and

---

[29] This is argued in both Ray E. Hiebert et al., eds., *The Political Image Merchants* (Washington: Acropolis Books, 1975) and Robert Agranoff, ed., *The New Style in Election Campaigns*, 2d ed. (Boston: Holbrook Press, 1976).

[30] Martz and Baloyra, *Electoral Mobilization*, p. 305.

[31] Blutstein, *Area Handbook*, p. 103.

TABLE 7–1

POLITICAL ADVERTISEMENTS ON VENEVISION, NOVEMBER 26, 1978

Starting Time of Set	Position in Set	Sponsor	Message
8:15	6	COPEI	Singers, "Vote for Herrera"
	8	Government	Nationalization of oil by Pérez
	10	AD	Piñerúa has already won
	11	Common Cause	Diego Arria talking with adoring people
8:30	4	MAS	José Vicente, alternative to two bad choices
	6	AD	Piñerúa has already won; scenes at Caracas rally
	11	Government	Government successes in Zulia
	12	Common Cause	Diego Arria says, "Give me your hand"
8:45	6	Common Cause	Diego Arria walking with people
	8	COPEI	Woman says things will be better with Herrera
	9	Government	Government successes in Yaracuy
	12	AD	Piñerúa has already won; walk through Caracas
9:00	3	MEP	Prieto accusing Pérez of sellout to rich
	5	AD	Piñerúa will govern for all Venezuelans
	8	MAS	MAS ball knocks AD and COPEI balls off screen
9:25	3	COPEI	Herrera will do more for development
	6	Common Cause	Diego Arria wants help building country
	8	Government	Nationalization of oil by Pérez
	10	AD	Piñerúa has already won
9:40	3	AD	Stamp ballot in upper left for Piñerúa
	5	MAS	MAS ball knocks AD and COPEI balls off screen
	7	COPEI	Government waste; where's the money?
	9	Common Cause	Cheerful song for Diego Arria
	11	COPEI	AD polls lie; COPEI will win

TABLE 7-1 (continued)

Starting Time of Set	Position in Set	Sponsor	Message
9:45	2	Common Cause	Diego Arria says, "Give me your hand"
	5	MEP	Government waste and corruption
	9	MIR	Martín says too much crime and police corruption
10:10	2	COPEI	Background of Herrera; experience and will
	4	MAS	MAS ball knocks AD and COPEI balls off screen
	5	AD	Piñerúa has already won; walk through Caracas
	7	MEP	Prieto accusing Pérez of sellout to rich
10:28	2	Cruzada Cívica	Martial music; will govern differently
	5	Government	"I am better off today"
	7	Common Cause	People walking with Diego Arria
	10	COPEI	Herrera, in formal suit, has the will
10:45	5	Common Cause	Diego Arria says, "Give me your hand"
	9	MAS	MAS ball knocks AD and COPEI balls off screen
	10	AD	Piñerúa has already won; walk through Caracas
11:07	3	Common Cause	People reaching up to Diego Arria
	5	COPEI	Herrera, walking, has the will
	9	MEP	Prieto accusing Pérez of sellout to rich

NOTE: A "set" is a group of advertisements, both commercial and political, shown consecutively. Thus, the COPEI spot in the 8:15 set was the sixth advertisement of that set; the first five were for commercial products.

the mountains and jungles which inhibit adequate television reception in many rural areas of the state.

Another survey, completed by the Gallup organization in late July 1978, found that one-quarter of the electorate was at least a little bothered by all of the television and radio propaganda for the candidates.[32] And if one-quarter of the electorate was annoyed a full four months before the election, it seems safe to assume that even more voters were annoyed by election day. In any event, that a large segment of the population expressed irritation at partisan political advertisements on television suggests that many Venezuelans were watching television frequently.

Like the print media, television was Caracas dominated, relatively nonpartisan, and generally free of government censorship. Most television receivers had access to each of the commercial channels (2 and 4) and to the government stations (5 and 8). All of these stations are located in Caracas, where all national programming is produced. The law requires half of all programs to be produced within the country. The other half is imported, mostly from the United States in the form of movies and series such as "Kojak," "Starsky and Hutch," and "Charlie's Angels." The shows produced in Venezuela are predominantly soap operas, talk shows, and the evening news. Reporting focuses on the capital, but some attention is given to happenings in major cities such as Maracaibo, Barquisimeto, and Valencia. Since Maracaibo's television channel closed in the early 1960s, no "interior" city has had its own television station. Programming is disseminated from Caracas by microwave or cable.

The commercial stations were nonpartisan during the campaign in that the news consisted of relatively straightforward reports of the parties' and candidates' activities, and the interview shows were open to candidates of all persuasions. Some talk show hosts, however, clearly favored one or another of the major candidates. Also, since the cost of television time for the presentation of campaign advertisements was high, the medium favored well-financed candidates and penalized poorer aspirants. Overall, the situation had not changed since 1973 when Martz and Baloyra wrote, "Partisanship on radio and television, then, existed more through the function of candidates' financial resources than through actual content of programming."[33] Handelman summarizes this situation for the first five months of the 1978 campaign:

> From April 1, the date on which Venezuela's current election laws allow extensive mass media advertising, through late August...the vast majority of television and other mass media advertisements were for AD candidate Luis Piñerúa. COPEI advertisements, sparse through the early months of the campaign, began to pick up somewhat in June, though

---

[32] *Semana*, no. 524 (August 13, 1978), pp. 14-17.
[33] Martz and Baloyra, *Electoral Mobilization*, p. 305.

not to AD's level. Nonparty candidate Diego Arria's entry into the race in late May was supported by an impressive television commercial campaign that nearly equaled COPEI's in quantity. Through August, neither Rangel nor any other third-party candidate had paid television exposure worth mentioning and Rangel particularly depended heavily on the optimum use of unpaid appearances on interview shows.[34]

In the final months of the campaign there began to be as many advertisements for COPEI as for AD, although AD retained a wide advantage when the Pérez administration's advertisements extolling the president's accomplishments are included. Of the minor party candidates, only the independently wealthy Diego Arria was able to use the airwaves as much as Herrera and Piñerúa used them.

Television is relatively free of censorship. Most of the laws that apply specifically to broadcasting, such as a 1937 regulation requiring prior government approval of all broadcasts, are not enforced.[35] Nevertheless, almost all of the laws restricting the print media also apply to broadcasting, and the government has occasionally clamped down on activities of which it did not approve. A recent example, again revolving around the kidnapping of William F. Niehous in 1976, culminated in the closing of one of the commercial television stations for three days. The Pérez administration invoked a 1963 statute regarding subversive propaganda to punish the station for airing an interview with a representative of the kidnappers. Admittedly, this action prompted a great deal of criticism of President Pérez from the media in general and from party leaders. Nothing of this kind took place during the 1978 campaign, but it set a precedent which may have a long-term influence on the willingness of station managers to tackle controversial projects.

During the campaign, the Supreme Electoral Council had the authority to regulate advertisements on television and radio as well as in the print media. Toward the end of the campaign the council did order two advertisements to be removed. One, prepared by COPEI, showed poor conditions in Piñerúa's home town and said that, if Piñerúa could not do more for his own home town, certainly he could not do much for Venezuela. The other, prepared by AD, implied that

---

[34] Howard Handelman, "The Making of a Venezuelan President 1978," *American Universities Field Staff Reports*, no. 45 (1978), p. 18.

[35] Pierce, *Keeping the Flame*, p. 173. Another example of a law which has not been implemented is a 1974 piece of legislation requiring all foreign films on television to be dubbed into Spanish in Venezuela. Viewers still hear Mexican or Puerto Rican accents.

Herrera was like an impetuous child shown making an obscene gesture at the Venezuelan people.

Much of the activity of the Supreme Electoral Council, however, involved advertisements not by the parties, but by the government. The government's extensive use of television during the campaign raises a serious issue regarding media and the campaign. Handelman notes:

> Ads promoting the Pérez administration's record were not only omnipresent but frequently appeared on television back-to-back with Piñerúa spots, which pledged to continue the good work of the government. When spokesmen for COPEI and MAS complained about this practice, Information Minister Celestino Armas replied that it wasn't the government's role to tell television stations in what order they should present their commercials.[36]

Six of the twenty-six government advertisements were so blatantly commercials for Acción Democrática that the Supreme Electoral Council ordered them removed from the airwaves, but the networks' willingness to cooperate with the government's advertising campaign calls into question the independence of the media. The government's involvement in the campaign, if not limited in future elections, may one day threaten the legitimacy of the electoral process and the political system itself.

Radio. Since the invention of the transistor, radio has been everywhere in Venezuela. There are over 2 million receivers and 150 radio stations.[37] Licenses for new stations are granted with every increase in the population of 150,000 in metropolitan areas and 50,000 in rural areas. This dense penetration of radio is confirmed by the Mycon survey of February 1979 in Monagas: even in this relatively undeveloped state, only 12 percent of respondents said they never or almost never listened to the radio, 41 percent listened to it one to two hours daily, 20 percent tuned in for three to four hours, and 27 percent listened for five or more hours.

Radio is less concentrated in Caracas than television or newsmagazines, and, as Blutstein notes, "Most stations program broadcasting according to the interests of the immediate area in which they can be heard."[38] Although there are four Caracas-based chains, three private and one government owned, most stations remain unaffiliated.

---

[36] Handelman, "Making of a President," p. 17.

[37] Blutstein, *Area Handbook*, p. 102.

[38] Ibid., p. 103.

Those affiliated with a chain seldom transmit all of the programs offered by Caracas. In 1978, this decentralization allowed the campaigners to target particular appeals to special regional audiences. For example, Acción Democrática, on learning that water shortages were of particular concern to the citizens of Monagas, ran radio spots on stations in the state capital, Maturín, that claimed Piñerúa would improve services offered by the government water corporation in Monagas.

Pierce characterizes Venezuelan radio as "a mixture of continual commercials, screaming and clownish newscasting, play-by-play sportscasting and specialized popular music."[39] The hundreds of brief newscasts that were to be heard on different stations during the campaign did not consistently praise one candidate while attacking another. Nevertheless, for every minute of news concerning the campaign or the candidates, several party or candidate commercials could be heard. Although the parties could have targeted different audiences by placing different types of advertisements on different types of stations, they usually ran their advertisements on all kinds of stations. The only obvious targeting nationally was the disproportionate placement of advertisements dealing with the needs of youth and young families on "Radio Youth" and other rock stations. These advertisements were either endorsements by prominent politicians, statements of support or opposition by ordinary citizens, or, most commonly, jingles, like the "Ballad of Luis Herrera":

> Enough of abuse
> and misfortune;
> enough of fear
> for fear of the truth.
> Luis Herrera will be
> a fearless president.
> Fearless Luis Herrera
> is bound to win.

> The country has the wealth;
> Luis Herrera
> has the will.

> Enough of promises,
> enough blah blah blah;
> enough of fear,
> for fear of the truth.
> Fearless Luis Herrera
> is bound to win.

---

[39] Pierce, *Keeping the Flame*, p. 161.

> The country has the wealth;
> Luis Herrera
> has the will.[40]

Jingles were also the staple of the soundtrucks, which can be considered the third significant broadcast medium in the campaign. A soundtruck is simply a vehicle equipped with portable broadcasting equipment. Figures on the numbers of soundtrucks and their frequency of use in 1978 are not available, but interviews with party leaders as well as personal observation suggest that their use was widespread, especially in the working-class areas of the large cities.[41] Soundtrucks serve two purposes. They are used to announce rallies and candidate appearances in order to boost the size of the crowd. At other times, they play jingles incessantly to remind citizens of the party's presence in their community. Party leaders believe that the appearance of strength is essential for winning votes and that soundtrucks enhance the appearance of strength.[42]

Conclusions

Six conclusions concerning the role of the media in the 1978 election seem warranted. First, and most important, the media successfully performed the function of providing conduits for the parties' and candidates' communications. Even minor parties had great opportunities (which they used) to make their positions known. Losing candidates could scarcely blame their defeat on a lack of communication to the electorate.

Second, the media enjoyed what was essentially freedom of expression. The discussion of some of the limitations on that freedom in this chapter should not obscure the fact that the government and the Supreme Electoral Council's use of censorship was highly restrained. Even the antisystem parties and candidates had their opportunities to attack the democratic regime. Only once, in the case of *Resumen's* attacks on President Pérez, did the government confiscate published materials. There were no comparable incidents involving the broadcast media.

---

[40] Edgar Alexánder, "The Ballad of Luis Herrera." The words appeared in Jesús Bustindui, "Guerra de jingles políticos reafirma talento del músico Venezolano," *El Mundo* (November 29, 1978), p. 49.

[41] In the state of Lara, each of the twenty-six *municipios* had at least one soundtruck. Interview with Homero Parra, head of the campaign for Acción Democrática in Lara, August 30, 1978.

[42] On the importance party strategists placed on the appearance of strength, see the chapters on the AD and COPEI campaigns.

Third, the media were generally nonpartisan, though not always evenhanded. What Martz and Baloyra wrote of 1973 remained true in 1978: "The large advantage of the two establishment parties lay not in legal inequities, nor even primarily in political partisanship on the part of management and staff of the media outlets; it was a matter of economic resources."[43]

Fourth, reflecting the primacy of Caracas in the Venezuelan financial, social, and political systems, the media are centered in the capital. The form and content of political advertisements, even those with regional messages, were determined by party elites in Caracas. The form and content of other media communications most often originated with print and broadcast communicators in Caracas. Even the stenciled graffiti, which might have been mistaken for spontaneous, local efforts, mostly had their origins in the capital.

Fifth, the widespread availability of television has the potential to alter both the party system and the type of candidate nominated. Television lessens the importance of the local party organization because the candidate is able to communicate directly with voters without involving local party workers. During the campaign several leaders of Acción Democrática privately expressed frustration that their organizational efforts were not producing votes for Piñerúa because Herrera performed better on television. Television's growing ability to bypass party organizations may contribute to a weakening of the parties, as it has in the United States.

Television may also force the parties to stress media image in choosing their presidential candidates. Several AD leaders murmured that, although they felt Piñerúa would make a fine president, the party should have nominated someone with a more attractive television presence. That the leaders emphasized the candidate's ability to communicate effectively on television suggests the great significance television will have in future Venezuelan election campaigns.

Sixth, the political significance of the media will have long-term effects of enormous importance. The media are one of the agents of socialization in Venezuelan culture. Their programs not only reflect values widely held in society, but also teach values. Implicitly, many of the television shows and magazines advance the ideals of a developed, consumerist society.[11] At the same time, both the print

---

[43] Martz and Baloyra, Electoral Mobilization, p. 305.

[44] See Richard Martin, Steven Chaffee, and Fausto Izcaray, "Media and Consumerism in Venezuela," Journalism Quarterly, vol. 56, no. 2 (Summer 1979), pp. 296-304; and Steven Chaffee and Fausto Izcaray, "Mass Communication Functions in a Media-Rich Developing Country," Communication Research, vol. 2 (October 1975), pp. 367-95.

and broadcast media promulgate democratic values. The success of the media in performing their role as a teacher of democratic values contributes to the likelihood that Venezuela will continue to hold free elections like that of 1978.

8

The Regional Dimension of Venezuelan Politics

David Blank

Definition of Venezuela's Regions

The regional scheme adopted in this chapter [1] divides Venezuela into the following components (see Figure 8–1):

Region 1. The Center Region comprises the four prosperous and heavily urbanized states of Aragua, Carabobo, the Federal District, and Miranda. The capital, Caracas, with a population close to 3 million in 1971, is located in this region. The Center Region's 3.9 million residents were 36.4 percent of the total population in 1971 and occupied less than 3 percent of the total national territory. [2]

Region 2. The Plains Region comprises the five rural states of Apure, Barinas, Cojedes, Guárico, and Portuguesa. This region had 1.1 million residents in 1971, 10.2 percent of the nation's total. None of these states had a city with a population in excess of 60,000 in 1971.

---

[1] This scheme is based on David J. Myers, "Urban Voting, Structural Cleavage, and Party System Evolution: The Case of Venezuela," *Comparative Politics*, vol. 8, no. 1 (October 1975), pp. 119-51, and Enrique A. Baloyra and John D. Martz, "Culture, Regionalism, and Political Opinion in Venezuela," *Canadian Journal of Political Science/Revue canadienne de science politique*, vol. 10, no. 3, pp. 527-72. See the latter's discussion of some of the existing regional typologies, pp. 537-41. The government's development regions were rejected as too numerous to be useful here. In addition, they ignore state boundaries, making calculation of regional election returns difficult. For the text of the three presidential decrees on the regionalization of public administration, see Allan R. Brewer-Carias and Norma Izquierdo Coser, *Estudios sobre la regionalización en Venezuela* [Studies of regionalization in Venezuela] (Caracas: Ediciones de la Biblioteca de la Universidad Central de Venezuela, 1977), pp. 161-92.

[2] Venezuela, Ministry of Development, *X censo de población, resumen general de la república* [Tenth census of population: general summary] (Caracas, 1974).

FIGURE 8–1
The Regions of Venezuela

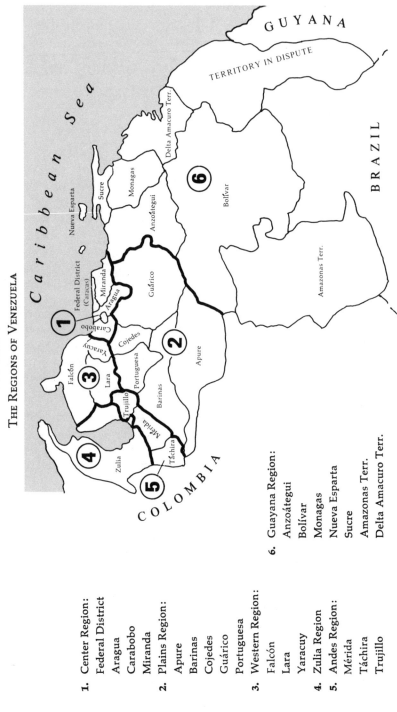

1. **Center Region:**
   Federal District
   Aragua
   Carabobo
   Miranda
2. **Plains Region:**
   Apure
   Barinas
   Cojedes
   Guárico
   Portuguesa
3. **Western Region:**
   Falcón
   Lara
   Yaracuy
4. **Zulia Region**
5. **Andes Region:**
   Mérida
   Táchira
   Trujillo
6. **Guayana Region:**
   Anzoátegui
   Bolívar
   Monagas
   Nueva Esparta
   Sucre
   Amazonas Terr.
   Delta Amacuro Terr.

Region 3. The Western Region comprises the three states of Falcón, Lara, and Yaracuy. It includes booming light-industry cities such as Barquisimeto in Lara State, whose population was over 300,000 in 1971. Barquisimeto's rapid industrial expansion is the result of government decisions to decentralize industrial production from the Center Region. The region's population was 1.3 million in 1971, 12.1 percent of the nation's total.

Region 4. The Zulia Region consists of a single state. Rich in oil, Zulia seems to be guaranteed a prosperous industrial future by the recent discovery of significant coal reserves and the national government's decision to construct a major iron and steel complex there. A major petrochemical plant is already under construction on the eastern side of Lake Maracaibo. In addition to the city of Maracaibo, whose population exceeded 650,000 in 1971, the city of Cabimas had a population of more than 110,000. The region's population was 1.3 million, 12.0 percent of the total, in 1971.

Region 5. The Andes Region comprises the three mountainous states of Mérida, Táchira, and Trujillo. The political importance of this region is illustrated by the fact that *caudillos* and elected presidents from the Andean state of Táchira ruled Venezuela for fifty-seven of the first seventy-nine years of this century. One city, San Cristóbal, near the Colombian border, had a population in excess of 150,000 in 1971. The region's population was 1.2 million, or 11.2 percent of the total, in 1971.

Region 6. The Guayana Region comprises the states of Anzoátegui, Bolívar, Monagas, Nueva Esparta, and Sucre and the two sparsely populated federal territories, Delta Amacuro and Amazonas. This region accounts for almost 60 percent of the national territory and in 1971 had 17.7 percent of the total population. The Guayana Region has frequently been referred to as the keystone of Venezuela's industrial future. The discovery of a major iron ore reserve in Bolívar State led to the creation by the government of the Venezuelan Guayana Corporation (CVG) to develop the resources of this region. The CVG is responsible for the construction and management of an integrated iron and steel plant, one of the world's largest hydroelectric dams (the Raúl Leoni–Guri dam), and an aluminum plant, of which it retains 50 percent ownership. This region's industrial future is further ensured by the very recent discovery of a major bauxite deposit and by the decision to accelerate research on the Orinoco heavy-oil belt, which contains some 1.8 trillion barrels of probable reserves. In addition, oil fields in the region (admittedly with limited

193

reserves) have been producing for the past thirty years. In order to develop the riches of the Guayana Region, the CVG has planned and developed a new industrial city, Ciudad Guayana, in Bolívar State, which already had a population exceeding 150,000 in 1971. In addition, plants to produce automobiles, buses, and tractors are being located in cities such as Cumaná (in Sucre State), with more than 119,000 people in 1971, and Ciudad Bolívar, with more than 100,000.

The Conceptual Problems of Regionalism

Political scientists disagree about the political role of regionalism in a culturally homogeneous nation. In culturally pluralistic nations, regionalism channels competition between geographically separated subnational groups that are divided along lines of race, religion, or language. But in Venezuela, almost all citizens share the same national identity and culture.[3]

According to some writers, regionalism is merely a "container" of political action, and other factors account for variations in the content of political action; regionalism by itself has no independent political force but merely identifies geographic subgroups within a nation, which may happen to have different political orientations. This view, however, overlooks the fact that people who live in the same territory often encounter the same historical problems and therefore develop similar political orientations regardless of their cultural identity and social status.[4] The emerging cleavage in the United States between the "frost belt" and the "sun belt" is a case in point: climate, terrain, and social history combine to give each of these regions an identity that has political consequences.

Another conceptual difficulty of regionalism is its multidimensionality. The first dimension of regionalism in Venezuela is the center-periphery cleavage: a relatively prosperous, supposedly modern, urban core (the Center Region surrounding Caracas) confronts a relatively poor, supposedly traditional, rural periphery. The basis of the center-periphery cleavage is the accelerating concentration of jobs, wealth, and people in the Center Region. The second dimension of regionalism reflects the historical rivalry that has existed among all Venezuela's regions.

---

[3] Baloyra and Martz state that regionalism "represents a conduit for the expression of 'the ethos or community norm of an area deriving from particular historical forces and events.'" Baloyra and Martz, "Culture, Regionalism, and Political Opinion," p. 540.

[4] Ibid. I accept this orientation rather than that which views regionalism as merely an inert container of political action.

In Venezuela, the center-periphery cleavage in part reflects the conflict between the raw-material-producing agricultural and mining states of the periphery and the governmental and private-sector bureaucracies of the Center Region. As they say in the oil-producing state of Zulia, Zulia produces just about all the national wealth, and Caracas consumes just about all of it. Venezuela's contemporary political party system emerged in large part as a result of this cleavage. David J. Myers describes the emergence of Acción Democrática in the 1930s and 1940s as "the vehicle through which 'peripherals' hoped to end five decades of rule by the center." [5]

The relationship between the urban center and the rural periphery was especially strained during the dictatorship of Marcos Pérez Jiménez (1952–1958). Pérez Jiménez dramatically increased the primacy of Caracas and the Center Region "by constructing more public works in the capital than all his predecessors combined." [6] The skilled manpower needed for these projects was provided by the immigration of many thousands of skilled workers (primarily from Spain, Portugal, and Italy) rather than by programs seeking to upgrade indigenous Venezuelans. The European immigrants and their families settled in the Center, enhancing its concentration of entrepreneurial skills while at the same time causing a perceptible ethnic differentiation between it and the periphery. In 1961, for example, 63 percent of the foreigners and naturalized Venezuelans lived in the Center Region. Also in 1961, foreigners and naturalized Venezuelans accounted for close to 20 percent of the population in metropolitan Caracas. Finally, the dictator encouraged the powerful foreign oil companies to locate their central administrative offices in Caracas, accentuating the relationship between the enhanced primacy of the urbanized Center Region and Venezuela's dependency on foreign companies and personnel for its economic development.

By 1958, the year Pérez Jiménez was overthrown and the first free elections under the present system were held, the Center Region

---

[5] The literature on the center-periphery conflict in Latin America is replete with references to the modern-traditional segmentation of national society on the one hand and to the exploitive, neocolonialist nature of this relationship on the other. See, for example, Fernando Travieso and Alberto Urdaneta, "Marco de referencia del desarrollo urbano en Venezuela" [Framework for urban development in Venezuela], *Cuadernos de la Sociedad Venezolana de Planificación*, nos. 84-86 (January-March 1971), p. 13; Fernando Travieso, *Ciudad, región y subdesarrollo* [City, region, and underdevelopment] (Caracas: Fondo Editorial Común, 1975). For the English language reader, there is David J. Myers, "Caracas: The Politics of Intensifying Primacy," *Latin American Urban Research*, vol. 6 (Beverly Hills, Calif.: Sage Publications, 1978). The quotation is from Myers, "Urban Voting," p. 126.

[6] Myers, "Caracas," p. 229.

housed over 30 percent of the nation's voters. It accounted for over 68 percent of its industrial employment in 1963. Given this reality, the democratic reform regime hesitated during its first decade to disrupt the accelerating primacy of the Center Region for fear of both economic dislocation and electoral reprisal. The concern of the democratic reform government to use state power to sponsor development and social justice had itself become a factor in the intensifying primacy of the Center Region. In order to deal with the increased government regulations, businessmen consistently favored locating in or near the capital. In order to deal with these businessmen and to represent the workers who flocked to the capital, politicians also tended to gear their careers toward Caracas. Central government planning, decision making, and budget control became all-important factors in the lives of most politicians, businessmen, and technicians. In the words of John Friedmann, a "symbiosis between economic and government organizations" occurred in Caracas despite their differing ideological outlooks and social origins. "Politicians, bureaucrats and businessmen mingle in exclusive clubs and the city's top restaurants, send their children to private schools . . . and form tight social networks of their own." [7]

As the democratic process has become more institutionalized and as the cost of concentrating population and jobs in the Center Region has begun to outweigh its advantages, the continuing efforts made by Venezuela's periphery to decentralize both power and employment have begun to bear fruit. One reason for this is that as democratic behavior and beliefs have become an integral part of the popular culture, the residents of Venezuela's periphery have become loyal and involved participants in politics. Rather than being "marginalized" or sinking into a self-defeating "culture of poverty," Venezuela's peripherals participate more in the life of the political parties, have higher rates of electoral turnout, and show higher levels of commitment to the democratic system than do residents of the urbanized Center Region. [8]

The creation of grass-roots regional development efforts since 1964 and the recent move toward municipal political autonomy reflect this enduring effort of peripherals to use the democratic process to redress the economic and political balance with the center. The

---

[7] John Friedmann, "The Spatial Organization of Power in the Development of Urban Systems," in John Friedmann and William Alonso, eds., Regional Policy Readings in Theory and Applications (Cambridge: MIT Press, 1975), pp. 272-73.
[8] Enrique A. Baloyra and John D. Martz, Political Attitudes in Venezuela: Societal Cleavages and Political Opinion (Austin: University of Texas Press, 1979), pp. 95-99.

assault on Center Region primacy is no longer limited to efforts to decentralize industrial employment from the Center Region. There is now a demand to disperse the public administration to eight peripheral cities. In addition some politicians and planners have suggested building a new capital city in the interior as a symbol of Venezuela's taking charge of its own destiny.[9]

The possibility that the political capital will be moved from Caracas is remote. There is, however, the precedent of Brazil in the 1950s. A number of influential politicians, such as the AD leader Enrique Tejera Paris, have advocated the construction of a new capital in the Orinoco River valley, and some technicians argue that the cost of supplying adequate electricity, clean water, and sewer and sanitation services to Caracas as it grows would alone justify relocating the capital. The planned east-west railroad connection from Ciudad Guayana to the booming city of Barquisimeto could very well become the spinal column of a new system of dynamic interior cities. This east-west rail link might also strengthen the political resolve of the periphery to end the Center Region's political domination.

The second dimension of regionalism has tended to reflect an east-west rivalry which continues to divide Venezuela's periphery. In the nineteenth century this rivalry took the form of a combative regionalism in which regionally based strongmen, or *caudillos*, fought among themselves for domination, and the victory of any one was associated with his region's domination of the others. The regimes of the great *caudillos* all had a regional basis.[10] The power base of José Antonio Páez (1830–1863) was the cowboy cavalry of the Plains Region; Antonio Guzmán Blanco (1870–1884) represented the emerging power of the export-oriented Center Region; and Juan Vicente Gómez (1908–1935) was the tyrant from the Andes Region as well as the "Tyrant of the Andes."

---

[9] For an excellent description of current Venezuelan regionalization policies, see the Venezuelan document, "The Venezuelan Experience in Regional and Urban Development," presented at the meeting of the ministers and heads of planning of Latin America and the Caribbean, April 13-16, 1977 (Caracas: CORDIPLAN, 1977). The planning faculty of the Simón Bolívar University under the direction of the influential AD politician Enrique Tejera Paris has already proposed moving the national capital to Cabruta, a small town on the Orinoco River. See the following magazine articles: "Caracas se muda a Cabruta" [Caracas moves to Cabruta], *Zeta* (August 20, 1978); and "Defensa territoria: Cabruta, capital geopolítica de Venezuela" [Territorial defense: Cabruta, geopolitical capital of Venezuela], *Elite* (June 16, 1978).

[10] Baloyra and Martz cite the voluminous literature on caudillism in their article "Culture, Regionalism, and Political Opinion," fn. 20, pp. 531-32. See especially Eric R. Wolf and Edward C. Hansen, *The Human Condition in Latin America* (New York: Oxford University Press, 1972), pp. 205-25.

The combative regionalism of the *caudillo* epoch has ended under the impact of petroleum money on the national treasury and the institutionalization of nationally oriented political parties. Contemporary regionalism in the Venezuelan context is competitive; the different regions vie with each other for development projects and national government investment. Despite the federal nature of the 1961 Venezuelan constitution, the national government, through its petroleum revenues, still accounts for 90 percent of total public-sector revenues. Most state and local sources of revenue are limited, and all states and local governments rely on "revenue-sharing" grants from the national government (called the *situado constitucional*) to meet even the most basic needs.

The origin of this contemporary regional rivalry was the central government's decision in 1960 to push the development of the resource-rich but sparsely populated Guayana Region. The Venezuelan Guayana Corporation (CVG), created in 1960, has spent about 10 percent of total government investment over the past generation. The CVG considers itself a national agency and not a champion of the Guayana Region. The oil-rich state of Zulia, which was experiencing a severe economic depression in the early 1960s, and the politically important but poor Andes Region resented the fact that the lion's share of government investment was earmarked for the sparsely populated Guayana Region.

For the purposes of this chapter, I concentrate the discussion of competitive regionalism on the response of Zulia State and the Andes Region to the central government's decision in 1960 to push the development of the Guayana Region. While this is not the whole story, these two western regions' attempts to overcome a policy of suspected "benign neglect" is illustrative of how Venezuelan democracy handles its challenges. As the maps showing the regional breakdown of presidential electoral results between 1963 and 1978 indicate, the electoral fault line between AD's dominance in the east and COPEI's increasing dominance of the west has followed the border separating the Andes Region and Zulia State from the rest of the periphery. I argue that while the partisan conflict between AD and COPEI fought out in the electoral arena has not been totally congruent with the competition for development between Zulia and the Andes in the west and Guayana in the east, the two have not been entirely divorced.

Venezuela, in its formulation of regional development policy, has sought "a delicate balance between national development criteria and those of the different regions."[11] A style of regional policy has resulted which mixes electoral significance, regional brokerage capabilities, and technical proficiency as a means of representing diverse regional interests before the national government and international investment agencies.

The discussion of regional planning that appeared in the Plan de la Nacion (1963–1966) illustrates the nature of the competition between western and eastern states for development. According to this National Plan, the argument in favor of concentrating development investment in the Guayana Region was that it was economically efficient in light of the need to accelerate national development. The argument in favor of diverting some of the development investment to the Andes Region was that it was in the interest of social equity and national integration. According to the planners of the Central Office of Coordination and Planning (CORDIPLAN) in 1963, there was a question whether poor regions would justify (in economic terms) much public investment in basic infrastructure. The Fifth National Plan (1976–1980) advocates the creation of a National Council of Regional Development in an effort to contain regional competition within a planning framework.

Brokerage politics tends to be nonideological in that all political factions in one region avidly support the allocation of a major public investment to their region.[12] Regional development politics also transcends the particularistic limitations of patron-clientelism since it concerns itself with major projects which bring indivisible benefits to an entire region. In 1964, a law was pushed through the national Congress establishing the Venezuelan Andean Corporation (CORPOANDES) as a potential rival to the CVG. Unlike the founding of CVG, that of CORPOANDES resulted from grass-roots political mobilization and pressure. In 1964, with the help of CORDIPLAN technicians, the state government in Zulia created its own state planning council (CONZUPLAN), and in 1969 it forced through a national law creating the Zulia Development Corporation (CORPOZULIA) based on the CORPOANDES model. In 1969, Presidential Decree Number 72 formalized the regionalization of Venezuela. Since 1969,

---

[11] John Friedmann, *Regional Development Policy: A Case Study of Venezuela* (Cambridge: MIT Press, 1966), p. 163. See also Lloyd Rodwin et al., *Planning Urban Growth and Regional Development: The Experience of the Guayana Program of Venezuela* (Cambridge: MIT Press, 1969).

[12] An excellent comparison between programmatic, brokerage, and patron-clientelist politics in the Latin American setting appears in Arturo Valenzuela, *Political Brokers in Chile: Local Government in a Centralized Polity* (Durham, N.C.: Duke University Press, 1977).

the entire country has been divided into development regions, each with its own development corporation and grass-roots regional council.

Partisan considerations have also not been absent from regional development. The fact that the eastern Guayana Region was AD's electoral stronghold probably entered into the decision to create the CVG. During the COPEI administration of President Caldera (1969–1974), major investments were made in Zulia State and in the Andes and reduced somewhat in Ciudad Guayana. Under the Caldera administration, a new planned industrial city, El Tablazo, based on petrochemical development, was to be built in Zulia State. The geography of the politics of regional development is not totally congruent with that of electoral politics. The concern of most politicians is microregional, that is, limited to their states or home districts.

The Regional Factor in Elections from 1958 to 1973

Between December 1958 and December 1973, Venezuelan voters elected four national presidents and the members of all legislative bodies in four consecutive general elections. The election law establishes a system of two separate party ballots, under which ticket-splitting is possible only between the "large ballot," used to elect the president by a simple plurality of popular votes, and the "small ballot," used to elect all legislative bodies according to the d'Hondt system of proportional representation.[13]

The role of regionalism in these four elections is examined here in the light of the two dimensions discussed above: the east-west rivalry and the center-periphery cleavage. Venezuela's party system experienced three dramatic transformations during the first fifteen years of the nation's contemporary democratic experience: essentially, the fragmentation and reconstitution of Acción Democrática as a major party, the continual growth of COPEI, the Social Christian party, to a position of national parity with AD, and the episodic emergence of new political parties and antiparty independent candidates. AD and COPEI have constituted Venezuela's democratic establishment since 1958; their showings at national elections between 1958 and 1978 are presented in Table 8–1 in order to provide a benchmark by which the reader can evaluate regional variations from the national norm.

A quick reading of Table 8–1 reveals that today's polarized two-party system emerged only in 1973. There are two regional explana-

---

[13] See the description of Venezuela's electoral system in David E. Blank, *Politics in Venezuela* (Boston: Little, Brown), pp. 87-96.

TABLE 8–1

AD and COPEI Vote, National Elections, 1958–1978
(in percentages)

Year	Presidential Elections			Legislative Elections		
	AD	COPEI	AD and COPEI	AD	COPEI	AD and COPEI
1958	49.18	15.17	64.35	49.45	26.75	76.20
1963	32.82	20.12	52.94	32.73	20.81	53.54
1968	28.24	29.13	57.37	25.52	24.01	49.53
1973	46.54	33.77	80.31	42.76	29.10	71.86
1978	43.34	45.24[a]	88.58	39.70	39.72	79.42

NOTE: The other parties receiving at least 10 percent of the vote were:

	Presidential Elections	Legislative Elections
1958	URD	URD
1963	URD, IPFN, FDP	URD, IPFN, FDP
1968	URD, MEP	MEP, CCN

Since 1968, only AD and COPEI have won more than 10 percent.

[a] The COPEI presidential candidate in 1978 received a total of 46.63 percent of the vote. The percentage recorded in this table is the share of the vote he received on the COPEI ballot.

SOURCE: Venezuela, Supreme Electoral Council, Public Relations, *Escrutinios de las elecciones desde 1946 hasta 1968; elecciones 1978; información general* [Electoral results 1946-1968; 1978 elections; general information] (Caracas: November 1978), various tables and *Boletín informativo, no. 13; elecciones 1978* [Information bulletin no. 13, 1978 elections] (December 12, 1978).

tions for this phenomenon. With regard to the historical east-west rivalry, COPEI had found it most difficult to compete successfully with AD as a serious national majority party in the east. Prior to 1973, one of the principal reasons for this regional failure of COPEI was the fact that the Democratic Republican Union (URD), a pre-1958 party led by the venerable politician Jóvito Villalba, maintained itself in the east as the electoral alternative to AD. The survival of the URD with significant support in the east denied COPEI national parity with AD. COPEI's eastern problem is illustrated in Figures 8–2 and 8–3, which portray the party's presidential vote in 1963 and 1968. Because of the essentially polarized nature of the 1973 elections and the fact that a COPEI Government was in power in 1973, COPEI's vote in the east approached 30 percent of the total. While the regional variations had decreased by 1973, COPEI's showing in the east was still relatively low.

FIGURE 8–2

VOTE FOR CALDERA (COPEI), DECEMBER 1, 1963

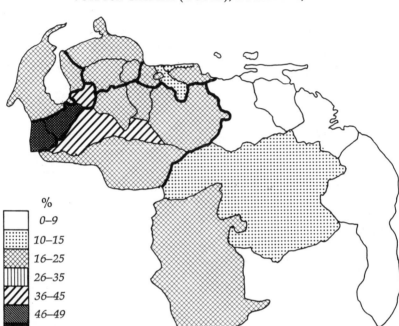

%
0–9
10–15
16–25
26–35
36–45
46–49
50+

COPEI's eastern problem shows that regionalism remained an important factor in Venezuela's electoral politics and was not simply a container of other variables. The synthesis of terrain and human interaction over time had given the eastern regions a unique political subculture. A group of Venezuelan social scientists who looked at the social repercussions of land tenancy as reported in the 1950 Census of Agriculture described the population of the eastern states as basically alienated and antiestablishment.[14] The dominant type of farm tenancy in these states, they found, was squatting; in states like Anzoátegui, Apure, Barinas, Bolívar, and Guárico, farm units falling into the squatter-occupant category in 1950 accounted for over 60 percent of the total. The study described the political subculture of

---

[14] George W. Hill, José A. Silva M., and Ruth Oliver de Hill, "Patterns of Land Tenancy and the Social Repercussions," in Dwight B. Heath and Richard N. Adams, eds., *Contemporary Cultures and Societies in Latin America* (New York: Random House, 1965), vol. 1, pp. 211-35.

FIGURE 8-3

VOTE FOR CALDERA (COPEI), DECEMBER 1, 1968

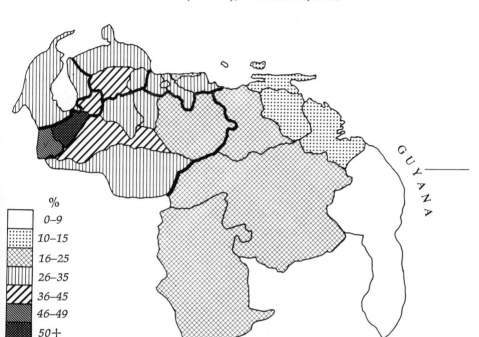

%
0–9
10–15
16–25
26–35
36–45
46–49
50+

these squatter-farmers, who had no legal claim to the land they occupied, as follows:

> Their social status in the community is uncertain. They cannot participate completely in their social institutions nor do they have the feeling of belonging to them, for they are constantly subject to being ousted by the owner—be this [an] individual, the municipality or [the] state. Their status not only relegates them to an asocial position but tends to make them belligerent and antisocial as well. These people are excluded by the laws of the country, all of which favor legal tenure, and as a consequence they learn to distrust and frequently defy them.[15]

Between 1899 and 1945, these freewheeling squatter-farmers and ranchers were subjected to Andean rule. Between 1908 and 1935, the Andean overlords in the east represented the Tyrant of the Andes,

[15] Ibid., p. 217.

Juan Vicente Gómez, and Andeans continued to dominate political life in the decade that followed. While the squatter society of the eastern plains had known a certain equalitarian anarchy, in the Andes Region the relationship between rich and poor was structured. One feature of agriculture in the Andes Region was sharecropping: the three states of the Andes had 26 percent of the nation's farms and over 42 percent of the sharecroppers in 1950. Also making for stability was the Catholic church hierarchy, which had considerably stronger roots in Andean society than in the east.

The people of the east greeted the AD's overthrow of Andean-born President Medina Angarita in 1945 as the downfall of the "hated Andean rule," and the east has remained AD's electoral stronghold ever since. Not surprisingly, it was in the Andes that COPEI had its first electoral success in challenging AD's hegemony during Venezuela's first democratic experiment (1945–1948). In both the October 1946 election for a constituent assembly and the December 1947 general election, COPEI outpolled AD in two Andean states, Mérida and Táchira. In the state of Trujillo, it received 35 percent of the vote in 1947. During the 1945–1948 period, COPEI was unquestionably the conservative opposition to AD. It was also the Andean party. Just as the east has remained faithful to AD, the Andes Region has stood by COPEI.

The second regional dimension, the center-periphery cleavage, had also persisted during the decade from 1958 to 1968. In the elections during this period, the voters of the urbanized Center Region rejected the two principal parties. In 1963 and to a lesser degree in 1968, the voters' rejection of both AD and COPEI took the form of support for independent antiparty electoral movements. The emergence of these antiparty electoral movements as vehicles through which urban middle-class voters expressed their resentment against the peasant-based populist AD and COPEI parties is treated at length in the literature. As I wrote some years ago, members of this urban middle class felt that their vote was "swamped" by demagogic politicians "who manipulated unsophisticated peasants in order to get elected."[16] David J. Myers drew a similar conclusion, stating that the post-1960 political parties and antiparty independent candidates "were vehicles through which literate and urban voters expressed [their] dissatisfaction with government policy, especially investment priorities, that favored peasants."[17]

---

[16] Blank, *Politics in Venezuela*, p. 142. See also Baloyra and Martz, "Culture, Regionalism, and Political Opinion," pp. 565-66.

[17] Myers, "Urban Voting," p. 128.

Although Rear Admiral Wolfgang Larrazábal was an independent, he ran on the URD ballot in 1958. His electoral campaign appeal was largely personal, and while he did receive 90 percent of his vote from the URD, the other 10 percent was from the Venezuelan Communist party (PCV) and the small National Independent Electoral Movement (MENI). His candidacy was a challenge to the pre-1958 political parties, AD and COPEI, and he received 34.5 percent of the vote nationwide; in the four-state Center Region he topped 61 percent of the vote.

The antiparty electoral challenge of the conservative author Arturo Uslar Pietri in 1963 was even more illustrative of the antiparty feelings of the Center Region. No existing political party endorsed his candidacy. Instead, he and his supporters formed their own Independents for a National Front (IPFN). Uslar Pietri was the electoral phenomenon of the 1963 election in the Center Region. While his support in the periphery states was very limited, he took 31.8 percent of the Center Region's presidential vote including a plurality in the Federal District, Aragua, and Miranda. Uslar's vote nationwide was 16.02 percent. Figure 8–4 shows the marked concentration of the IPFN's electoral appeal in the Center Region.

The candidate who received the plurality of the vote in the 1963 election in the fourth Center Region state, Carabobo, was none other than Larrazábal, the electoral phenomenon of 1958. Larrazábal was the candidate of a new political party, the Popular Democratic Force (FDP). Between them these two anti-established-party candidates totaled 51.3 percent of the Center Region's vote while receiving only 25.5 percent of the vote nationwide.

In 1958 and 1963, the Center Region's hostility was AD's principal electoral problem. By 1963, one-third of all presidential ballots were cast in this region, and AD's share of this sizable regional vote was a paltry 18.7 percent. In a sense, AD and COPEI were being blamed by the urbanized voters of the Center for the political turmoil and economic dislocations the nation was experiencing. Figure 8–5 shows the regional variations in AD's presidential vote in 1963.

While the Center Region's receptivity to independent candidates and new political parties continued in 1968, its deviation from the national norm was not as overwhelming as it had been in 1958 and 1963. The independent presidential candidacy of Miguel Angel Burelli Rivas was in fact supported by three smaller political parties: the URD, the FDP, and the National Democratic Front (the FND, out of Uslar Pietri's IPFN). Burelli gained a narrow plurality of the region's vote; however, the 28.3 percent he received in the region

FIGURE 8–4

VOTE FOR USLAR (IPFN), DECEMBER 1, 1963

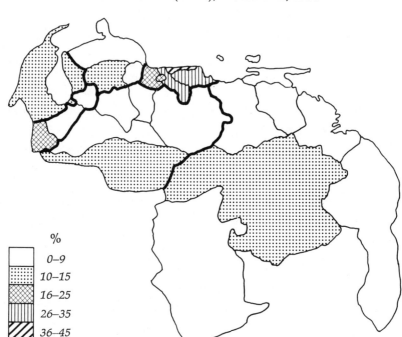

%	
	0–9
	10–15
	16–25
	26–35
	36–45

was not too far out of line with the 22.2 percent he received nationwide. Similarly, the 23.7 percent of the regional vote AD received was more or less in line with the 28.2 percent it received nationwide. COPEI's regional vote, 27.0 percent, was about identical to its national vote. This was also true for the People's Electoral Movement (MEP), an offshoot of AD.

The most interesting vehicle of Center Region electoral protest in 1968 was the Nationalist Civic Crusade (CCN), the movement of those who sought the return to power of former dictator Marcos Pérez Jiménez. Because Pérez Jiménez was barred from running for president, the CCN contested only the legislative election—and polled 10.9 percent of the small-card vote nationwide. In the Center Region, its share of the vote was 20.3 percent. In addition, 65 percent of its national vote came from the four states of the Center. The CCN also did well in Pérez Jiménez's home state of Táchira and in other urbanized states. Outside the Center Region, only Zulia and Táchira gave the CCN over 10 percent (see Figure 8–6).

FIGURE 8–5

Vote for Leoni (AD), December 1, 1963

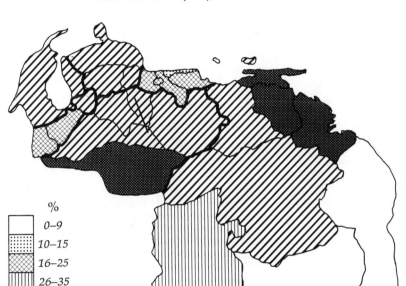

%

	0–9
	10–15
	16–25
	26–35
	36–45
	46–49
	50+

In 1973, AD won all four Center Region states in its triumphant return to power. It also ended COPEI's domination of the Andes: its presidential candidate, Carlos Andrés Pérez, was a native son of the Andean state of Táchira. The only state in the country that AD did not win was Zulia, native state of the MEP presidential candidate, Jesús Angel Paz Galarraga.

Regionalism, the 1978 Elections, and the Future

By the 1978 general elections, a number of factors had combined to diminish the electoral impact of regionalism. First, the continuing mass migration of rural people to Venezuela's cities and almost a generation of agrarian reform had eliminated the rural basis of the regional subcultures reflected in the 1950 Census of Agriculture. Sharecroppers, who had formed a notable feature of Andean society in 1950, and squatter-farmers, who in some Plains Region states had accounted for 60 to 70 percent of farmers, were no longer significant

FIGURE 8–6

VOTE FOR THE CCN, LEGISLATIVE ELECTION, DECEMBER 1, 1968

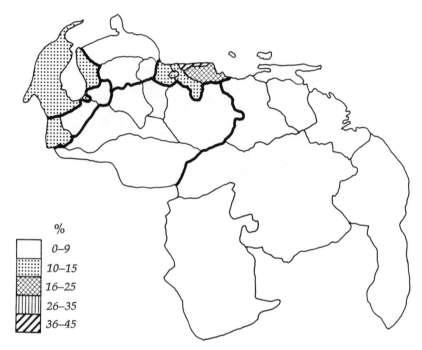

%	
0–9	
10–15	
16–25	
26–35	
36–45	

elements of the rural population. Since 1950 Venezuela has been transformed into an urban nation: in 1950, 53 percent of the population lived outside urban areas (that is, settlements with at least 2,500 people); by 1961, this figure had been reduced to 37.5 percent; and by 1971, it had shrunk to a mere 28.0 percent. The accelerating growth of large cities is even more impressive. In 1971, there were ten cities with populations in excess of 100,000, including metropolitan Caracas; their combined population was 4.4 million, or 41.3 percent of Venezuela's total population. In 1950, the same urban centers had accounted for only 1.4 million people, or 27.8 percent of the nation's total population. In fact, in 1950, excluding metropolitan Caracas, only two cities—Maracaibo in Zulia State and Barquisimeto in Lara State—had had populations in excess of 100,000 (see Table 8–2).

Venezuela's tranformation into a nation of large-city dwellers is reflected in the fact that by 1978 fewer of its people were gainfully

TABLE 8-2
POPULATION OF MAJOR VENEZUELAN CITIES, 1950 AND 1971

City	1950	1971
Metropolitan Caracas	695,586	2,183,935
Maracaibo	235,750	651,574
Valencia	88,701	367,171
Barquisimeto	105,108	330,815
Maracay	64,535	255,134
San Cristóbal	53,933	151,717
San Félix de Guayana	3,803	143,540[a]
Cumaná	46,312	119,751
Cabimas	42,294	118,037
Cuidad Bolívar	31,504	103,728
Total, large cities	1,367,526	4,425,402
Total, Venezuela	5,034,838	10,721,522

[a] Ciudad Guayana has developed since 1960 as a "planned" industrial city under the auspices of the Venezuelan Guayana Corporation.

SOURCE: Venezuela, Ministry of Development, X censo de población, resumen general de la república [Tenth population census, general summary], table 9, p. 57.

employed in agriculture, as peasants, commercial farmers, or agricultural workers, than were reported working in the public sector (which by then embraced the iron ore and petroleum industries): about 25 percent of the labor force was in the public sector, while just 20 percent worked in agriculture. Concomitant with the trend toward urban living has been the increased concentration of population in the Center Region. In 1958, 31.4 percent of valid presidential votes were cast in the four states of the Center Region. In 1978, this figure increased to 39.6 percent. At the same time, literacy has increased significantly: in 1950, a bare majority (51.2 percent) of adult Venezuelans were literate; by 1971, over 77 percent had basic reading and writing skills.

And of course, people's political orientations and aspirations have not remained unchanged. In 1958, politics was based largely on grass-roots brokers and their organized electoral clients or "blockets."[18] The main features of the 1958 electoral campaign were mass rallies and local grass-roots efforts. By 1963, television had made its first impact. One political observer felt that the vote that year for the

[18] John Duncan Powell, "Peasant Society and Clientelist Politics," American Political Science Review, vol. 64, no. 2 (June 1970), p. 416.

antiparty independent Arturo Uslar Pietri came mainly from the large cities covered by television. By 1978, television coverage extended to the entire nation. More important, in 1958 the residents of stable farm communities and small towns had known their local political brokers as intimate friends and neighbors. In many instances these men had begun their political careers during the 1945–1948 democratic experiment and had maintained more or less clandestine party organizations—COPEI in the Andes Region, AD in the Plains and Guayana—during the military regime. By 1978, local political leaders were usually strangers with whom the average urban voter had no regular or personal contact.

The mass media had become the principal channel for political communication by 1978. Journalistic estimates of the cost of the 1978 campaign for all of the political parties range from $80 million to about $120 million. Using the figure $100 million, divided by 5 million votes cast, the average campaign expenditure per voter was about $20. Local Venezuelan political leaders found that they had to compete with U.S. media experts for the attention of the principal candidates. Some commentators even complained about the de-Venezuelanization of the 1978 campaign and exaggerated the role U.S. media experts were playing. COPEI's successful presidential candidate, Luis Herrera Campíns, hired media consultant David Garth at $10,000 per month; AD's candidate, Luis Piñerúa Ordaz, used the firm of Joseph Napolitan, who had advised AD in its successful 1973 campaign; while the well-financed independent Diego Arria used the services of John Deardourff.[19]

The two principal political parties took 88.6 percent of the vote in the 1978 presidential election but only 79.4 percent in the legislative election. The results did not tell the entire story of the presidential race. A popular Venezuelan television personality, Renny Ottolina, had announced his independent candidacy in late 1977. In March 1978, Ottolina was killed in the crash of a small chartered plane. After his death, his Movement for National Integrity (MIN) evaporated. While one can only speculate on the impact of his candidacy had he lived, it seems likely that Ottolina would have done at least as well as Uslar Pietri did in 1963. The MIN received over 84,000 votes on the legislative ballot. This was largely a sympathy vote, concentrated almost exclusively in the Federal District and the other Center Region states.

---

[19] See an article in Caracas's English language newspaper, "Mystery Media Man Goes Public; Garth: 'Herrera Was a Man of Steel,'" *Caracas Daily Journal*, December 13, 1978, p. 4. In many ways these foreign media consultants had become campaign issues as well as campaign aides.

Diego Arria, a former cabinet member in the Government of President Carlos Andrés Pérez, announced his independent presidential candidacy following the death of Ottolina. Arria had previously created a party called Causa Común, and he attempted to project himself as the independent voter's candidate. However, Arria's close ties to the incumbent AD president denied his campaign any aura of independence. Despite a relatively well financed campaign, he received less than 2 percent of the national vote and less than 3 percent of the vote in the Center Region.

Because of the two-party domination of the presidential vote, it is appropriate to analyze the outcome in terms of the difference between the AD and COPEI votes in the states rather than the share of a state's vote each party received. A glance at Figure 8–7 reveals that the regional variation between the east and the west was not absent in 1978. AD was still dominant in the Plains Region and Guayana Region; however, COPEI was now clearly the number two party in these states, receiving from 35 to 40 percent of the vote. For the first time, there would be COPEI senators from the east and sizable COPEI factions in all the eastern state assemblies. In 1968, when COPEI's leader, Rafael Caldera, had been elected president by a narrow margin, the party's vote on the legislative ballot had been appreciably less than AD's. This not only had denied President Caldera control over the national Congress from 1969 to 1973 but also had caused COPEI's grass-roots organizations to remain weak in the east. This was not true in 1978, when COPEI was able to defeat AD narrowly on the legislative ballot in the nation as a whole and to run a close second on the legislative vote in the east.

COPEI's reasonably successful electoral penetration of the east had a number of explanations. The URD, which had long been the regional nemesis of COPEI, formed an electoral alliance with COPEI in 1978. While the URD had been reduced to a minor role in 1973 when its leader, Jóvito Villalba, had received only 3 percent of the presidential vote, the URD and Jóvito Villalba helped open up the east to COPEI. Villalba's home state of Nueva Esparta is a case in point. Piñerúa took more votes on the AD ticket than Herrera did on the COPEI ticket, but Luis Herrera's vote on the URD ballot brought that state into his column.

At the western border of the east-west regional division, the one Plains state that voted for COPEI's Luis Herrera was his home state of Portuguesa. Indicative of the role that favorite-son and local-personality factors have played in Venezuela's elections is the fact that the man elected to be Portuguesa's national senator on the AD

211

FIGURE 8–7

DIFFERENCE BETWEEN HERRERA (COPEI) AND PINERUA (AD),
BY STATE, DECEMBER 3, 1978

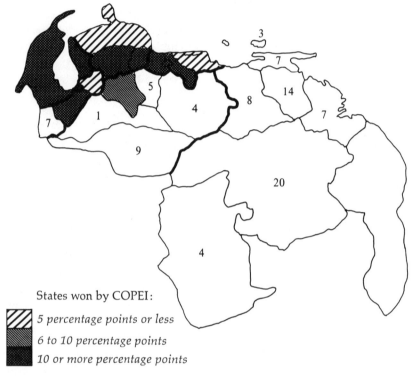

States won by COPEI:

5 percentage points or less
6 to 10 percentage points
10 or more percentage points

States won by AD:

Percentage point difference between
AD and COPEI shown on map.

ballot was Pablo Herrera Campíns, Luis Herrera's younger brother. For similar reasons, AD also was able to breach the east-west barrier. Táchira, long an electoral citadel for COPEI, gave a plurality of its presidential vote to AD's Luis Piñerúa Ordaz. One can reasonably speculate that this represented the state's vote of confidence in its native son, President Carlos Andrés Pérez, rather than a vote for the AD. Táchira's loyalty to its native sons is confirmed by the election of Ramón J. Velásquez to the Senate. Velásquez is a distinguished independent political figure who is considered the father of CORPOANDES. Although he served as a cabinet minister in the

COPEI administration of Rafael Caldera, he supported the AD candidate, his fellow Táchira native son Carlos Andrés Pérez, in 1973, and in 1978, Velásquez once again agreed to lend his prestige to the AD legislative ballot. Táchira, the home state of Venezuela's Andean rulers (1899–1945) and of former dictator Pérez Jiménez, also gave considerable electoral support to the CCN in 1968 and to the IPFN in 1963. The "paired" defections of Portuguesa and Táchira aside, however, the east-west regional variation was maintained, albeit much reduced.

In many ways, the campaign in the oil-rich state of Zulia, the second largest state in population following the Federal District, was decisive. COPEI's electoral plurality of over 66,000 votes in the state on the presidential ballot accounted for one-third of Luis Herrera's national plurality. The campaign in Zulia was a debacle for AD. The election returns from Zulia also demonstrate the degree to which regional development politics is separate from partisan electoral politics. Zulia's fifteen-year struggle to receive major industrial investments on a par with those made by the national government through the CVG in the Guayana Region had finally culminated in victory. In the midst of the 1978 campaign, the national Congress had unanimously passed major appropriations guaranteeing the development of the recently discovered coal reserves in Zulia and the installation of a steel plant that by 1990 would equal the CVG-SIDOR plant planned for Ciudad Guayana in the east. President Carlos Andrés Pérez had visited Zulia to deliver the authorizations personally to CORPOZULIA's president, Fernando Chumaceiro. Why then did this most favored state so overwhelmingly reject AD?

For one thing, Chumaceiro had insisted that CORPOZULIA's management be completely nonpartisan and that all its projects be shown to be both economically feasible and technically well designed. He had relied on a multiparty bloc within the state, rather than on any one party, to boost CORPOZULIA's proposals. Moreover, political parties in Venezuela are not expected to determine the location of major industrial projects, but their constituents do tend to hold them accountable for the delivery of basic public services such as education, public safety, street cleaning, and garbage collection. While the AD administration had succeeded in bringing large-scale capital-intensive projects to Zulia, it had failed to perform well in administering the small, everyday duties of government. One COPEI leader suggested to the author that the AD state administration in Zulia during the 1974–1978 period had been considered especially inept while the COPEI state administration of Hilarión Cardozo (1969–1973) had been considered especially able.

The vote in the Center Region, which accounted for almost 40 percent of the total, was perhaps the most severely contested. In both the Federal District and Miranda State, where the metropolitan area of Caracas is located, the election was almost a dead heat. In the Federal District, the difference between COPEI's and AD's presidential vote was a mere 0.24 percentage points. In Miranda State, the difference was 1.50 percentage points. On the other hand, Carabobo State gave COPEI's Luis Herrera his largest margin, a 16.2 percentage point advantage over Piñerúa. Herrera's advantage in Aragua State was in excess of 10 percentage points. In both Zulia and the Center Region, a considerable number of voters who did not support COPEI in the legislative ballot vote did vote for Luis Herrera on either the URD or the FDP ballot.

The published results of the 1978 elections and my own field research suggest that there were two critical causes of COPEI's victory over AD. The first of these was that the modern, urban middle class found in the Center Region, Zulia, and Lara State continued to prefer COPEI to AD. Second, the fragmented parties of the left appeared to have only one common objective: the AD's defeat. If one accepts the proposition that the cumulative effect of petrodollars on the metropolitan area of Caracas in the form of public works projects and employment explains why AD ran nearly neck and neck with COPEI in the Federal District and in Miranda State, one can conclude that COPEI's critical electoral advantage lay along the axis of large cities extending from Maracaibo, in Zulia, through Barquisimeto, in Lara, to Maracay and Valencia in the Center Region. Perhaps only the concentration of government money and patronage in the capital prevented Caracas from joining this apparent axis of anti-AD cities in the presidential vote.

In 1978, the death of Renny Ottolina and the failure of Diego Arria to project his independent image made COPEI the only electoral option available to this modern urban sector. As a result, COPEI gained over 50 percent of the vote in Zulia, Lara, and Carabobo and 48.9 percent of the vote in Aragua. When one adds the vote that Luis Herrera received here on the URD, FDP, and OPINA ballots, his victory in these urbanized states of the Western and Center Regions is even more impressive.

Gleaned from a careful reading of the Venezuelan press in December 1978 and January 1979 and from extensive interviews with a variety of AD and COPEI leaders, the following facts, perceptions, and plain rumors help account for the urban middle class's resolve to defeat AD in 1978 in order to prevent it from becoming a hegemonic party like Mexico's PRI.

• The urban middle class was exasperated by the accelerating inflation that was eroding Venezuela's gains from its petrobillions.

• This sector was offended by the great increase in government corruption and public employee indifference and absenteeism that accompanied the influx of petrodollars. This had resulted in a massive breakdown of many vital public services in urban Venezuela at a time when the middle-class voter would have expected the quality of these services to be improving.

• The literate urban Venezuelan was also made uneasy by the possible involvement of the Government in a murder (the Carmona case), the closing down of a prestigious magazine, *Resumen*, and the imprisonment, on what were felt to be specious grounds, of two opposition politicians. The seizure of the October 1978 issue of *Resumen* and the exiling of its editor were especially damaging to AD's electoral chances.

• The personal life of President Carlos Andrés Pérez offended the more respectable elements of the urban middle class.

There was a major breakdown in both the electrical and the water supply systems of Caracas in late December 1978. About one-half of the metropolitan area was without piped water for several days. Had these breakdowns occurred prior to the election, it seems very likely that AD's defeat in the Federal District would have been even more decisive. While the urban middle class was not enthusiastic about COPEI's Luis Herrera, his insistence upon government austerity, combined with his reputation as a good family man, certainly helped make him the presidential choice of the urban middle class in 1978. On the other hand, it is not at all certain that those in the middle class who advocate austerity would be eager to sacrifice much of their own standard of living. If President Herrera should implement a rigorous program of government austerity and honesty, many in the urban middle class might well seek an independent electoral hope in 1983 or perhaps even long for the return of the big-spending AD politicians.

The left, though fragmented into four political parties, was one element in AD's defeat. While the four leftist presidential candidates gained a total of only 8.2 percent of the presidential vote, their parties did appreciably better in the legislative vote, where they took 12.8 percent. The difference between their legislative vote, 672,110, and their presidential vote, 436,730, was 235,380. There is every indication that a great many of these votes were cast for Herrera in the presidential election by leftists whose priority was to see AD defeated. The anti-AD focus of the leftist campaigns was epitomized

TABLE 8–3

VOTE FOR THE LEFT IN URBAN STATES, 1978 LEGISLATIVE ELECTION

(in percentages)

Party	Federal District	Aragua	Cara-bobo	Miranda	Zulia	Lara	Sucre	Táchira	Bolívar
MAS	10.7	9.9	7.3	7.9	3.1	4.5	4.6	3.8	4.3
VUC	1.9	1.7	1.2	1.2	0.3	0.7	0.5	0.3	1.0
MEP	1.6	1.3	1.5	1.4	4.6	1.9	2.9	2.6	1.5
PCV	1.0	1.0	1.9	0.8	0.7	1.7	0.9	0.4	0.4
MIR	3.1	1.0	2.7	2.2	1.4	6.1	2.4	1.0	2.5
Causa Radical	0.7	—	—	—	—	—	—	—	3.0
Total	19.0	14.9	14.7	13.6	10.6	14.8	11.3	8.1	12.7

NOTE: Urban states are those containing at least one city whose population in 1971 exceeded 100,000.
SOURCE: Venezuela, Supreme Council, *Boletín informativo, no. 13.*

by MEP, whose candidate, recognizing the futility of his own play for the presidency, concentrated his campaign on lashing out at the corruption of AD leaders and their betrayal of the democratic revolution promised in 1958. Prieto, who is a former party president of AD, insisted that he was more an *adeco* than "the gang" who remained in control of the party. One AD leader expressed the view that Prieto's campaign was especially damaging to the party; Prieto acted as a sort of "kamikaze pilot," he said, crashing into AD with an impact far beyond the few votes he won.[20]

The leftist vote was almost exclusively concentrated in the large cities—in the Center Region and the states with large cities. One leader of the Movement toward Socialism acknowledged this fact, pointing out that in 1978 the left had penetrated the large cities of the periphery for the first time and was no longer limited to the Center Region (see Table 8–3). There was also an interesting regional variation in the relative strength of the various leftist parties. While MAS was by far the dominant party on the left in the country as a whole, MEP was the dominant leftist group in Zulia State, while the Movement of the Revolutionary Left was dominant in Lara. There was also one party, Causa Radical, that concentrated its electoral effort in a single metropolitan Caracas working-class neighborhood and in the planned industrial city Ciudad Guayana.

[20] Interview with a respected AD leader, December 18, 1979. See also *Zeta*, November 12, 1979.

The results of Venezuela's first off-year municipal elections, held in June 1979, illustrate the continuing evolution of the political party system. For the first time, the Christian Democrats emerged as a potential majority party, winning 50 percent of the vote. AD's share of the vote declined to a mere 30 percent, while that of a newly organized united leftist coalition rose to 18.5 percent. If this leftist coalition continues, it may emerge as a significant third force, holding the balance of power in Venezuelan politics. There are signs of a new realignment of Venezuelan politics as AD has moved to the left in order to reclaim its image as being the "party of the people." Under the Pérez administration (1974–1979) it had increasingly become identified with the new entrepreneurial groups. In late October 1979, AD labor leaders joined with leftist student and political leaders in organizing a noisy and somewhat violent demonstration against the COPEI administration's wage and price policy. The same AD labor leaders had been rather quiet during the Pérez administration.

A reinvigorated grass-roots political life should also bring about a more sensitive concern for the human factor in the nation's development. This should strengthen the regional factor in Venezuelan politics. While the cultural basis for regionalism appears to be declining, regions as places where people have their intimate attachments and associations and where they share the same social space and experience the same shortages will remain a vital element in democratic politics. Regions may be perceived in Caracas as instruments for disaggregating national politics and plans, but from the perspective of the average Venezuelan, regions are the primary instrument for effective democratic participation.[21]

---

[21] For a provocative plea for the recovery of territorial life see John Friedmann and Clyde Weaver, *Territory and Function: The Evolution of Regional Planning* (Berkeley: University of California Press, 1979).

9

The Elections and the Evolution of Venezuela's Party System

David J. Myers

On the evening of December 3, 1978, Carlos Andrés Pérez invited some of his closest associates from government, business, and the media to the presidential palace at Miraflores. Together they watched television coverage of the election returns and received advance releases from the Supreme Electoral Council and the Ministry of the Interior. By 9:00 P.M. this inner circle knew that Herrera's lead was insurmountable. Soon afterwards, the president's guests began excusing themselves. Many, particularly the businessmen, returned to their own executive offices to ponder how the unexpected turn of events would affect their interests during the coming five years. Soon after their departure the streets of Caracas filled with motor caravans of jubilant Social Christians, and spontaneous celebrations continued in the capital and other large cities until dawn.

About midnight crowds began to swell around the residence of Luis Herrera Campíns in the Sebucan zone of eastern Caracas. Adoring supporters broke into loud cheers when the president-elect appeared briefly and thanked them for their efforts in his behalf.[1] This tumultuous scene was carried by television into the homes of all who had remained awake into the small hours of the morning. On Monday afternoon Luis Herrera held a nationally televised press conference in which he promised to govern in the interests of all Venezuelans. On Tuesday Carlos Andrés Pérez sent his personal secretary, Carmelo Lauría, to convey the Government's good wishes and to discuss the most pressing details of the transition of power. Soon afterwards, Herrera received a telegram of congratulations from the defeated Acción Democrática candidate, Luis Piñerúa Ordaz. Beginning on

---

[1] Detailed accounts of Herrera's press conference appeared in the December 5, 1978, issues of *El Nacional* and *El Universal*.

Tuesday, Herrera also received a steady stream of visitors representing Venezuela's political, business, and communications establishments. Carlos Delgado Chapellin, president of the Supreme Electoral Council, officially ratified Herrera's victory on the Saturday following the election by proclaiming the Social Christian candidate president-elect of Venezuela.

Delgado Chapellin's declaration confirmed that pluralistic democracy in Venezuela had assumed a new shape. Single-party dominance, as it existed in Mexico, was ruled out, and rightist populism, long a threat to political stability, had disappeared as a viable political option. Electoral politics was dominated by two roughly equal political parties, and for the first time the Social Christians appeared to be the stronger. The radical Marxists on the left remained an alternative, but only in the long or medium run. The June municipal elections confirmed these trends: on June 3, 1979, the Social Christians and radical Marxists did a bit better than in December, and Acción Democrática did substantially worse.

The period beginning with the opening of the presidential election campaign on April 1, 1978, and lasting through the aftermath of the June 1979 municipal elections demonstrated the dynamic character of Venezuelan electoral politics. It also held important implications for the future of the party system in Venezuela. The following analysis of these implications will address four basic questions: how the change of power from Pérez to Herrera took place; the conduct of the municipal election campaign and its outcome; the implications of events between April 1978 and June 1979 for both the major political parties and the radical Marxist left; and finally, what those events tell us about the evolving operational characteristics and viability of the political party system.

From Carlos Andrés Pérez to Luis Herrera Campíns

The Pérez Presidency in Perspective. Carlos Andrés Pérez, while more impetuous than Rómulo Betancourt, resembles his former mentor in attaching great importance to his place in history. Pérez accepted the difficult job of suppressing Castroite guerrillas during the tense days of 1962, 1963, and 1964, and he performed well. During the Leoni administration Pérez ably led his party's congressional delegation, and between 1969 and 1972 he served as its secretary general. His reorganization of Acción Democrática laid the groundwork for the successful presidential campaign of 1973. In his own view, however, Carlos Andrés Pérez would be remembered most for the contributions made during his presidency.

Pérez's nationalization of petroleum placed the nation's single most important natural resource under the formal control of all Venezuelans. He used revenues from rising petroleum prices for large-scale development projects like new steel factories, additional hydroelectric dams, and innovative advances in transportation including the Caracas subway. Carlos Andrés Pérez argued that in giving priority to such projects, ones that added to the nation's productive capacity, he was ending Venezuela's economic dependence on its dwindling petroleum reserves. Also, he warned that the payoffs from this investment strategy would not immediately be evident to the average Venezuelan.[2]

Carlos Andrés Pérez had reason to be apprehensive about the immediate political consequences of his investments. As of 1978 many of their anticipated benefits were yet to be experienced. Opposition charges that Acción Democrática had squandered public funds struck a responsive chord. Such charges were to be expected from the Social Christians and from the extreme left. What Pérez could not understand, and what kindled his anger to an unprecedented degree, was the unwillingness of his own party's senior leadership to defend the accomplishments of his administration. He was even more outraged by insinuations from these same leaders that his Government had been unacceptably corrupt.

In one form or another, payoffs and kickbacks are part of the accepted way of doing business with the government in most countries most of the time, and Venezuela had long been in the mainstream. The amount of clandestine payments from contractors to officials historically had depended on the size of the contract in question. The Pérez Government let more contracts for greater sums than any Government in Venezuelan history. If standard operating procedures were followed between 1974 and 1979—and there is no evidence that they were not—the monetary value of these practices would have been greater than in the past. Defenders of Carlos Andrés Pérez argued privately that from this perspective his Government was at least as honest as the two immediately preceding it.[3] Pérez's allies

---

[2] This was the basic theme of informal remarks by Carlos Andrés Pérez to regional social, economic, and political leaders at a private gathering in Carora, Lara State, on November 27, 1978. The author was present during these remarks.
[3] For a useful scholarly discussion of the importance of corruption in politics, see James C. Scott, *Comparative Political Corruption* (Englewood Cliffs, N.J.: Prentice-Hall, 1972). Corruption in previous Venezuelan Governments is discussed in "Con sus acusaciones, Lauría se ganó por vida el odio de Caldera" [Lauría's accusations have won him Caldera's lifelong hatred] and "Rómulo Betancourt: toda una vida en lucha contra la corrupción" [Rómulo Betancourt: a lifelong struggle against corruption], in *Resumen*, no. 275 (February 11, 1979), pp. 4-6, 11-14.

within the party believed that the public charges of unprecedented corruption made by Piñerúa and his supporters had been a major factor in Acción Democrática's loss of the presidency.[4]

The Pérez faction also affirmed that defending and explaining what had been done between 1974 and 1978 constituted a first step in developing a modern ideology for Acción Democrática. They pointed out that the party's historic ideology had evolved as a reaction to the primitive and repressive regime of Juan Vicente Gómez. They considered that most of its tenets and accompanying programs either had been implemented or had become obsolete. In any case, they failed to address the needs of a people who lived overwhelmingly in the cities, enjoyed rising living standards, and took for granted the competitive democratic political environment. Pérez and his supporters argued that some mixture of developmentalism and populism would be the most effective intellectual brew for maintaining effective linkages between Acción Democrática and the Venezuelan people. Developmental populism could also be shaped to provide theoretical justification for integrating the national bourgeoisie and the growing middle class into Acción Democrática's historic clientele.

While governing, the Pérez faction lacked time for attending to matters of ideological reformulation, and Piñerúa's victory in the 1977 presidential primaries guaranteed that the party would not undertake ideological reformulation along the lines Pérez desired. Acción Democrática devoted most of its energy during the second half of 1977 and all of 1978 to the presidential election campaign. Soon after the December elections, however, Pérez served notice that he would return to the party and fight for his point of view. During his final months as president, Pérez's behavior was conditioned strongly by his intention of strengthening his position in anticipation of exercising a dominant role in the party.[5]

Pérez had to maintain the image of a president responsible for initiating unparalleled economic development if he were to achieve his ambitions within Acción Democrática. This influenced several important decisions taken during the final months of his administration. First, when investments by the country's leading commercial bank, the Banco Nacional de Descuento (BND), were found to be over-

---

[4] Interview on February 26, 1979, with a high-ranking official of the Pérez Government. Compare "AD no esperaba la derrota" [AD didn't expect defeat], *Zeta*, no. 248 (December 10, 1978), pp. 14-15.

[5] This was the conventional wisdom around national party headquarters during the author's visits in February and March 1979. Speculation on Pérez's impending challenge to Betancourt's domination of the party appeared in "Pérez Lives," *Latin America Political Report*, vol. 13 (January 12, 1979), p. 13.

221

extended, Carlos Andrés Pérez intervened personally. Using his statutory authority, the president named businessman Pedro Tinoco interim chairman at the BND and guaranteed its deposits. This halted a run on the bank. Depositors returned funds that had been withdrawn when it became public knowledge that bank executives had invested disproportionately in unsound business ventures controlled by the BND's largest stockholder, J. J. González Gorrondona.[6] Collapse of the BND would have shaken the entire Venezuelan banking community, undermined international confidence, and compromised the image Carlos Andrés Pérez desired to project.

Pérez also signed contracts for two important projects long talked about but never undertaken. The first was the Caracas-Ciudad Guayana railroad. Its construction would irrevocably commit Venezuela to developing a modern railroad system. The second, the Zulia steel complex, would add significantly to Venezuela's capacity for exporting steel.[7] It would also generate thousands of jobs in a populous region with many of the votes Acción Democrática would need if it were to recapture the presidency in 1983.

In the final major decision of his presidency, Carlos Andrés Pérez ordered his minister of mines and energy, Valentin Hernández Acosta, to raise the price of Venezuelan crude an average of $1.20 a barrel over the rate currently authorized by the Organization of Petroleum Exporting Countries.[8] This reminded the Venezuelan people that Pérez had nationalized petroleum and pursued an aggressive pricing policy. The president also hoped it would blunt the criticism that he had not taken into account how the Government would pay for the many development projects contracted for between 1974 and 1979.

Herrera Sets His Course. Between his election on December 3, 1978, and his inauguration on March 12, 1979, Luis Herrera refrained from commenting publicly on the final actions of the Pérez administration. The president-elect concentrated on choosing those with whom he would govern and on arranging that his departure from the Social Christian party would not open the way for Rafael Caldera to gain control of the party apparatus. Herrera spent long hours convincing his supporters that until the June 3 municipal elections many of them would have to remain in the party, since victory in the municipal

---

[6] "State Takes Over Venezuela's Leading Commercial Bank," *Latin America Economic Report*, vol. 6 (December 15, 1978), p. 1.

[7] "Difficult Decisions Face Venezuelan Government," *Latin America Economic Report*, vol. 6 (December 22, 1978).

[8] "Oil Companies Fail to Halt Venezuelan Increase," *Latin America Economic Report*, vol. 7 (March 9, 1979), p. 1.

elections was essential if his mandate for the 1979–1984 constitutional period were to be strong. Herrera thus labored to secure talented individuals for his cabinet without weakening the Social Christian electoral organization, which soon would be called upon to conduct a municipal election campaign.[9]

In selecting the cabinet, President-elect Herrera demonstrated an intention to work with experienced and technically proficient individuals, but not necessarily ones well known to the public. Another important criterion was that these individuals be primarily loyal to him. The cabinet, therefore, contained few well-known figures from the Caldera administration. The key post of minister of the interior went to the president-elect's confidant and campaign manager, Rafael Montes de Oca. The almost equally important office of secretary for the presidential staff went to another longtime supporter within 'the Social Christian party, Gonzalo García Bastillos. Luis Ugüeto, a young entrepreneur with strong links to the banking sector, received the powerful Ministry of the Treasury. Supporters of former President Caldera who made it to the cabinet obtained posts of lesser importance; thus, Enrique Pérez Olivares became governor of the Federal District, and the post of minister for the development of intelligence was specially created for Luis Alberto Machado. Luis Herrera also established the new cabinet-level positions of minister of state for female participation in development and minister of state for relations with eastern Venezuela. Cynics pointed out that the former was tokenism in an otherwise exclusively male cabinet, while the latter would concentrate on undermining Acción Democrática's historic position as the east's strongest political party. On the other hand, Herrera's defenders argued that the new president intended to emphasize the role of women in national life and that the ministry dealing with eastern Venezuela would focus on raising living standards in that comparatively poor region of the country.[10]

In his inaugural speech, as in the naming of his cabinet, Luis Herrera Campíns demonstrated that he was his own man. Prior to the inauguration, a great deal of speculation had circulated that because the Social Christians were a minority in Congress, the new president would seek some kind of arrangement with Acción Democrática. Between 1969 and 1974 Rafael Caldera had followed this

---

[9] "Los problemas políticos de Herrera Campíns estarán en COPEI" [Herrera Campíns's political problems will be in COPEI], Zeta, no. 266 (March 18, 1979), pp. 6-8. Compare Jesús Sanoja Hernández, "Rompecabezas en el gabinete" [Head knocking in the cabinet], Semana, no. 552 (March 25, 1979), pp. 24-25.
[10] The complete listing of the Herrera cabinet appears in Latin America Political Report, vol. 13 (March 23, 1979), p. 91.

strategy in order to get his programs through an opposition-controlled Congress. Within minutes of having accepted the presidential sash of office from Carlos Andrés Pérez, however, Herrera surprised everyone by strongly attacking the Pérez administration. He charged that his predecessor's reckless spending had mortgaged Venezuela's future. Herrera drew partisan cheers from COPEI supporters when he promised to end the practice of using presidential influence to circumvent standards and individual rights. This played to earlier Social Christian charges that the outgoing Acción Democrática administration had covered up corruption and used executive power to bend if not break legal norms.[11]

Acción Democrática rallied around Carlos Andrés Pérez after the new president's unanticipated attack. Rafael Poleo, editor of the magazine *Zeta* and a strong Acción Democrática supporter, wrote that the mere contracting of a large debt does not imply that an administration has "mortgaged" the country's future.[12] Other columnists favorable toward Acción Democrática argued that Carlos Andrés Pérez had greatly added to the base for industrialization with the credits he had negotiated. They proclaimed that in the long run his policies would end Venezuela's extreme dependence on petroleum revenue for economic prosperity.

Herrera's inaugural address, in summary, revealed the gulf that separated him from Acción Democrática. At least for the immediate future, cooperation between the country's two largest political parties to pass legislation was not feasible. In addition, Herrera's charges seemed to be a strategy calculated to place Acción Democrática on the defensive during the approaching municipal election campaign. It also challenged the image of dynamic developmentalism that Carlos Andrés Pérez had labored to create.

To open a breach with Acción Democrática appeared to be President Herrera's strategic choice. His difficulties with the military, however, while not wholly unanticipated, became more serious than expected. The officer corps had been favorably disposed toward Acción Democrática since the early 1960s. At that time two Acción

---

11 "Un discurso que divide al país" [A speech that divides the country], *Auténtico*, no. 93 (March 26, 1979), pp. 20-21; "El primer mensaje" [First message], *Bohemia*, no. 834 (March 19-25, 1979), pp. 12-14; "Presidente Herrera alza banderas populistas" [President Herrera raises the populist banner], *Semana*, no. 552 (March 25, 1979), pp. 34-36; and "Todos miraron hacia Pérez" [Everyone looks to Pérez], *Zeta*, no. 262 (March 18, 1979).

12 Rafael Poleo, "No explican" [They don't explain], *Zeta*, no. 263 (March 25, 1979), p. 5. Scattered columns in *El Nacional* and *El Universal* during the week of March 14 to 21 carried defenses of the Pérez administration.

Democrática administrations had worked with the military to defeat the Castroites' and other radical leftists' attempts to overthrow the constitutionally elected government. President Rafael Caldera, seeking to undermine Acción Democrática's strength in the army, had favored an alternative group of officers headed by General Martín García Villasmíl.[13] García Villasmíl's policies and appointments had convinced Acción Democrática officers that he was planning a coup. After presenting their evidence to Raúl Leoni, the former president had met with then-President Caldera. On the following day Caldera had dismissed General García Villasmíl.

President Carlos Andrés Pérez had worked with one of the most talented pro–Acción Democrática generals as his minister of defense, Fernando Paredes Bello. Initially, President-elect Herrera planned to name a pro–Social Christian general from Maturín, Tomás Abreu Rascaniere, to this position. Abreu Rascaniere, however, was relatively junior. Sixteen senior general officers sent word to Herrera that they would sign a formal letter of protest if he named Abreu Rascaniere. A surprised and frustrated Herrera decided to retain Fernando Paredes Bello through July 4, 1979. Since many of the pro–Acción Democrática senior officers from the guerrilla era were due to retire between mid-1979 and the end of 1980, Herrera believed that time would favor his efforts to reshape the military.[14]

Soon after his inauguration, the new president began following policies signaling to the officer corps that the soon-to-retire senior officers belonged to a bygone era. Some of these policies aimed at enhancing Herrera's support among radical leftists, who, as discussed earlier, had tipped the close presidential elections to the Social Christians. Herrera's most dramatic gesture was to extend blanket amnesty to guerrillas still actually fighting, including the well-known leader Julio Escalona. On more than one occasion Escalona had boasted of having inflicted substantial losses on pursuing army units. Nevertheless, President Herrera publicly assured all Venezuelans that the military supported his pacification strategy. In private, however, many high-ranking officers who had risked their lives and lost comrades in

---

[13] Interview with Admiral Diez Ugüeto, January 6, 1973.

[14] A detailed discussion of turbulence in the military during May 1979 appeared in "Informe político: es profundo el disgusto militar par la política de pacificación" [Military disgust over the pacification policy is profound], *Zeta*, no. 273 (June 3, 1979), pp. 6–7. See also "Fernando Paredes Bello: un ministro sin querer está entre la espada y la pared" [A minister who doesn't want to be between the rock and the hard place], *Resumen*, no. 284 (April 15, 1979), pp. 5–6, and "¿Quién designa al ministro de la defensa?" [Who will designate the defense minister?], *Resumen*, no. 288 (May 13, 1979), p. 16.

the antiguerrilla campaigns expressed serious misgivings about the president's decision.[15]

The returning guerrillas received permits to hold public rallies in major cities throughout the country. These rallies became forums for boasting of martial exploits and belittling the armed forces. Not surprisingly, guerrilla leaders charged the military with ineptitude and corruption. The officer corps, in addition to being forced to endure the public bravado of their hated enemies, found themselves confronted with a major problem of a different kind. In the Congress, radical leftists and Social Christians joined in voting to investigate alleged kickbacks in the purchase of naval frigates from Italy.[16] The vote added to the officers' frustration with the new Government. General Arnaldo Castro Hurtado, the army commander, resigned in disgust.

The details of what happened following the resignation of Castro Hurtado remain unclear. Within several hours of his departure, however, a long line of high-ranking officers visited the general's home in the Prados del Este zone of Caracas. Rumors raced through the capital that a takeover by the military was under way. The coup never occurred. Some recounted that former Presidents Rómulo Betancourt and Carlos Andrés Pérez personally intervened to guarantee political stability and constitutional continuity. Others stated that the senior officers backed down when they encountered strong opposition among middle-ranking officers and from the private sector. Only those intimately involved knew the whole story, and they remained silent.

While President Herrera wrestled with the military and attempted to get his administration under way, the political parties immersed themselves in the campaign for the first municipal elections held apart from national elections in thirty-one years.

The Municipal Elections

The Reform of 1978. On August 18, 1978, the Organic Law of the Municipalities was published in the National Register. This was the most significant institutional innovation in Venezuelan democracy since the promulgation of the 1961 constitution. The 1961 constitution anticipated such a law, but disagreement among the political parties over the nature and extent of the powers to be granted to local government delayed its passage for seventeen years. Carlos Andrés Pérez's

[15] Informal conversations with several high-ranking members of Acción Democrática in May 1979.

[16] "Seis fragatas, dos presidentes y muchos genoveses" [Six frigates, two presidents, and a lot of men from Genoa], *Resumen*, no. 289 (May 20, 1979), pp. 11-15.

election as president, concurrent with Acción Democrática's attainment of majorities in both houses of Congress, gave the ruling party's experts in municipal affairs an opportunity to transform their ideas into law. The Organic Law of the Municipalities went through several drafts, with the Social Christians agreeing to the final version. Radical leftists also felt the new law was an improvement. Nevertheless, they would have preferred provisions allowing for even greater citizen participation.[17]

For two decades, municipal elections had been held at the same time as presidential, congressional, and state legislative balloting. A single ballot, the small card, had elected party lists of candidates for legislative bodies at the national, state, and local levels. The candidates on the municipal council lists were often unknowns or party hacks. It didn't matter. The municipal political system provided for minimal citizen involvement in local decision making, and voters focused on the congressional candidates when they bothered to acquaint themselves with the lists at all. More often their attention centered on the presidential race.

The August 18 law provided new mechanisms for citizen participation and new ways of holding municipal politicians responsible for their performance in office.[18] In regard to the former, the most important departure mandated open council meetings at which citizens speaking on behalf of community organizations would have the right to address sessions of the municipal councils directly. Procedures here were modeled on a colonial local government institution known as the *cabildo abierto*.

The Supreme Electoral Council held the power to decide for how long and by what procedures councilmen would be elected. However, the municipal law clearly intended that local elections would be separated from state and national voting in order to allow citizens the opportunity to pass judgment on local officials. Precedents for this procedure existed. In modern times separate municipal elections had been held during the administration of President Isaías Medina (1941–1945) and in 1948. The military did not permit separate municipal elections during their decade in power (1948–1958). They treated

---

[17] The August 18, 1978, and August 19, 1978, issues of El Nacional and El Universal contain detailed information on the "Ley Orgánica de Régimen Local." Also see Allan R. Brewer-Carias, "La participación política a nivel local" [Political participation at the local level], Resumen, no. 277 (February 25, 1979), pp. 13-22, and Emilio Pacheco, "La izquierda y las elecciones municipales" [The left and the municipal elections], SIC, no. 415 (May 1979), pp. 208-9.

[18] A useful summary of local government history is Arturo Sosa A., "El poder municipal en el proceso histórico venezolano" [Municipal power and Venezuelan history], SIC, no. 415 (May 1979), pp. 202-50.

local political institutions as implementing arms of the national government. In contrast, the political party elites who dominated politics after the January 23, 1958, revolution believed that strong local government could play a major role in consolidating the democratic system.

Between 1959 and 1979, except for the special deliberative body in the Federal District, all municipal councils were composed of seven members. Rural municipalities, even those with populations below 2,500, had councils the same size as Maracaibo, a city approaching one million inhabitants. The new law mandated seven councilmen for all municipalities of less than 50,000. Above 50,000 the number of councilmen depended on population. Under this system Maracaibo was allocated seventeen councilmen.

Whether a municipality received seven or seventeen councilmen, all were elected at large on the basis of proportional representation. Thus individual councilmen did not represent any specific geographic area, and voters in casting their ballot accepted the entire list of councilmen set forth by the party of their choice. If the party received 40 percent of the total vote, for example, and if the municipality qualified for ten councilmen, the first four councilmen on the party's list would be elected. The new procedures significantly increased local autonomy. Continuing national party control over the order in which candidates were listed, however, provided an important mechanism for enforcing party discipline on elected local officials.

The COPEI Campaign. In the early phases of the 1978 presidential election campaign the Social Christians organized a group to evaluate potential candidates for the municipal councils. Herrera's campaign manager, Rafael Montes de Oca, held periodic conversations with state and local party officials during this period about the composition of the municipal council lists.[19] Late in June, however, it became clear that Congress would approve the revised organic municipal charter, and that municipal elections would take place subsequent to the presidential voting. This change stopped work on the municipal council lists since candidates would now have to undergo closer scrutiny than if they were part of a ballot that included state and national legislative candidates. A separate municipal election campaign would have to be planned. However, neither the Social Christians nor any other political party could design its municipal election campaign strategy until the chief executive had been elected and the political party balance in

---

[19] Interview with Valmore Acevedo Amaya, the Social Christian expert on local government. It appeared in *Resumen*, no. 282 (April 1, 1979), pp. 14-15.

Congress determined. Luis Herrera Campíns's victory, the emergence of the Social Christians as Venezuela's strongest political party, and the weak showing of third parties set the tone for municipal election campaign maneuvering.

President-elect Herrera, as mentioned earlier, felt that a Social Christian victory in the municipal elections would strengthen his mandate. A strong Acción Democrática showing, on the other hand, would embolden the opposition party to use its leverage in Congress and in the state legislatures to block Social Christian reforms.[20] Having tied the Social Christians in the small-card vote of December 3, Acción Democrática had enough legislative strength to demand programs of its own and protection for bureaucrats appointed by the AD administration as the price for passing legislation; negotiating of this kind had become accepted practice during the Caldera presidency between 1969 and 1974, when the Social Christians were a minority in Congress. Herrera believed that control over the municipal councils would place him in a significantly better bargaining position than the one enjoyed by Rafael Caldera.

Luis Herrera Campíns kept an eye on plans for the municipal election campaign, but after being proclaimed president-elect he focused on organizing his administration. The Social Christian party's secretary general, Pedro Pablo Aguilar, participated more actively in developing the campaign, but as suggested earlier, he was engaged with followers of former President Caldera in a struggle to control the party machinery. Aguilar chose Manuel Selva, a Herrera loyalist with technical training from the German Christian Democrats, to plan and oversee the municipal election campaign. He was assisted by José Curiel, Caldera's successful campaign manager from 1968, and by the North American consultant David Garth. Selva, Curiel, and Garth believed that since the municipal elections were to be held within eleven weeks of President Herrera's inauguration, the new Government would still be enjoying its honeymoon during the voting. Thus, if the general good will that they expected to develop toward the new chief executive were transformed into votes for Social Christian municipal council lists, the party could win a decisive victory.[21]

The initial stage of strategy implementation involved convincing voters that the new president wanted to know their opinions about

[20] A useful analysis of the implications of controlling the executive but not the Congress was made by Rafael Caldera in his April address to the Social Christian party. This address is reprinted in *Resumen*, no. 285 (April 22, 1979), pp. 9-15.

[21] Author's observation of the precampaign maneuvering inside COPEI during March 1979. See the discussion in "Caldera no salió tan mal" [Caldera didn't come out all that badly], *Zeta*, no. 271 (May 20, 1979), p. Z-21.

municipal problems. Selva ordered the printing of hundreds of thousands of copies of a political questionnaire which invited respondents to indicate which local services were functioning acceptably and which needed President Herrera's special attention. The questionnaire was distributed in March, long before the official opening of the municipal election campaign on May 1. During the campaign itself Social Christian candidates cited the results of this survey when stressing the importance of improving such services as water, electricity, and garbage collection.

Selva decided that local Social Christian candidates would emphasize that Acción Democrática was to blame for whatever problems existed in their respective municipalities. Garth advised that voters could again be swayed by the charges made against Acción Democrática during the presidential election campaign: corruption, party cronyism, and personal favoritism. In contrast, the Social Christians were to portray themselves as honest, efficient, and capable of bringing the changes needed to revitalize municipal government. The voters also were reminded that a Social Christian–dominated council would surely be more efficient in obtaining support from the national government for local projects than one controlled by the opposition.

Finally, the Social Christian campaign organization for the municipal election was without peer. Herrera had been careful to keep in place most of the key individuals who had guided his successful presidential campaign.[22] Those continuing in the party believed that the new administration would find an acceptable place for them if they performed well during the municipal election campaign. Consequently, morale in the Social Christian party was high.

The AD Campaign. Acción Democrática, in contrast, acted like a badly shaken prizefighter in the months between Piñerúa's unexpected defeat and the municipal election disaster that came in June. In retrospect, Carlos Andrés Pérez's 1973 victory looked extremely impressive to his fellow party members. Pundits speculated that Acción Democrática was Pérez's for the taking, that Rómulo Betancourt was finished as an active party leader, and that Piñerúa and his supporters would be eased out of the important positions they controlled in the party apparatus. However, an alternative interpretation argued that Piñerúa's defeat was a repudiation of the Pérez administration. Those taking this position, the Betancourt/Piñerúa faction, urged the party

---

[22] For example, most of the team assembled by Manuel Selva in the Secretariat of Organization for the presidential election campaign of 1978 remained for the 1979 municipal elections. See "Informe político" [Political note], in Zeta, no. 274 (June 10, 1979), p. Z-7.

to return immediately to its historic concern for the have-nots and to its social democratic ideological origins.[23]

Inside Acción Democrática, Alejandro Izaguirre remained secretary general. However, Luis Alfaro Ucero, a close confidant of Betancourt and Piñerúa, appeared to exercise more influence from his position as national secretary of organization. In a heroic attempt to strengthen Acción Democrática's infrastructure for the municipal election campaign, Alfaro began intervening in what he perceived to be the weaker state party organizations. Supporters of Carlos Andrés Pérez, however, charged that Alfaro Ucero was attempting to purge them from state and local leadership positions. They mounted a major campaign to remove Alfaro as national secretary of organization. This paralyzed the party and led to public speculation that Acción Democrática might divide yet again. However, in early March the party's National Executive Committee decided to delay consideration of any major organizational changes until after the June 3 municipal voting.[24]

The decision to keep all national leaders in their present positions freed Alfaro Ucero to resume preparations for the municipal elections. The national organization secretary and his deputy, Luis Raúl Matos, worked incessantly to prepare the party for a second round of campaigning. However, loss of the presidency had badly demoralized state and local leaders. Fearful that they would lose their patronage jobs with the government, many were scrambling to find alternative means of employment. Others, alienated because of continuing tension between the Pérez and Betancourt/Piñerúa factions, decided to sit out the campaign. With each report from the field, Acción Democrática's national leaders became more pessimistic.

Carlos Andrés Pérez saw the growing gloom at party headquarters as an opportunity to assert leadership and demonstrate his continuing appeal. Public opinion polls still indicated that he was the country's most popular politician.[25] Pérez thus decided to take personal charge of the approaching municipal election campaign. He devoted his full attention to this task upon leaving office. Octavio Lepage, Acción Democrática's secretary general during the successful 1973 election campaign and Pérez's minister of the interior, became official head of the campaign. Correspondingly, Luis Alfaro Ucero and the regular party organization assumed a subservient role.

---

[23] Both sentiments were expressed to the author in numerous conversations with Acción Democrática leaders in February 1979.

[24] A detailed discussion appears in *Zeta*, no. 263 (March 25, 1979), pp. 12-13.

[25] Polling done by the author in Monagas and Aragua during April 1979 continued to show Carlos Andrés Pérez as Venezuela's most popular politician.

The Pérez gamble rested on an assumption that his prestige and charisma could restore party morale and avert electoral disaster. No Acción Democrática leader believed that his party could retain control of municipal councils in the populous cities of the Western and Center Regions. These municipalities provided the winning margin for Herrera in December. Medium-sized municipalities in the east and in the Plains Region, on the other hand, continued to vote for Acción Democrática, and the party remained the strongest political force in most rural municipalities. If it could duplicate its December small-card vote in June, it would elect a majority of the country's municipal councilmen. This was the goal Carlos Andrés Pérez set for Acción Democrática in the municipal elections.[26]

As we have seen, Pérez wanted to make the municipal elections into a popularity contest between himself and Luis Herrera. He hoped that in such a confrontation Acción Democrática's municipal council slates might reap the benefit of his greater popularity. The former president's second strategy was to attack the Social Christian party for not having been able to get the national government running. Acción Democrática's campaign slogan reflected the latter strategy: "Confronting a Government that can't get started, a council in action," it proclaimed, and party propaganda pictured a frustrated driver unable to start his car. The campaign was effectively mounted, and Pérez attracted cheering crowds as he toured the country.[27]

The Radical Left. The two major political parties' increasing share of the total legislative and presidential vote surprised and frustrated radical leftist political leaders. Instead of doubling its 1973 support as it had hoped to do, the Movement toward Socialism increased its vote by less than two points, to just below 6 percent of the total. While the Movement of the Revolutionary Left grew marginally, to 2 percent, the People's Electoral Movement shrank from 5 percent in 1973 to the size of the MIR. The Communist party remained at 1 percent. Thus, every radical left party except the MAS feared for its very life, and this last perceived itself as stuck on an unacceptably low electoral plateau.

Radical leftists shared the perception that their potential clientele was far greater than the 10 percent of the vote they obtained on the December small-card ballot. Teodoro Petkoff of the MAS long had argued that if leftists could only work together, their share of the total vote would increase dramatically. Historically, personalistic

---

[26] "Informe político," in *Zeta*, no. 271 (May 20, 1979), pp. Z-6–Z-8.
[27] Ibid.

rivalries and ideological disputes had blocked cooperation on the left since the first election after the overthrow of General Marcos Pérez Jiménez. Increasing domination by the Social Christians and Acción Democrática, however, finally spurred radical leftists to forge a new dimension of unity in early 1979.[28]

Personalist rivalries and ideological disputes ran sufficiently deep to prevent the formation of a single radical left political party. Instead, radical leftists presented voters with a unified slate containing candidates from the four participating political parties. Voting for any of the four counted as support for the list of municipal council candidates. Position on the lists and the number of candidates allotted to each participating party depended on a complex formula whose basic component was the percentage of the small-card vote received in the December 1978 election. Radical leftists hoped that their new-found unity would make the voters see them as a viable alternative to the two major parties.

The Outcome. On the evening of June 3, 1979, soon after the polls closed, it was evident that the Social Christians had won the largest and broadest electoral victory in their history as a political party. In every state except Monagas and Sucre, the Social Christians would hold a majority of the municipal council positions. Only in a few districts of the east did Acción Democrática control the municipal councils. The party's 30 percent of the total national vote was below what its most pessimistic leaders had anticipated. Even the municipal council of Maturín, long considered the most *adeco* of Venezuelan cities, fell to the Social Christians.[29]

Radical leftists also enjoyed unprecedented electoral success. Nationally their lists obtained 18 percent of the total municipal vote. Their support was concentrated in Caracas and other urban clusters of the Center Region and in the cities of Lara and Zulia. These advances prompted a jubilant Teodoro Petkoff to proclaim that two-party dominance had passed into the history books.[30] Others, alarmed at the growth in radical left voting, warned that unless Acción Demo-

[28] See Pacheo, "La izquierda," pp. 208-9; "La izquierda cuenta con la abstención [The left is counting on abstentions], *Auténtico*, no. 103, pp. 48-49; and "La izquierda junta pero no unida" [The left together but not united], *Zeta*, no. 271 (May 20, 1979), pp. 18-19.
[29] A readily available source in English is "Venezuela: Local Landslide," *Latin America Political Report*, vol. 13, no. 22 (June 8, 1979), p. 172. Also see "C. A. Pérez el gran derrotado . . . ," *Resumen*, no. 293 (June 17, 1979), pp. 6-9, and "Todo el poder y toda la responsabilidad para COPEI" [All the power and all the responsibility for COPEI], *Zeta*, no. 274 (June 10, 1979), pp. Z-6-Z-7.
[30] *Resumen* (June 17, 1979), p. 9.

crática could pull itself together quickly it would cease to be regarded as a viable contender for power. This prompted Valmore Acevedo Amaya, the Social Christian secretary for municipal affairs, to muse that for the good of Venezuelan democracy he hoped that Acción Democrática would survive as a major political force.[31] Five years earlier, of course, Acción Democrática pundits were saying the same thing about the Social Christians.

Some evidence suggests that the Social Christians won the municipal election, and Acción Democrática lost, because Carlos Andrés Pérez chose to make himself and his administration the major campaign issue. Robert O'Connor's chapter on the electorate demonstrates that while the former president was Venezuela's most popular politician, he also evoked more negative emotions than any other major party leader. Unfortunately for Acción Democrática, Pérez detractors outnumbered Pérez enthusiasts among the large undecided group prior to the December balloting.[32] When asked to express their opinion of the former president for a second time within six months, the voters gave a verdict even more devastating for Pérez and Acción Democrática. Apparently they believed that the former chief executive had had his chance—and now Herrera deserved his.

Radical leftists vigorously attacked Acción Democrática and the Social Christians during the municipal election campaign. Their theme, that the two major political parties were so entrenched that only a third alternative could make the councils representative of popular opinion, struck a responsive chord. Also, many dissatisfied voters who were unwilling to support radical leftists for national office seemed inclined to give them a chance at the local level. Nevertheless, a single municipal election, especially one held under procedures never before used, was inconclusive for demonstrating that voters now saw the radical left as a viable contender for power. It was also insufficient evidence that a rough parity between the Social Christians and Acción Democrática had given way to COPEI dominance.

The Future of Venezuelan Political Parties

Balloting in December 1978 gave the Social Christians and Acción Democrática even greater dominance than they had exercised following the general collapse of third parties in the 1973 presidential voting.

---

[31] This statement was made tongue in cheek.

[32] Future work by the author and Robert O'Connor will analyze Mycon public opinion data to describe and explain more fully the choices of Venezuelan voters in the 1979 municipal elections.

The unanticipated support for the radical left unity list in the June 1979 municipal elections, however, cautions against the assumption that two-party dominance will persist throughout the 1980s. Whether Acción Democrática and the Social Christians continue to divide between 80 and 90 percent of the total vote will depend on two sets of variables. The first, the external variables, include such factors as the persistence of a strong global market for petroleum and Venezuela's continuing ability to produce, the maintenance of reasonable levels of efficiency in the state corporations, the cultivation of minimal standards for public morality, and the stimulation of a climate of opinion in which the rights of unpopular minorities are protected.[33]

The internal variables encompass three basic kinds of problems: those associated with leadership and succession; those deriving from the importance of sustaining a viable political ideology in the face of rapidly changing social and economic realities; and those involving the ability of party elites to adapt organizational and political campaigning technology from the North Atlantic democracies. The eighteen months of electioneering discussed in this volume reveal much more about the internal than about the external variables. In examining the future of Venezuelan political parties, consequently, the following discussion focuses on internal variables.

The Social Christians: An Unparalleled Opportunity. Leadership and succession problems in the Social Christian party never had been so serious as following the election of Luis Herrera Campíns. While COPEI was evolving into one of the country's two major political parties, Social Christian leaders were surprisingly successful in muting tensions and rivalries among themselves. Fear that a major division would reduce the party to electoral impotence influenced their behavior. In addition, significance should be attached to the fact that many early Social Christian leaders had attended either San Ignacio, the Jesuit high school in Caracas, or Colégio La Salle, the capital's other prestigious Catholic high school. Graduates of these institutions saw themselves as guardians of a Christian civilization that increasingly was threatened by the rising tide of atheistic Marxism. This perception helped hold the Social Christians together. Finally, much of the credit for the steady Social Christian growth between 1958 and 1973 belongs to Rafael Caldera. His skill in unifying diverse ideo-

---

33 For a detailed discussion of the external factors affecting Venezuelan democracy, see John D. Martz and David J. Myers, "Venezuelan Democracy and the Future," in John D. Martz and David J. Myers, eds., *Venezuela: The Democratic Experience* (New York: Praeger, 1977).

logical, regional, and generational interests earned him the well-deserved title of "co-godfather"—along with Rómulo Betancourt—of Venezuelan democracy.

Don Herman's chapter in this book recounts how Caldera's control of the party slipped during 1974 and 1975. The alliance of Herrera and Aguilar supporters that crushed the former president's candidate for Social Christian party secretary general in December 1975 saw its efforts vindicated by the electoral successes of December 1978 and June 1979. Herrera and Aguilar's position in the party became stronger than ever. Correspondingly, they hoped to pressure Caldera into accepting the honorific but relatively powerless role of party elder statesman.

Rafael Caldera had other ideas. Dissatisfied with his place in history, the Social Christian party founder hoped for a second term in which to implement reforms that opposition control of the Congress during his first administration (1969–1974) had forced him to abandon. In addition, continuing domination of the party machinery by Pedro Pablo Aguilar and Luis Herrera Campíns guaranteed that no one else from the Caldera faction had any chance of securing the Social Christian presidential nomination for 1983. With Caldera serving as president between 1984 and 1989, on the other hand, his faction would have a good opportunity to regain the upper hand.[34]

After the June municipal elections political infighting intensified within the Social Christian party. Each faction maneuvered to elect its candidate secretary general. While Pedro Pablo Aguilar intended to remain in office, Caldera hoped to replace him with Eduardo Fernández, a longtime associate. Abdón Vivas Terán, leader of the small but vocal Social Christian left, also announced his candidacy. The course of this competition during July 1979 suggested to Caldera that Eduardo Fernández's chances of ousting the incumbent were questionable. Consequently, José Curiel, another Caldera loyalist, offered a compromise. Pedro Pablo Aguilar could remain secretary general, but Eduardo Fernández and Abdón Vivas Terán would occupy the two sub–secretary general positions, each with considerable autonomy from Pedro Pablo Aguilar. The new team would have two basic

---

[34] A useful discussion of how the Caldera–Pedro Pablo/Herrera factions grew out of struggles in the Social Christian youth movement appeared in "En la JRC producería el primer choque entre Calderistas y Herrera-Pablistas" [Inside the JRC occurred the first clashes between supporters of Caldera and Herrera], Zeta, no. 276 (June 24, 1979), pp. 22-26. Also see "Pedro Pablo el silencioso fabricante de victorias" [Pedro Pablo, the silent architect of victories], Zeta, no. 274 (June 10, 1979), pp. 18-22.

objectives: supporting the Government of Luis Herrera Campíns and electing Rafael Caldera president in 1983.[35]

At the Social Christian national convention in November 1979, Eduardo Fernández unexpectedly ousted Pedro Pablo Aguilar as the party's secretary general. Fernández's winning margin, 87 votes out of roughly 1,600, revealed that the two Social Christian factions were roughly equal in strength. Despite his ouster as secretary general, Pedro Pablo retained control of a majority of COPEI state party organizations and seemed determined to run for the presidency in 1983. However, Caldera's prestige within the party and among critically important independent voters is unequaled by any other Social Christian leader. Should the party founder threaten to split his creation if denied its 1983 presidential nomination, Pedro Pablo Aguilar and Luis Herrera Campíns will be hard pressed to prevail.[36] A breakaway Social Christian party with Caldera as its presidential candidate would return Acción Democrática to power. It would also erode, if not destroy, the Social Christians' position as one of the country's two major political organizations. Many Social Christian leaders who are now in their forties and early fifties have expected to have a realistic chance to become president. At a minimum they anticipate high governmental responsibility. They will not throw the opportunity away.

For the time being, ideological problems are less serious for the Social Christians than those of leadership and succession. Initially the party contained an important rightist faction that favored Catholic corporatism. Luis Herrera's candidacy demonstrated that Social Christian rightists had become an inconsequential minority within the party. Present Social Christian ideology derives from the progressive social thinking of Jacques Maritain and the papal encyclical *Rerum Novarum*. Rafael Caldera's voluminous writings have discussed Maritain and *Rerum Novarum* in terms of the Venezuelan situation. Broad enough for all but the most radical leftists and rightists, these interpretations have been a major source of Social Christian unity.

The thrust of Caldera's writing has enabled Venezuela's Social Christians to assume a position considerably to the left of their

---

[35] See "COPEI: ahora puede dividirse" [COPEI: a division is possible], *Zeta*, no. 276 (June 24, 1979), pp. 18-22; and "Pedro Pablo comienza hacerle concesiones a Rafael Caldera" [Pedro Pablo is beginning to make concessions to Rafael Caldera], *Zeta*, no. 277 (July 1, 1979), pp. 6-7.

[36] The "Brasero" section in *Zeta*, no. 281 (July 29, 1979), p. 15, contains several short news items suggesting that Pedro Pablo retains control over the party apparatus. Also see "Apoyo a Pedro Pablo y a Jaime Lusinchi" [Help for Pedro Pablo and for Jaime Lusinchi], *El Universal*, July 29, 1979.

European counterparts without denying their Roman Catholic heritage.[37] Caldera emphasizes domestic and international social justice, family ties and individual rectitude, and participation in local and national political decisions. Caldera's progressive implementation of these positions caused the Social Christians' leading rightist, Germán Borregales, to form his own political party, the Movement for National Action (MAN).[38] Never more than a gadfly organization, the MAN disappeared in 1974, after losing its only congressman.

The major challenge to Caldera's reformist social justice position within the Social Christian party comes from the small but vocal "Christian left." This intellectual current includes such important party leaders as Abdón Vivas Terán, José Rodolfo Cárdenas, and Donald Ramírez. Christian leftists argue that all productive facilities must be thought of as "community property." Given its attitude toward free enterprise, which ranged from overt hostility to grudging acceptance, the Christian left's continuing presence within the Social Christian party strongly influenced the private sector's tilt toward Acción Democrática in 1973 and 1978.[39]

Despite impatience with Caldera's reformism and pragmatism, Christian leftists have not broken with the Social Christian party, except in isolated instances. The party founder's interpretation of social justice has been sufficiently anti–status quo for Christian leftists to support it as the best alternative in an imperfect world. Also, Christian leftists consider that Luis Herrera Campíns will move increasingly toward a social communalism and that a second Caldera Government would not reverse "advances" of this nature. Therefore, although important internal ideological differences exist, the Social Christian party does not appear on the brink of an important division.

The presidential and municipal election campaigns of 1978 and 1979 suggest that the Social Christians made progress in adapting organizational and electoral technology from the North Atlantic democracies to their needs. David Garth's ability to work closely

---

[37] A useful summary of the history of Social Christian ideology appears in Miguel Jorrín and John D. Martz, *Latin American Political Thought and Ideology* (Chapel Hill: University of North Carolina Press, 1970), pp. 416-20.

[38] Germán Borregales, *COPEI hoy: una negación* [COPEI today: a negation] (Caracas: Ediciones Garrido, 1968).

[39] The position of the Social Christian left is skillfully presented in José Rodolfo Cárdenas, *El combate político* [The political struggle] (Caracas: Editorial Doñá Bárbara, 1966). Luis Herrera's vagueness on many propositions of his party's left comes through in Alfredo Peña, *Conversaciones con Luis Herrera Campíns* [Conversations with Luis Herrera Campíns] (Caracas: Editorial Ateneo, 1978). Also see "Ideología," in J. E. Rivera Oviedo, *Los social cristianos en Venezuela* [The Social Christians in Venezuela] (Caracas: Ediciones Centauro, 1977).

with Luis Herrera Campíns is a most impressive example of successful electoral technology transfer. On the other hand, many in the Social Christian campaign organization resented Garth. It was the latter's relationship with Herrera that enabled him to carry the day. This raises the question whether the Social Christian party as a whole is really disposed to accept foreign electoral technology.[40]

Evidence from a different source, the German Christian Democrats, indicates that Venezuela's Social Christians as a whole are ambivalent about using foreign consultants and techniques. Social scientists from Germany's Konrad Adenauer Institute who worked in the last three Venezuelan presidential election campaigns report that Social Christian leaders often reacted to their advice as if it were an unwanted intrusion into Venezuelan affairs. On the other hand, these German social scientists seem to have convinced their Venezuelan colleagues that efficiently using foreign electoral technology can mean the difference between victory and defeat. As the Social Christians prepared for the 1978 presidential election campaign, they did consult with the Germans, but only when they wanted specific answers to technical problems. Whenever possible the Germans were kept at arm's length. The Germans, defensive because Herrera eventually turned to David Garth, argue that Venezuelan reluctance to incorporate them into an integrated strategy group kept the Social Christians' presidential election effort disorganized until well after the official opening of the campaign.

Resentment stemming from the feeling that the North Atlantic nations long had exploited Venezuela hobbled Social Christians in their efforts to make the best use of the technology they were importing. However, the Social Christians' principal adversary, Acción Democrática, exhibited the same mixed feelings about the presence of foreign electoral consultants and social scientists. The future advantage that foreign electoral technology will give the Social Christians thus depends on three factors: the receptivity of its own leaders and party workers to that technology, the quality of the technology transferred, and the relative willingness of opposition parties to seek out and incorporate similar organizational and campaigning technology. In addition, the Social Christians must decide the extent to which they will develop and maintain an infrastructure of Venezuelans trained in receiving and applying technological advances from abroad.

---

[40] Author's interview on July 25, 1979, with a social scientist from the Konrad Adenauer Institute who had worked with the Venezuelan Social Christians during the past three years.

To summarize, never has the future been brighter for Venezuela's Social Christians. For the first time they appear stronger than Acción Democrática. Luis Herrera Campíns occupies the presidency and Pedro Pablo Aguilar dominates the party organization. Having led the Social Christians to unprecedented electoral victories in 1978 and 1979, Herrera and Aguilar will spare no effort in seeking to make their party a permanent majority. Currently, the central problem for the Social Christians is the growing effort by former President Rafael Caldera to secure the 1983 presidential nomination and regain control of the party organization. Short of this effort's leading to a division of the party, the Social Christian presidential nominee stands at least an even chance of being elected in 1983. The other basic factor influencing his prospects will be the Herrera Government's performance.

Acción Democrática: The Need to Rebuild. Following the Social Christian victory in June 1979, Acción Democrática entered a phase, which continues as of this writing, of soul searching and reassessment. The Betancourt/Piñerúa and Pérez factions each argued that their party somehow had lost touch with the Venezuelan people. However, no consensus existed about how this had occurred, which policies had led to unprecedented electoral disaster, or the nature of the corrective measures to be adopted.

Three years of infighting between supporters of Piñerúa/Betancourt and Pérez impaired Acción Democrática's effectiveness in the presidential and municipal election campaigns.[41] Defeat in the former demoralized the Piñerúa/Betancourt faction, while the June debacle discredited Carlos Andrés Pérez and his followers. On the positive side, the two setbacks convinced both factions that coexistence and cooperation would be imperative if the party hoped to recapture the presidency in 1983. Though personal rivalry continued, Acción Democrática seemed to be safe from yet another split.

During July and August 1979, Jaime Lusinchi and Arturo Hernández Grisanti emerged as strong contenders for the position of party secretary general.[42] Support for the two did not correspond

---

[41] "C. A. Pérez el gran derrotado por segunda vez . . ." [C. A. Pérez: the big loser for a second time], *Resumen*, no. 293 (June 17, 1979), pp. 6-11; and "Carlos Andrés sobrevivió al plomo grueso del CPN" [Carlos Andrés survives the lead weight of the National Political Committee], *Zeta*, no. 26 (June 24, 1979).

[42] "Hernández Grisanti puede ser secretario general por el rechazo adeco a Carlos Andrés Pérez" [Hernández Grisanti may become secretary general because of AD's rejection of Carlos Andrés Pérez], *Zeta*, no. 278 (July 8, 1979); and "La indecisión de Izaguirre fortalece la oportunidad de Hernández Grisanti" [The indecision of Izaguirre strengthens the opportunity of Hernández Grisanti], *Zeta*, no. 281 (July 29, 1979), pp. 6-7.

exactly to the Piñerúa/Betancourt and Pérez cleavage. Nevertheless, there was a long history of personal dislike and programmatic difference between Hernández Grisanti and Pérez. Neither Hernández Grisanti nor Lusinchi enjoyed the broad support commanded by incumbent party Secretary General Alejandro Izaguirre. Izaguirre spent much of June in the United States undergoing medical tests. He remained acceptable to Piñerúa, Betancourt, and Pérez, but it was unclear whether he desired to remain in office or whether he was physically capable of serving another term. Consequently, the structure of Acción Democrática's national leadership following the loss of power remained a major unresolved question as the party struggled to develop a strategy for conducting democratic opposition during the opening phase of the Herrera Government.

Another leadership problem concerned generational circulation within the party. With the notable exception of Carlos Andrés Pérez, those exercising the greatest power belonged to the founding generation of 1928. Even given the longevity and extraordinary vigor of this group, its domination would end during the 1980s. Most in the generation that normally would be competing for control of the party, those in their late forties and fifties, abandoned Acción Democrática in the divisions of 1961 (MIR), 1962 (Acción Democrática/Oposición), and 1967 (MEP). Some exceptional individuals in their late thirties and early forties held cabinet or subcabinet positions in the Pérez administration. They looked forward to commensurate responsibility within the party as it conducted the opposition. Nevertheless, while the health of the founding generation held, the careers of individuals in this generation remained subject to continuing approval from their elders.

Rivalry between Caracas and the interior also contributed to leadership problems within Acción Democrática. Historically, the party's national leaders were political bosses in important states or regions. These regional political elites moved to Caracas where they represented their region's interests in the party's National Executive Committee, while continuing to dominate their respective localities. The recent growth of Maracaibo, Valencia, Barquisimeto, Maracay, Barcelona, and San Cristóbal, however, facilitated in each of these urban centers the growth of an influential and autonomous local professional class. Leaders in the regional big city party organizations increasingly resisted being rubber stamps for those living in Caracas.

Growing local autonomy and the importance of equitable representation for each region in the national party leadership presents yet another important challenge to Acción Democrática, as well as to other political parties. For example, Acción Democrática's present

241

national leaders are drawn disproportionately from the east. The Western and Center-West Regions are underrepresented. This helped Acción Democrática in the former but may have cost Piñerúa heavily in the latter. Consequently, Acción Democrática is considering how to give greater national prominence to talented leaders from the Western and Center-West Regions. This suggests that elites in the interior cities are increasingly successful in playing off the parties against each other by using their influence with local voters for leverage.[43]

Earlier analysis hinted that ideological differences entered into the struggle for control of Acción Democrática. The founding generation was influenced profoundly by Karl Marx in its initial diagnosis of Venezuela's problems and in its early programs. After flirting with Marxism-Leninism, however, Acción Democrática became a mortal enemy of international communism, whose subservience to the Soviet Union outraged the Venezuelan nationalism of Acción Democrática's founders. Eventually they settled on domestic redistributive and development policies closely paralleling those advocated by Mexico's Revolutionary Institutional party. For reasons not entirely clear, however, Acción Democrática and the Mexican party never developed a close relationship. Instead, especially during the 1970s, Acción Democrática sought out and solidified a broad range of ties with Europe's Social Democrats.

As Acción Democrática approached the 1980s, its overarching ideological problem was that the programs that had allowed it to capture broad popularity in the 1940s were largely accomplished.[44] The first Betancourt Government (1945–1947) modernized the bureaucracy and the second (1959–1964) initiated agrarian reform. Raúl Leoni's administration (1964–1969) pushed development of the interior and obtained final acceptance from business of organized labor's legitimacy. Leoni also contributed mightily to consolidating pluralistic democracy when in defeat he turned the government over to his constitutionally elected successor, Rafael Caldera. Finally, President Carlos Andrés Pérez (1974–1979) realized the decades-old dream of nationalizing petroleum.

The most important issues of the 1980s were not foreseen when the party doctrine was first formulated. They include such thorny matters as setting the terms of transferring needed technology from

---

[43] The growing importance of regional leaders not residing in Caracas came up repeatedly in conversations between the author and assorted Acción Democrática leaders during 1978 and early 1979.

[44] For a useful historical summary of Acción Democrática's ideology, see Jorrín and Martz, *Latin American Political Thought*, pp. 360-72.

the North Atlantic areas to Venezuela, striking an acceptable balance between the public and private sectors, and determining the geographic priorities for investing ever-increasing petroleum revenues and maintaining environmental standards without slowing the growth of job-creating industrialization. Within Acción Democrática almost everyone recognized that these issues were more complex than those who had formulated party doctrine in the 1940s and 1950s had ever imagined. Nevertheless, the majority faction argued that the party must return to its ideological and programmatic roots. This involved becoming more than ever a spokesman for the have-nots. Correspondingly, the majority advocated holding disparities in income within a narrow range until all Venezuelans enjoyed a decent standard of living. If this meant imposing higher taxes on the upper middle class and the economic elite, the party's only choice was to accept whatever consequences flowed from pursuing such a policy.

During the Pérez Government, an alternative position that had been gaining strength since the Leoni years became official policy. Advocates of this position remained committed to economic justice and social equality. However, their medium-range formula for achieving long-range goals differed substantially from that of the founding generation. The Pérez position assumed that the most important immediate priorities were to create new industrial facilities and to upgrade the work force. These objectives could be achieved most rapidly by providing economic incentives for businessmen to invest and for talented youth to acquire needed skills. Initially this would do little for the poorest and least talented groups. It might even exacerbate existing social and economic inequalities. In the long run, however, increasing economic productivity from an expanded middle class would generate the wealth needed to abolish poverty.[45]

One important policy flowing from Carlos Andrés Pérez's ideology of economic development was minimal taxation for the technical and professional middle class. Similarly, if businessmen reinvested profits in job-producing facilities, they could expect substantial reductions in their taxes. Over and over this approach was reflected in decisions by President Pérez that encouraged the private sector to enter new areas of the economy and in government projects whose immediate benefits were to employ limited numbers of highly trained and well-paid technicians. In the eyes of Acción Democrática's founding generation, this approach alienated many have-nots and working poor who historically had been the party's mainstay.

---

[45] The Pérez position is summarized by Luis Esteban Rey, "AD, CAP y el Desarrollismo" [AD, CAP, and developmentalism], *SIC*, no. 414 (April 1979).

After the June municipal elections, advocates of policies that would more immediately benefit the poor consolidated their domination within the party organization. Nevertheless, partisans of the developmentalist ideology associated with Carlos Andrés Pérez remained influential and aggressive. Their establishment of and continuing involvement in a major new Caracas newspaper, *El Diario de Caracas*, was only one indication that they intended to remain an important force within the party. Consequently, Acción Democrática's ability to formulate an acceptable synthesis between its two ideological tendencies will largely determine its effectiveness as a party during the 1980s.

In matters of adapting modern electoral technology, Acción Democrática had met both success and failure. Its most impressive success had come during the 1973 electoral campaign, when Carlos Andrés Pérez and Octavio Lepage, then party secretary general, had skillfully integrated technical advice from consultant Joseph Napolitan and pollster George Gaither. Next to this effort the more lavishly financed campaign of Lorenzo Fernández, the Social Christian presidential candidate, had appeared clumsy and almost amateurish. When Acción Democrática had returned to power in March 1974, the party had held a substantial lead over its major rival in the use of modern electoral techniques.[46]

Once in power, Acción Democrática had allowed the infrastructure used by Napolitan and Gaither for transferring electoral technology to dissolve. Efforts were made to develop a comparable one following Piñerúa's selection as the Acción Democrática presidential nominee, but organizational problems prevented the party from effectively employing the technical information it was receiving. In response, even prior to the June electoral disaster, Acción Democrática's national Organization Secretariat moved to rebuild the party's ability to use electoral and organizational technology from abroad. Notably, it reopened contacts with Napolitan and obtained technicians familiar with polling techniques from Germany's Social Democrats. Organization Secretary Luis Alfaro Ucero hoped above all to develop new ways of appealing to the middle class, whose support for Luis Herrera Campíns, according to Robert O'Connor's analysis, had contributed mightily to Acción Democrática's loss of the presidency.

---

[46] The best account of the campaign organizations and strategies employed in the 1973 presidential election campaign is John D. Martz and Enrique Baloyra, *Electoral Mobilization and Public Opinion: The Venezuelan Campaign of 1973* (Chapel Hill: University of North Carolina Press, 1976).

In the aftermath of the election Acción Democrática also renewed its long neglected relationship with Mexico's Revolutionary Institutional party. Like their Venezuelan counterparts, Revolutionary Institutional party technicians needed new techniques that would enable them to retain support among the peasants while strengthening their appeal to the growing middle class. Finally, Acción Democrática sent promising young professionals abroad to study polling and campaigning techniques at assorted universities in the industrial democracies. Whether the one-time majority party would develop the infrastructure necessary for effectively using the skills of these individuals in the 1982 municipal and 1983 presidential election campaigns remained an open question.

The Left: The Continuing Struggle for Unity. Political parties on the radical left command far fewer resources than either the Social Christians or Acción Democrática. They have less access to technical expertise from Europe and North America than either of the major political parties. Nevertheless, the Movement toward Socialism enjoys important support among Venezuelan social scientists. Political scientists, sociologists, and economists usually invest considerable time and effort in MAS election campaigns. MAS also receives assistance from Western European Communist parties. The Italian Communist party has been particularly generous in providing the MAS with expertise in the areas of publicity and party organization. Following the June municipal elections, Eurocommunists were more optimistic about the future of the MAS than at any time since the founding of the party.[47]

Ideological disputes between parties of the far left appear less intense since most remaining guerrilla leaders accepted President Herrera's offer of amnesty. By 1979 there was little sympathy for the armed insurrection that had so divided radical leftists during the 1960s and 1970s. While the situation could change overnight, President Herrera was probably correct when he argued that for the foreseeable future the radical leftists would concentrate on increasing their appeal at the polls. The municipal campaign revealed general agreement among radical leftists on the need to "socialize" most means of production and to pursue a more radical program of redistributing wealth.[48] If history is any guide, however, ideological

---

[47] "El MAS precipita la inflación" [The MAS is causing inflation], *Auténtico*, no. 107 (July 2, 1979), pp. 11-13.

[48] "La izquierda junta pero no unida" notes in passing that the longstanding struggle between the Márquez and Petkoff factions continues undiminished. Also see "AD recibe sonrisas de la izquierda" [AD gets smiles from the left], *Zeta*, no. 281 (July 29, 1979), p. Z-9.

disputes will be less important than personal differences in determining the extent to which Venezuela's radical leftists can sustain a unified front.

The two most important political parties of the radical left, the MAS and the MIR, have continuing leadership problems. Since its founding the MAS has been divided between supporters of Pompeyo Márquez, José Vicente Rangel, and Teodoro Petkoff.[49] Márquez loyalists have forced the nomination of Rangel as the party's presidential candidate in the past two elections. Petkoff, considerably younger than either Rangel or Márquez, grudgingly went along with Rangel's candidacy. Petkoff's strategy has been to avoid an open break with Márquez in the expectation that during the 1980s he will inherit a vigorous and unified political party. If the health of Márquez and Rangel holds, however, this strategy could force Petkoff to wait until the 1990s. Since it is dubious that Petkoff will bide his time for an entire decade, the struggle within MAS for control of the party during the 1980s will be intense. Even though a division would reduce each faction to microparty status, it is a real possibility.

MIR doubled its share of the total vote in the December 1978 election. Nevertheless, the party remains only marginally viable. Its two leaders, Américo Martín and Moisés Moleiro, each seek unchallenged domination over the incipient MIR party organization. Their rivalry takes the form of ideological disagreement: Martín, the party's founder and presidential candidate, advocates a vaguely pragmatic radical socialism, while the party secretary general, Moleiro, favors a more orthodox Marxist-Leninist approach that includes closer ties with Eastern Europe and the Soviet Union.[50] Moleiro, however, denies that he would accept subservience to international communism in the traditional manner of the Venezuelan Communist party. For its part, the PCV seems unable to break out of the extreme electoral impotence to which it was relegated following the Soviet invasion of Czechoslovakia and the splitting away of the MAS.

To summarize, events between April 1978 and June 1979 indicate that radical leftists can count on between 10 and 20 percent of the total vote in Venezuela. Robert O'Connor's analysis suggests

---

[49] See John Martz's chapter on the minor parties. A useful and perceptive account of the byzantine politics of the radical left appears in "Los que no quieren ser devorados" [Those who don't want to be devoured], Zeta, no. 273 (June 3, 1979), pp. Z-34–Z-35.

[50] Martín and Moleiro both have published extensively. For example, see Moisés Moleiro, La izquierda y su proceso [The left and its process] (Caracas: Ediciones Centauro, 1977), and Américo Martín, El estado soy yo [I am the state] (Valencia: Vadell Hermanos, 1977).

that even a unified radical left will find it impossible to leap the 20 percent barrier unless political attitudes change significantly. However, following the June municipal elections the radical left appeared less, rather than more, united. Leaders of the MIR, PCV, and MEP complained that the MAS had benefited disproportionately from the unification of radical leftist municipal council slates. Given these complaints and the personalistic rivalries we have noted, it is unlikely that the radical leftists will achieve the degree of unity that characterized their 1979 municipal election campaign in time for either the 1982 municipal elections or the 1983 presidential contest.

Operational Characteristics of the Party System

This chapter will now discuss five operational characteristics of Venezuela's party system suggested by events between April 1978 and June 1979, namely, its structure, its locus of competition, its evolving patterns of accountability, its impact on democratic institutionalization, and its linkages with the international environment. To identify and analyze these characteristics is the first step in developing a dynamic model of Venezuela's party system. Formal model building, however, is a task reserved for subsequent scholarship.

The Dynamic Two-and-a-Quarter-Party System. Venezuela's party system has undergone several metamorphoses. It began as a single-party-dominant system in which Acción Democrática regularly received more than 70 percent of the total vote. In 1958 Acción Democrática remained the strongest single political party, but it commanded just under 50 percent of the total vote. Fragmentation subsequently transformed the party system into one in which no political party commanded a majority. During the fifteen years of the multiparty system (1959–1974), Venezuela was governed by assorted formal and informal party coalitions built around Acción Democrática and the Social Christians.

The fragmentation of the party system peaked in the 1968 election, when Social Christian Rafael Caldera captured the presidency with only 29 percent of the total vote. Caldera depended upon Acción Democrática support to get his programs through Congress. At the beginning of the 1973 presidential election campaign, however, there was considerable speculation that Acción Democrática and the Social Christians might do worse in the approaching elections than they had done five years earlier. Leaders in the two parties feared that if the trend toward fragmentation continued, even in coalition they would be unable to control Congress, the state legislatures, and the municipal councils.

Not only did the 1973 election returns provide a pleasant surprise for Acción Democrática and Carlos Andrés Pérez, they also reshaped the party system. Voting in 1978 and 1979 confirmed that the new configuration was a two-and-a-quarter-party system. Within this system a rough parity prevails between the Social Christians and Acción Democrática. Either is capable of winning the presidency with between 40 and 50 percent of the total vote. The quarter belongs to parties on the radical left, especially the Movement toward Socialism and the Movement of the Revolutionary Left. While radical left political parties together receive between 10 and 20 percent of the total vote, none of them alone breaks the 10 percent barrier.

The basic structural dynamic of the two-and-a-quarter-party system is that each of the major actors attempts marginally to strengthen parties on the radical left. The goal is to reduce the other major actor, by bleeding off some of its support to radical leftists, to a position where it cannot mount an effective challenge for the presidency. Decades of cooperation and controlled competition between Acción Democrática and the Social Christians have made each more comfortable with the other than with any radical leftist party. Neither major actor wants the other to be replaced as the second political force by a radical left party. The desired state of affairs is what the Social Christians achieved in the June municipal elections, when they took just over half of the vote and the other major actor won 30 percent. Radical leftists divided the remaining 20 percent.

The two-and-a-quarter-party system forces the radical leftists to play a waiting game. Their hope is that some cataclysmic event will destroy one or both of the major political parties and leave the radical leftists to pick up the pieces. Barring such an eventuality, the radical leftists must content themselves with marginal increments in their support facilitated by dissatisfaction with the big two. Also, the inability of the radical left to gain power while the two-and-a-quarter-party system persists weakens their cohesion; apparently it is sometimes more desirable to be number one in a political organization that receives 2 percent of the total vote than to be number two or three in one that receives 7 percent.

Competition for the Left-Center Position. Venezuelans expect the state to be heavily involved in economic activity, including—as in the United States—massive water projects like hydroelectric dams and irrigation facilities, road and port development, and mail delivery, but also including steel production, mineral and petroleum extraction, and commercial fishing. Private enterprise is still involved in some of these activities, and it dominates construction, ranching, commerce, and assorted light industries, but few Latin American countries consign more of their total economic activity to the public sector than Venezuela.

Conventional wisdom in the United States supports the sentiment that the government which governs least governs best. In the political arena, this is reflected in movements advocating reductions in government expenditures, lower taxes, and the simplification of bureaucracy. Their professed aim is to "get the government off the back of the average citizen." In most cases they believe that the interest of the collectivity is best served by giving free reign to individual interests. Venezuelans generally feel otherwise. The most recent political party to defend private economic activity against state regulation, the Development Movement in 1973, polled only 1 percent of the total vote.

One explanation for public suspicion of private enterprise derives from the early history of capitalism in Venezuela. Until recently most important businesses were controlled from abroad, and government was the mechanism used to keep foreigners from exploiting the economy for their selfish ends. Another source of hostility to private enterprise is the feudal communalism that structured colonial society and oriented thought in Venezuelan universities until its replacement by Marxism. Feudal communalism is a spiritual predecessor of the community property ideology so prevalent among contemporary youth in the Social Christian party.

For the Social Christians, as well as for Acción Democrática, private enterprise exists only because it serves the interests of the collectivity as determined by the state.[51] The burden of proof is on the businessmen to convince elected officials that their economic activities should not be regulated or taken over directly by government. The Social Christians and Acción Democrática accuse each other of being too favorably disposed toward private interests and brand one another as "rightist," each seeking to monopolize the political space occupied by a majority of the electorate, the center left.

In attempting to maneuver to the left of each other, Acción Democrática and the Social Christians take care not to appear too far to the left. Being too far to the left is associated with communism, and the Venezuelans are anticommunist. Part of this aversion to communism stems from the Venezuelan Communist party's

---

[51] For a perceptive discussion of government-business relations in Venezuela, see José Antonio Gil Yepes, *El reto de los elites* [The challenge of the elites] (Madrid: Editorial Tecnos, 1979).

long history of subservience to the Soviet Union. Another element is the party's involvement in the unpopular guerrilla movement of the 1960s. Other political parties on the radical left also find this perception limiting. As suggested earlier, however, they can only wait and hope that a cataclysmic event or the gradual discrediting of the two major political parties will move the voters further to the left.

Increasing Accountability for Performance while Governing. Until recently the prevailing political mythology in Venezuela had it that Acción Democrática voters were the majority and that they were unswervingly loyal to the party. Events in 1967–1968 cast doubt on these assumptions. Following the party's much discussed third split, the Social Christian Rafael Caldera was elected to the presidency by the narrowest of margins. This demonstrated that Acción Democrática was not invulnerable and that the party would surrender power upon losing an open and fair election. The overwhelming victory of Carlos Andrés Pérez in 1973, however, suggested that Acción Democrática was unbeatable unless weakened by the breaking away of an important faction. Many observers speculated that, having learned the lessons of 1968 and 1973, Acción Democrática would be able to govern throughout the closing decades of this century.

In this context, Herrera's victory was at least as important as Rafael Caldera's. Herrera defeated a unified Acción Democrática that controlled the presidency and enjoyed unprecedented resources with which to dispense patronage. His election demonstrated that neither of the major political parties could count upon the voters' automatically renewing its mandate. Indeed, the 1978 election was the third consecutive election the opposition had won.

In light of the relative narrowness of their December victory, President Herrera and the Social Christians moved cautiously but deliberately to create the impression that better than Acción Democrática they reflected the interests and aspirations of the Venezuelan people. The president's initial strategy included a careful analysis of conditions in the bureaucracy, the government corporations, and the private sector—allegedly intended to produce evidence to document the charge that Herrera had found the country's political and economic institutions in an extremely precarious situation. The new administration clearly intends to discredit Acción Democrática and the Pérez Government.

Herrera also is building bridges to his left and to his right. He believes that an expanded base of support, along with continuing petroleum revenues, will enable him to preside over a stable political environment and a steadily improving economy. This approach will be publicly contrasted with the supposedly impetuous and misguided policies of Pérez. If successful, the Social Christians expect to be able to convince the voters that they are better able to manage the country's political and economic affairs than their major rival.

Herrera's strategy assumes a large floating vote that supports the democratic system but is not irrevocably committed to either Acción Democrática or the Social Christians. His advisers believe that these voters made the difference in his narrow victory over Piñerúa and that they switched to the Social Christians in substantial numbers for the June 1979 municipal voting. The long-term strategy is to integrate the floating voters into the Social Christian party. In the short term, however, the party hopes to convince independents that their interests are better served by a Social Christian Government than by one over which Acción Democrática presides. Of course, Acción Democrática intends to demonstrate just the opposite. The point is that the leaders of each of the major political parties understand that their hard core supporters alone are not sufficiently numerous to win elections. Victory will go to the party that better demonstrates its responsiveness to an increasingly independent and pragmatic electorate.

Interparty Elite Cooperation in Defense of Democracy. Seven honest elections and twenty years of unbroken constitutional rule are an unprecedented achievement for Venezuela. Nevertheless, democracy remains a precariously rooted plant. For each year of representative democracy, the country has experienced almost seven of authoritarian rule. Through municipal reform both Acción Democrática and Social Christian leaders have made a major effort to secure so great a commitment to representative democracy at the grass roots that any other form of government would be unthinkable.

The resignation of General Arnaldo Castro Hurtado as army chief of staff following President Herrera's decision to grant amnesty to leftist guerrillas suggests that the two major political parties have good reason to be concerned about the long-range viability of the democratic system. On that May 1979 evening when rumors of a military coup were sweeping Caracas, the two "godfathers" of Venezuelan democracy had to intervene to calm the troubled waters. Betancourt and Caldera's cooperation in dealing with the military shows that the Acción Democrática and Social Christian elites have been able to set aside their differences to defend the democratic system.

How far the younger leaders in the two major political parties are willing and able to cooperate is an important unknown. Those in their forties remember *adecos* and Social Christians fighting side by side against the dictatorship of General Marcos Pérez Jiménez. For those under thirty-eight, however, memories of bitter interparty rivalry and political infighting seem stronger than ones of the joint struggle against a corrupt regime. It remains an open question whether these younger leaders will be inclined to cooperate in defense of a democratic system that remains more precariously institutionalized than either of the two major political parties cares to admit.

Technological and Programmatic Dependence on the North Atlantic Democracies. The dependence of Venezuelan political parties on campaign technology, organizational methods, and programmatic appeals developed in Western Europe and North America is amply documented in this volume. It remains to point out here that the likelihood that this operational characteristic of the party system will change any time soon is remote. Venezuelan political parties lack the resources and inclination to develop an indigenous electoral technology that would be more effective than methods imported and adapted from the industrial democracies.

The Social Christian party's experience with Garth suggests that, in the short run, imported technology can provide a winning advantage. Like most democratic political parties, Acción Democrática, the Social Christians, and the Movement toward Socialism are preoccupied with winning elections. In the long run, however, winning will require party leaders to blend foreign technology with techniques and appeals that are uniquely Venezuelan. The ability of the political party leaders to accomplish this will be an important consideration determining whether the democratic system survives, and in what form. During the middle third of this century Rómulo Betancourt and Rafael Caldera created such a blend while continuing to involve themselves in daily political affairs. Their legacy, to a large extent, sustains the party system's two most important members. Those who value the democratic experience can only hope that a new generation of political party leaders will carry this tradition forward.

Appendix A
The Venezuelan Ballot, 1978

The Venezuelan ballot used in 1978 measures roughly fifteen by twenty inches and is printed in brilliant color on heavy black paper. It is folded when the voter receives it, and he refolds it before placing it in the ballot box. To cast a vote for president, the elector stamps one of the large boxes; to vote for a party's list of candidates for all national and state legislative offices, he stamps one of the small boxes. The small boxes in the bottom half of the ballot that are numbered but show no party symbol are slots that were not assigned to any party. The history of this ballot and the system used for assigning places on the ballot to parties are described in chapter 2.

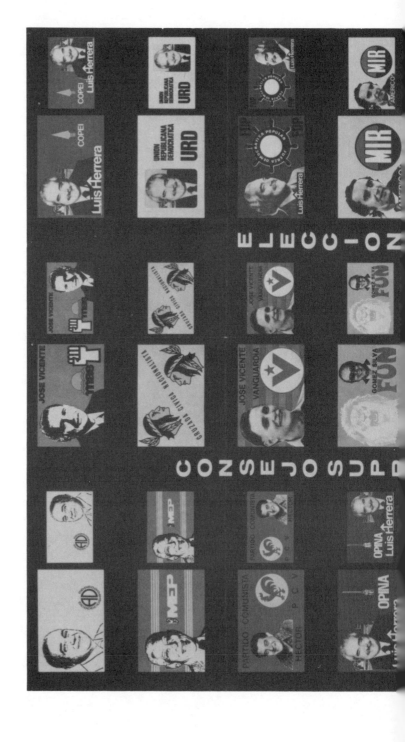

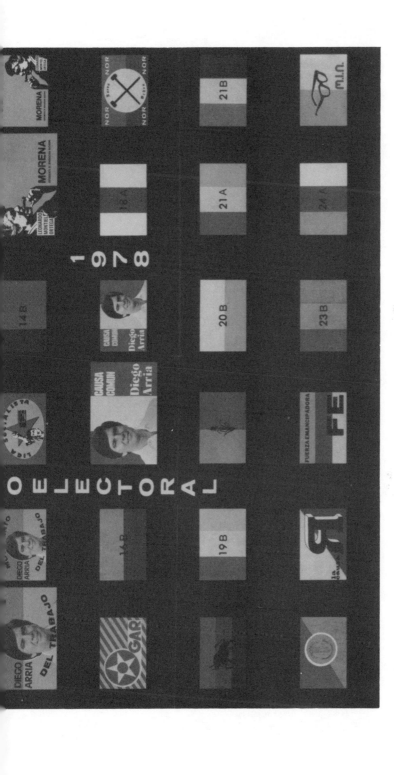

Appendix B

Venezuelan Election Returns, 1973 and 1978

Compiled by Richard M. Scammon

CHAMBER OF DEPUTIES, 1973: POPULAR VOTE, PERCENTAGE, AND SEATS, BY DISTRICT

District	Total Valid Vote	AD	COPEI	MAS	MEP	CCN
Federal District	808,935	306,397	242,430	90,958	15,715	55,059
Percentage		37.9	30.0	11.2	1.9	6.8
Seats	37	16	13	5	—	3
Anzoátegui	204,397	102,202	41,999	6,922	17,863	4,522
Percentage		50.0	20.5	3.4	8.7	2.2
Seats	9	6	2	—	1	—
Apure	56,256	35,300	13,532	502	1,786	1,516
Percentage		62.7	24.1	0.9	3.2	2.7
Seats	3	2	1	—	—	—
Aragua	235,562	93,979	72,782	13,648	8,933	16,038
Percentage		39.9	30.9	5.8	3.8	6.8
Seats	7	4	3	—	—	—
Barinas	82,817	46,427	26,088	2,166	1,476	2,209
Percentage		56.1	31.5	2.6	1.8	2.7
Seats	3	2	1	—	—	—
Bolívar	162,072	89,269	38,874	6,873	3,592	4,686
Percentage		55.1	24.0	4.2	2.2	2.9
Seats	7	5	2	—	—	—
Carabobo	280,761	114,851	87,683	13,967	11,311	20,128
Percentage		40.9	31.2	5.0	4.0	7.2
Seats	9	5	4	—	—	—
Cojedes	40,409	22,866	9,295	707	1,622	1,585
Percentage		56.6	23.0	1.7	4.0	3.9
Seats	2	2	—	—	—	—
Falcón	170,344	76,628	48,670	4,279	10,098	2,233
Percentage		45.0	28.6	2.5	5.9	1.3
Seats	7	4	2	—	—	—
Guárico	123,528	67,210	29,880	4,002	4,823	6,172
Percentage		54.4	24.2	3.2	3.9	5.0
Seats	6	4	2	—	—	—
Lara	277,043	121,946	91,821	22,091	11,915	7,892
Percentage		44.0	33.1	8.0	4.3	2.8
Seats	10	5	4	1	—	—

URD	FDP	PCV	MIR	OPINA	PNI	IP	Other[a]
16,231	12,074	7,433	15,927	10,020	6,712	4,816	25,163
2.0	1.5	0.9	2.0	1.2	0.8	0.6	3.1
—	—	—	—	—	—	—	—
13,838	3,447	5,203	1,995	847	816	1,131	3,612
6.8	1.7	2.5	1.0	0.4	0.4	0.6	1.8
—	—	—	—	—	—	—	—
1,105	906	304	89	21	100	—	1,095
2.0	1.6	0.5	0.2	—	0.2	—	1.9
—	—	—	—	—	—	—	—
6,343	3,652	3,490	1,905	2,867	2,667	740	8,518
2.7	1.6	1.5	0.8	1.2	1.1	0.3	3.6
—	—	—	—	—	—	—	—
895	971	549	449	70	322	310	885
1.1	1.2	0.7	0.5	0.1	0.4	0.4	1.1
—	—	—	—	—	—	—	—
4,747	2,442	3,734	1,499	1,346	1,096	391	3,523
2.9	1.5	2.3	0.9	0.8	0.7	0.2	2.2
—	—	—	—	—	—	—	—
6,225	4,587	5,378	2,933	3,309	2,952	1,558	5,879
2.2	1.6	1.9	1.0	1.2	1.1	0.6	2.1
—	—	—	—	—	—	—	—
3,020	417	188	48	110	139	—	412
7.5	1.0	0.5	0.1	0.3	0.3	—	1.0
—	—	—	—	—	—	—	—
19,634	1,609	2,420	1,157	453	630	308	2,225
11.5	0.9	1.4	0.7	0.3	0.4	0.2	1.3
1	—	—	—	—	—	—	—
5,793	1,546	706	527	177	375	731	1,586
4.7	1.3	0.6	0.4	0.1	0.3	0.6	1.3
—	—	—	—	—	—	—	—
2,646	2,615	4,503	3,274	2,034	1,545	1,592	3,169
1.0	0.9	1.6	1.2	0.7	0.6	0.6	1.1
—	—	—	—	—	—	—	—

District	Total Valid Vote	AD	COPEI	MAS	MEP	CCN
Mérida	135,753	61,625	53,742	3,821	4,860	5,836
Percentage		45.4	39.6	2.8	3.6	4.3
Seats	6	3	3	—	—	—
Miranda	382,119	167,484	119,390	23,208	7,479	22,151
Percentage		43.8	31.2	6.1	2.0	5.8
Seats	12	7	5	—	—	—
Monagas	122,958	70,149	30,621	4,010	6,239	1,223
Percentage		57.1	24.9	3.3	5.1	1.0
Seats	5	4	1	—	—	—
Nueva Esparta	54,742	16,539	9,322	2,467	8,985	420
Percentage		30.2	17.0	4.5	16.4	0.8
Seats	2	1	—	—	—	—
Portuguesa	120,927	59,135	33,778	3,916	8,276	6,316
Percentage		48.9	27.9	3.2	6.8	5.2
Seats	5	3	2	—	—	—
Sucre	186,284	96,617	34,183	5,090	16,648	2,630
Percentage		51.9	18.3	2.7	8.9	1.4
Seats	8	5	2	—	—	—
Táchira	166,677	79,702	58,861	3,984	1,942	15,863
Percentage		47.8	35.3	2.4	1.2	9.5
Seats	9	5	3	—	—	1
Trujillo	151,965	78,887	54,403	3,098	6,199	2,829
Percentage		51.9	35.8	2.0	4.1	1.9
Seats	6	4	2	—	—	—
Yaracuy	91,123	45,881	29,476	4,298	2,385	2,105
Percentage		50.4	32.3	4.7	2.6	2.3
Seats	4	3	1	—	—	—
Zulia	518,688	190,945	198,036	12,569	60,384	8,076
Percentage		36.8	38.2	2.4	11.6	1.6
Seats	24	10	11	—	3	—
Fed. Ter. Amazonas	9,088	4,620	2,513	51	931	55
Percentage		50.8	27.7	0.6	10.2	0.6
Seats	1	1	—	—	—	—

URD	FDP	PCV	MIR	OPINA	PNI	IP	Other[a]
702	715	674	1,146	777	254	348	1,253
0.5	0.5	0.5	0.8	0.6	0.2	0.3	0.9
—	—	—	—	—	—	—	—
6,952	4,825	2,859	4,450	5,656	5,464	2,535	9,666
1.8	1.3	0.7	1.2	1.5	1.4	0.7	2.5
—	—	—	—	—	—	—	—
5,805	746	1,217	853	287	168	783	857
4.7	0.6	1.0	0.7	0.2	0.1	0.6	0.7
—	—	—	—	—	—	—	—
14,065	159	913	228	53	317	370	904
25.7	0.3	1.7	0.4	0.1	0.6	0.7	1.7
1	—	—	—	—	—	—	—
2,487	849	3,571	418	247	462	—	1,472
2.1	0.7	3.0	0.3	0.2	0.4	—	1.2
—	—	—	—	—	—	—	—
17,448	2,723	2,376	1,121	186	784	4,636	1,842
9.4	1.5	1.3	0.6	0.1	0.4	2.5	1.0
1	—	—	—	—	—	—	—
914	234	594	656	394	384	254	2,895
0.5	0.1	0.4	0.4	0.2	0.2	0.2	1.7
—	—	—	—	—	—	—	—
1,014	1,051	575	511	1,472	360	—	1,566
0.7	0.7	0.4	0.3	1.0	0.2	—	1.0
—	—	—	—	—	—	—	—
1,538	1,158	1,128	1,119	205	305	281	1,244
1.7	1.3	1.2	1.2	0.2	0.3	0.3	1.4
—	—	—	—	—	—	—	—
7,342	7,844	4,823	3,169	2,205	4,701	6,311	12,283
1.4	1.5	0.9	0.6	0.4	0.9	1.2	2.4
—	—	—	—	—	—	—	—
740	19	43	—	2	26	14	74
8.1	0.2	0.5	—	—	0.3	0.2	0.8
—	—	—	—	—	—	—	—

CHAMBER OF DEPUTIES, 1973: POPULAR VOTE, PERCENTAGE, AND SEATS, BY DISTRICT (continued)

District	Total Valid Vote	AD	COPEI	MAS	MEP	CCN
Fed. Ter. Delta						
Amacuro	17,317	6,780	3,135	129	4,730	123
Percentage		39.2	18.1	0.7	27.3	0.7
Seats	1	1	—	—	—	—
Total, Venezuela	4,399,765	1,955,439	1,330,514	232,756	218,192	189,667
Percentage		44.44	30.24	5.29	4.96	4.31
Direct seats	183	102	64	6	4	4
National seats	17	—	—	3	4	3
Total seats	200	102	64	9	8	7

a Other vote includes: 15,537 FUN; 12,588 MAN; 12,238 PSD; 11,313 FND; 8,324 MPJ; 7,341 Desarrollo Comunidad; 6,220 MDI; 3,658 PRN; 3,489 URI; 2,309 FE; 1,575 ARPA; 1,459 ALCINA; 4,262 minor local parties.

SOURCE: Consejo Supremo Electoral, *Resultados Electorales 1973.*

URD	FDP	PCV	MIR	OPINA	PNI	IP	Other[a]
978	170	73	538	13	39	419	190
5.6	1.0	0.4	3.1	0.1	0.2	2.4	1.1
—	—	—	—	—	—	—	—
140,462	54,759	52,754	44,012	32,751	30,618	27,528	90,313
3.19	1.24	1.20	1.00	0.74	0.70	0.63	2.05
3	—	—	—	—	—	—	—
2	—	2	1	1	1	—	—
5	—	2	1	1	1	—	—

District	Total Valid Vote	Pérez	Fernández	Paz	Rangel	Villalba	Others
Federal District	802,098	346,962	318,916	17,058	72,614	19,949	26,599
Percentage		43.3	39.8	2.1	9.1	2.5	3.3
Anzoátegui	205,617	112,776	54,023	18,795	5,845	12,103	2,075
Percentage		54.8	26.3	9.1	2.8	5.9	1.0
Apure	56,327	37,022	15,845	1,456	461	1,117	426
Percentage		65.7	28.1	2.6	0.8	2.0	0.8
Aragua	231,402	104,272	90,336	9,661	11,297	7,082	8,754
Percentage		45.1	39.0	4.2	4.9	3.1	3.8
Barinas	82,485	48,236	29,091	1,537	1,624	1,169	828
Percentage		58.5	35.3	1.9	2.0	1.4	1.0
Bolívar	162,412	95,971	48,239	4,940	5,724	4,937	2,601
Percentage		59.1	29.7	3.0	3.5	3.0	1.6
Carabobo	278,147	125,590	111,368	14,055	11,348	6,598	9,188
Percentage		45.2	40.0	5.1	4.1	2.4	3.3
Cojedes	40,307	24,400	11,015	1,420	534	2,500	438
Percentage		60.5	27.3	3.5	1.3	6.2	1.1
Falcón	171,342	86,015	56,966	10,253	3,487	12,290	2,331
Percentage		50.2	33.2	6.0	2.0	7.2	1.4

(Table continued on next page)

PRESIDENT, 1973: POPULAR VOTE TOTALS AND PERCENTAGES, BY DISTRICT (continued)

District	Total Valid Vote	Pérez	Fernández	Paz	Rangel	Villalba	Others
Guárico	122,776	71,592	36,366	4,159	3,135	6,184	1,340
Percentage		58.3	29.6	3.4	2.6	5.0	1.1
Lara	277,418	129,436	106,530	14,668	18,184	2,392	6,208
Percentage		46.7	38.4	5.3	6.6	0.9	2.2
Mérida	133,500	65,684	57,934	3,923	3,294	594	2,071
Percentage		49.2	43.4	2.9	2.5	0.4	1.6
Miranda	379,633	186,799	147,706	7,092	18,171	7,353	12,512
Percentage		49.2	38.9	1.9	4.8	1.9	3.3
Monagas	123,400	72,710	35,428	6,235	2,704	5,486	837
Percentage		58.9	28.7	5.1	2.2	4.4	0.7
Nueva Esparta	54,877	18,508	10,963	7,668	2,093	15,147	498
Percentage		33.7	20.0	14.0	3.8	27.6	0.9
Portuguesa	119,133	61,663	38,504	11,055	3,411	2,581	1,919
Percentage		51.8	32.3	9.3	2.9	2.2	1.6
Sucre	187,989	103,406	46,213	15,582	3,985	17,415	1,388
Percentage		55.0	24.6	8.3	2.1	9.3	0.7
Táchira	155,198	83,794	63,727	2,272	2,826	964	1,615
Percentage		54.0	41.1	1.5	1.8	0.6	1.0
Trujillo	152,372	82,572	58,486	5,722	2,133	748	2,711
Percentage		54.2	38.4	3.8	1.4	0.5	1.8

	Total						
Yaracuy	92,148	49,206	33,989	2,922	3,177	1,362	1,492
Percentage		53.4	36.9	3.2	3.4	1.5	1.6
Zulia	520,228	210,130	226,306	59,143	9,933	4,466	10,250
Percentage		40.4	43.5	11.4	1.9	0.9	2.0
Fed. Ter. Amazonas	9,127	5,105	2,854	533	89	450	96
Percentage		55.9	31.3	5.8	1.0	4.9	1.1
Fed. Ter. Delta Amacuro	17,333	8,894	4,823	1,678	186	1,591	161
Percentage		51.3	27.8	9.7	1.1	9.2	0.9
Total, Venezuela	4,375,269	2,130,743	1,605,628	221,827	186,255	134,478	96,338
Percentage		48.7	36.7	5.1	4.3	3.1	2.2

NOTE: The Pérez vote includes 2,128, 161 AD; 2,168 PRN; 414 AD-PRN. The Fernández vote includes 1,544,223 COPEI; 35,165 FDP; 3,394 MPJ; 20,350 IP; 2,496 COPEI-FDP-MPJ-IP. The Paz vote includes 191,004 MEP; 30,235 PCV; 588 MEP-PCV. The Rangel vote includes 161,780 MAS; 23,943 MIR; 532 MAS-MIR.

[a] Other vote includes: 33,977 Miguel Angel Burelli (OPINA); 29,399 Pedro Tinoco (PNI and Movimiento Desarrollista); 11,965 Martín García Villasmil (PSD); 9,331 Germán Borregales (MAN); 6,176 Pedro Segnini La Cruz (FND); 3,754 Raimundo Verde Rojas (MDI); 1,736 Alberto Solano (FE).

SOURCE: Consejo Supremo Electoral, *Resultados Electorales 1973*.

CHAMBER OF DEPUTIES, 1978: POPULAR VOTE, PERCENTAGE, AND SEATS, BY DISTRICT

District	Total Valid Vote	COPEI[a]	AD	MAS
Federal District	905,899	308,102	326,585	94,039
Percentage		34.0	36.1	10.4
Seats	32	13	13	3
Anzoátegui	243,358	83,429	108,325	11,662
Percentage		34.3	44.5	4.8
Seats	9	4	5	—
Apure	64,137	27,277	33,115	1,310
Percentage		42.5	51.6	2.0
Seats	3	1	2	—
Aragua	314,119	126,165	109,311	31,201
Percentage		40.2	34.8	9.9
Seats	9	5	3	1
Barinas	103,559	45,931	47,363	4,556
Percentage		44.4	45.7	4.4
Seats	4	2	2	—
Bolívar	214,763	64,779	107,560	9,251
Percentage		30.2	50.1	4.3
Seats	7	3	4	—
Carabobo	375,819	162,402	120,204	27,593
Percentage		43.2	32.0	7.3
Seats	11	6	4	1
Cojedes	50,126	19,422	23,039	2,475
Percentage		38.7	46.0	4.9
Seats	2	1	1	—
Falcón	194,294	76,742	78,790	8,359
Percentage		39.5	40.6	4.3
Seats	7	3	4	—
Guárico	146,116	60,053	67,035	6,845
Percentage		41.1	45.9	4.7
Seats	5	2	3	—
Lara	341,310	154,223	119,618	15,327
Percentage		45.2	35.0	4.5
Seats	11	6	4	1

MIR	MEP	Causa Común	URD	MIN	PCV	VUC	Other[b]
27,853	14,843	30,396	12,830	30,943	9,154	13,626	37,528
3.1	1.6	3.4	1.4	3.4	1.0	1.5	4.1
1	—	1	—	1	—	—	—
5,505	9,268	3,079	7,741	1,476	3,649	1,708	7,516
2.3	3.8	1.3	3.2	0.6	1.5	0.7	3.1
—	—	—	—	—	—	—	—
348	690	107	311	45	200	131	603
0.5	1.1	0.2	0.5	0.1	0.3	0.2	0.9
—	—	—	—	—	—	—	—
4,794	4,853	6,178	3,422	7,783	4,115	5,267	11,030
1.5	1.5	2.0	1.1	2.5	1.3	1.7	3.5
—	—	—	—	—	—	—	—
1,408	784	323	598	293	712	489	1,102
1.4	0.8	0.3	0.6	0.3	0.7	0.5	1.1
—	—	—	—	—	—	—	—
5,316	3,160	4,535	1,660	1,046	1,693	2,158	13,605
2.5	1.5	2.1	0.8	0.5	0.8	1.0	6.3
—	—	—	—	—	—	—	—
10,114	5,734	5,615	5,136	14,933	6,865	4,648	12,575
2.7	1.5	1.5	1.4	4.0	1.8	1.2	3.3
—	—	—	—	—	—	—	—
192	627	279	1,670	181	267	294	1,680
0.4	1.3	0.6	3.3	0.4	0.5	0.6	3.4
—	—	—	—	—	—	—	—
2,867	8,757	1,925	5,955	1,922	1,737	1,190	6,050
1.5	4.5	1.0	3.1	1.0	0.9	0.6	3.1
—•—	—	—	—	—	—	—	—
897	1,945	1,290	1,659	472	672	712	4,536
0.6	1.3	0.9	1.1	0.3	0.5	0.5	3.1
—	—	—	—	—	—	—	—
20,758	6,351	4,432	2,970	1,543	5,688	2,564	7,836
6.1	1.9	1.3	0.9	0.5	1.7	0.8	2.3
—	—	—	—	—	—	—	—

Chamber of Deputies, 1978: Popular Vote, Percentage, and Seats, by District (continued)

District	Total Valid Vote	COPEI[a]	AD	MAS
Mérida	158,703	76,968	61,588	6,431
Percentage		48.5	38.8	4.1
Seats	6	3	3	—
Miranda	512,447	196,256	194,866	39,995
Percentage		38.3	38.0	7.8
Seats	15	7	7	1
Monagas	137,938	49,051	71,856	5,698
Percentage		35.6	52.1	4.1
Seats	5	2	3	—
Nueva Esparta	73,867	20,960	27,191	4,852
Percentage		28.4	36.8	6.6
Seats	2	1	1	—
Portuguesa	146,504	63,325	59,154	7,199
Percentage		43.2	40.4	4.9
Seats	5	3	2	—
Sucre	201,590	59,916	99,687	9,339
Percentage		29.7	49.5	4.6
Seats	8	3	5	—
Táchira	198,980	82,823	97,310	7,129
Percentage		41.6	48.9	3.6
Seats	8	4	4	—
Trujillo	163,039	74,740	68,812	4,857
Percentage		45.8	42.2	3.0
Seats	6	3	3	—
Yaracuy	107,510	50,151	39,294	4,486
Percentage		46.6	36.5	4.2
Seats	4	2	2	—
Zulia	597,107	281,394	222,183	18,399
Percentage		47.1	37.2	3.1
Seats	22	12	9	—
Fed. Ter. Amazonas	9,737	4,436	4,705	344
Percentage		45.6	48.3	3.5
Seats	1	—	1	—

MIR	MEP	Causa Común	URD	MIN	PCV	VUC	Other[b]
3,792	1,982	1,407	608	813	1,177	640	3,297
2.4	1.2	0.9	0.4	0.5	0.7	0.4	2.1
—	—	—	—	—	—	—	—
11,391	7,357	14,517	5,889	16,677	3,986	6,150	15,363
2.2	1.4	2.8	1.1	3.3	0.8	1.2	3.0
—	—	—	—	—	—	—	—
1,573	1,659	649	3,349	317	1,264	732	1,790
1.1	1.2	0.5	2.4	0.2	0.9	0.5	1.3
—	—	—	—	—	—	—	—
880	3,341	431	11,805	621	920	338	2,528
1.2	4.5	0.6	16.0	0.8	1.2	0.5	3.4
—	—	—	—	—	—	—	—
2,941	2,433	854	1,548	304	4,716	820	3,210
2.0	1.7	0.6	1.1	0.2	3.2	0.6	2.2
—	—	—	—	—	—	—	—
4,906	5,897	951	10,583	485	1,772	1,084	6,970
2.4	2.9	0.5	5.2	0.2	0.9	0.5	3.5
—	—	—	—	—	—	—	—
1,989	1,714	2,248	1,016	415	715	672	2,949
1.0	0.9	1.1	0.5	0.2	0.4	0.3	1.5
—	—	—	—	—	—	—	—
1,738	6,374	1,214	1,464	673	718	537	1,912
1.1	3.9	0.7	0.9	0.4	0.4	0.3	1.2
—	—	—	—	—	—	—	—
5,425	936	1,181	1,580	412	1,202	575	2,268
5.0	0.9	1.1	1.5	0.4	1.1	0.5	2.1
—	—	—	—	—	—	—	—
8,466	26,837	8,193	7,342	3,336	4,081	1,945	14,931
1.4	4.5	1.4	1.2	0.6	0.7	0.3	2.5
—	1	—	—	—	—	—	—
18	104	6	58	4	7	17	38
0.2	1.1	0.1	0.6	—	0.1	0.2	0.4
—	—	—	—	—	—	—	—

Chamber of Deputies, 1978: Popular Vote, Percentage, and Seats, by District (continued)

District	Total Valid Vote	COPEI[a]	AD	MAS
Fed. Ter. Delta Amacuro	20,089	9,280	9,330	222
Percentage		46.2	46.4	1.1
Seats	1	—	1	—
Total, Venezuela	5,281,011	2,097,825	2,096,921	321,569
Percentage		39.72	39.71	6.09
Direct seats	183	86	86	7
National seats	16	—	—	4
Total seats	199	86	86	11

[a] In each of three states—Nueva Esparta, Yaracuy, and Zulia—one COPEI deputy was elected on a joint URD-COPEI ticket.

[b] The only "Other" party to obtain a seat was the Socialist League, which won 30,453 votes and was awarded one seat in the national distribution. The remaining "Other" vote was as follows: 26,014 MORENA; 23,029 MDT; 13,614 FDP; 13,170 FUN; 12,919 Causa Radical; 10,861 CCN; 9,049 GAR (Grupo de Acción Revolucionaria); 7,950 OPINA; 6,746 IPDC (Independientes pro Desarrollo de la Comunidad); 2,045 ORA (Organización Renovadora Auténtica); 1,207 FE; 1,049 MAI Bolívar (Movimiento de Arrase Independiente); 1,368 minor local parties.

Source: Acción Democrática, Secretaria de Organización. The Supreme Electoral Council still had not issued final official returns for the 1978 elections as this book was going to press. The figures given here are taken from a computer printout issued by Operación Satélite, the AD's poll-watching program in 1978. They are derived from totals reported to the AD research center in Caracas by the official AD observer in each polling place, who copied them from the final tallies, which he was entitled to sign before they were sent to the Supreme Electoral Council. (See the account of procedures for counting the votes, pp. 51 and 52.)

MIR	MEP	Causa Común	URD	MIN	PCV	VUC	Other[b]
243	758	7	49	5	28	10	157
1.2	3.8	—	0.2	—	0.1	—	0.8
—	—	—	—	—	—	—	—
123,414	116,404	89,817	89,243	84,699	55,338	46,307	159,474
2.34	2.20	1.70	1.69	1.60	1.05	0.88	3.02
1	1	1	—	1	—	—	—
3	3	—	3	—	1	1	1
4	4	1	3	1	1	1	1

President, 1978: Popular Vote Totals and Percentages, by District

District	Total Valid Vote	Herrera	Piñería	Rangel	Arria	Prieto	Martín	Others[a]
Federal District	911,931	389,117	374,876	86,311	30,007	7,173	13,254	11,193
Percentage		42.7	41.1	9.5	3.3	0.8	1.5	1.2
Anzoátegui	245,414	105,599	118,954	9,718	3,065	3,514	2,130	2,434
Percentage		43.0	48.5	4.0	1.2	1.4	0.9	1.0
Apure	64,736	28,808	34,603	677	105	135	91	317
Percentage		44.5	53.5	1.0	0.2	0.2	0.1	0.5
Aragua	316,559	152,174	121,146	26,221	6,652	2,670	2,316	5,380
Percentage		48.1	38.3	8.3	2.1	0.8	0.7	1.7
Barinas	104,088	49,096	49,770	3,211	278	313	629	791
Percentage		47.2	47.8	3.1	0.3	0.3	0.6	0.8
Bolívar	217,432	77,909	119,618	10,172	4,719	996	2,353	1,665
Percentage		35.8	55.0	4.7	2.2	0.5	1.1	0.8
Carabobo	379,494	201,586	134,962	23,683	6,291	2,882	4,278	5,812
Percentage		53.1	35.6	6.2	1.7	0.8	1.1	1.5
Cojedes	50,655	22,868	24,809	1,743	282	347	151	455
Percentage		45.1	49.0	3.4	0.6	0.7	0.3	0.9
Falcón	196,165	92,142	88,336	6,223	2,113	4,177	1,075	2,099
Percentage		47.0	45.0	3.2	1.1	2.1	0.5	1.1
Guárico	147,406	67,222	71,172	5,370	1,241	741	396	1,264
Percentage		45.6	48.3	3.6	0.8	0.5	0.3	0.9

Lara	344,512	178,055	130,097	13,904	4,816	3,805	9,189	4,646
Percentage		51.7	37.8	4.0	1.4	1.1	2.7	1.3
Mérida	159,747	83,591	66,316	4,635	1,328	1,001	1,500	1,376
Percentage		52.3	41.5	2.9	0.8	0.6	0.9	0.9
Miranda	515,046	231,963	220,425	34,528	14,192	3,569	4,958	5,411
Percentage		45.0	42.8	6.7	2.8	0.7	1.0	1.1
Monagas	138,908	57,254	74,822	3,799	629	912	579	913
Percentage		41.2	53.9	2.7	0.5	0.7	0.4	0.7
Nueva Esparta	74,334	36,948	30,217	4,217	574	1,522	404	452
Percentage		49.7	40.7	5.7	0.8	2.0	0.5	0.6
Portuguesa	148,626	73,321	63,973	4,966	920	1,250	1,290	2,906
Percentage		49.3	43.0	3.3	0.6	0.8	0.9	2.0
Sucre	203,362	81,030	108,593	7,173	793	2,782	1,578	1,413
Percentage		39.8	53.4	3.5	0.4	1.4	0.8	0.7
Táchira	200,192	88,403	102,046	4,665	1,922	834	785	1,537
Percentage		44.2	51.0	2.3	1.0	0.4	0.4	0.8
Trujillo	164,978	81,441	74,219	3,341	1,034	3,058	744	1,141
Percentage		49.4	45.0	2.0	0.6	1.9	0.5	0.7
Yaracuy	108,847	57,404	42,924	3,443	1,106	596	1,843	1,531
Percentage		52.7	39.4	3.2	1.0	0.5	1.7	1.4
Zulia	602,574	313,704	240,808	15,591	8,886	16,406	2,546	4,633
Percentage		52.1	40.0	2.6	1.5	2.7	0.4	0.8

(Table continued on next page)

PRESIDENT, 1978: POPULAR VOTE TOTALS AND PERCENTAGES, BY DISTRICT (continued)

District	Total Valid Vote	Herrera	Piñerúa	Rangel	Arria	Prieto	Martín	Others[a]
Fed. Ter. Amazonas	10,109	4,651	5,027	315	12	60	13	31
Percentage		46.0	49.7	3.1	0.1	0.6	0.1	0.3
Fed. Ter. Delta Amacuro	20,190	8,901	10,383	351	22	245	202	86
Percentage		44.1	51.4	1.7	0.1	1.2	1.0	0.4
Total, Venezuela	5,325,305	2,483,187	2,308,096	274,257	90,987	58,988	52,304	57,486
Percentage		46.6	43.3	5.2	1.7	1.1	1.0	1.1

NOTE: The Herrera vote includes 2,409,478 COPEI; 57,755 URD; 8,776 FDP; 7,178 OPINA. The Rangel vote includes 249,478 MAS; 24,779 VUC. The Arria vote includes 72,234 Causa Común; 18,752 MDT.

The national totals published in the *Gaceta Oficial de la República de Venezuela* on December 12, 1978, were as follows: 2,487,318 Herrera; 2,309,577 Piñerúa; 275,942 Rangel; 89,651 Arria; 59,747 Prieto; 52,286 Martín; 29,305 Mújica; 13,918 Ortega; 8,337 Silva; 6,081 Castillo.

[a] Other vote includes: 28,967 Héctor Mújica (PCV); 13,859 L. Montiel Ortega (MRN); 8,641 A. Gomez Silva (FUN); 6,019 P. Salas Castillo (CCN).

SOURCE: Acción Democrática, Secretaria de Organización (see source note to preceding table).

Contributors

DAVID BLANK is professor of political science at the University of Louisville. He has written several monographs and books on Venezuelan politics.

DONALD L. HERMAN is professor of political science at Grand Valley State Colleges. In addition to articles on Latin American politics, he has published *The Comintern in Mexico*, *The Communist Tide in Latin America: A Selected Treatment* (editor), and *Christian Democracy in Venezuela*.

JOHN D. MARTZ is professor of political science at The Pennsylvania State University. He was editor of the *Latin American Research Review* from 1975 to 1980, and his publications include several articles and four books on Venezuelan politics.

DAVID J. MYERS is associate professor of political science at The Pennsylvania State University. His publications include *Democratic Campaigning in Venezuela: Caldera's Victory* and *Venezuela: The Democratic Experience* (coeditor and contributor).

ROBERT E. O'CONNOR is associate professor of political science at The Pennsylvania State University and codirector of Mycon, a political consulting firm which worked with Acción Democrática during the 1978 election campaign. He has published monographs and articles on public opinion and public policy.

RICHARD M. SCAMMON, coauthor of *This U.S.A.* and *The Real Majority*, is director of the Elections Research Center in Washington, D.C. He has edited the biennial series *America Votes* since 1956.

HENRY WELLS is professor of political science at the University of Pennsylvania. He has served as an election observer for the Organization of American States and is the author of *The Modernization of Puerto Rico* as well as articles on Latin American politics.

Index

Spanish names of parties and movements appear in the list of abbreviations at the front of the book.

JRC (COPEI Revolutionary Youth): 19, 149

Larrazábal, Wolfgang: 7, 11, 19, 31
  candidacies: 8, 10, 18, 118, 205
Lauría, Carmelo: 28, 218
Law of Journalism: 174
Law of Parties: 154
Leandro Moro, Reinaldo:
  campaign strategies: 112–13, 116, 120–21, 127, 128, 131
  party activities: 99, 101–3, 109
  senatorial candidacy: 118
Leftist movements: 13, 149
  congressional representation, 1974–1984: 168
  election results: 166–67, 215–16
  Herrera, support for: 93, 127–28, 150
  legalization of parties: 12
  municipal elections: 217, 232–34
  problems: 245–47
  resistance to: 8–9, 249–50
  rivalry and fragmentation: 9, 18, 28, 154–55, 158, 164, 168–69
  role in two-party polarization: 248
  Senate and Chamber of Deputies, seat distribution, 1969 and 1974: 155
  support for: 82–88 passim
  urban terrorism: 9
  viability of: 217, 219
  see also Communist party of Venezuela; Movement of the Revolutionary Left; Movement toward Socialism; People's Electoral Movement
Legislative Assemblies: 34, 36
Leoni, Raúl: 10, 12, 18, 27, 41, 115
Lepage, Octavio: 94, 96, 231, 244
Levine, David: 8
Liga Socialista: 164
López Contreras, Eleazar: 4, 30
Lusinchi, Jaime: 42, 96–97, 102, 114, 240–41

Machado, Eduardo: 13, 157
Machado, Gustavo: 6, 13, 157, 168
Machado, Luis Alberto: 223
Magazines. See Newsmagazines
MAN (Movement for National Action): 154, 238
Marginados, definition of: 142
Maritain, Jacques: 237
Márquez, Pompeyo: 22, 156, 161, 168, 246

Martín, Américo: 168–69, 246
  candidacy: 85, 93n, 157, 162, 167
Martz, John D.: 106, 171, 176, 181, 184, 189
Marxist movements. See Leftist movements
MAS. See Movement toward Socialism
Matos, Guanipo: 148
MDI (Independent Democratic Movement): 16–17, 154
Media:
  candidates' access to: 46
  role in campaigns: 188–89
  see also Newsmagazines; Newspapers; Radio broadcasting; Television broadcasting
Medina Angarita, Isaías: 4, 91, 204
MENI (National Independent Electoral Movement): 205
MEP. See People's Electoral Movement
Merc-Analysis polling firm: 121
Meridiano: 172, 173
Mesa electoral, definition of: 33
Mesa Espinosa, Salóm: 177–78
"Mexicanization" of party system: 10, 60, 219
Military:
  AD, support for: 224–25
  electoral procedures, role in: x, 52-54
  Herrera relations with: 224–26
  as ineligible to vote: x–xi, 37
MIN (Movement for National Integrity): 159, 164, 210
Minor parties. See Antiparty candidacies; Leftist movements; Rightist movements
MIR. See Movement of the Revolutionary Left
Moleiro, Moisés: 246
Molina Gásperi, Manuel: 129
Montes de Oca, Rafael: 136, 138, 141, 223, 228
Montiel Ortega, Leonardo: 17, 160–61, 166, 169
Morales Bello, David: 95
MORENA (Movement for National Renewal): 161, 169
Movement for National Action (MAN): 154, 238
Movement for National Integrity (MIN): 159, 164, 210
Movement for National Renewal (MORENA): 161, 169
Movement of the Revolutionary Left (MIR): 14, 92
  campaign strategy: 162

A NOTE ON THE BOOK

The typeface used for the text of this book is Palatino, designed by Hermann Zapf. The type was set by Hendricks-Miller Typographic Company, of Washington, D.C. Braun-Brumfield, Inc., of Ann Arbor, Michigan, printed and bound the book, using paper manufactured by the S. D. Warren Company. The cover and format were designed by Pat Taylor, and the figures were drawn by Hördur Karlsson.

The manuscript was edited by Claudia Winkler of the AEI Political and Social Processes Studies staff and by Gertrude Kaplan of the AEI Publications staff.

Democracy at the Polls

A Comparative Study of Competitive National Elections

Edited by David Butler, Howard R. Penniman, and Austin Ranney

This comprehensive cross-national study examines national elections in twenty-eight democracies. It provides both a catalog of information—on matters like electoral systems, candidate selection, party organization and ideology, campaign practices, media access, campaign financing, and voter turnout, for countries as diverse as Israel, India, Venezuela, and Japan, as well as the Anglo-American and European democracies—and an analysis of underlying patterns. The long-term effects of electoral rules on the shape of political life; the oddness, in a world context, of many features of electoral politics in the United States; the frequency with which elections decide major constitutional issues, alter party systems, or redirect policy; and the prevalence of the "new politics" of opinion research and media professionals are some of the themes that emerge. In addition, several of the chapters offer reflections on the problems, methods, and purpose of comparative electoral studies.

The contributors, aside from the editors, are Ivor Crewe, Leon D. Epstein, Dennis Kavanagh, Anthony King, Jeane J. Kirkpatrick, Arend Lijphart, Khayyam Zev Paltiel, Anthony Smith, and Donald E. Stokes. *1981/Political and Social Processes Study/3405–5 Cloth $16.25/ 3403–9 Paper $8.25*

AEI's *At the Polls* Studies

Australia at the Polls: The National Elections of 1975, Howard R. Penniman, ed. (373 pp., $5)

The Australian National Elections of 1977, Howard R. Penniman, ed. (367 pp., $8.25)

Britain at the Polls: The Parliamentary Elections of 1974, Howard R. Penniman, ed. (256 pp., $3)

Britain Says Yes: The 1975 Referendum on the Common Market, Anthony King (153 pp., $3.75)

Canada at the Polls: The General Elections of 1974, Howard R. Penniman, ed. (310 pp., $4.50)

France at the Polls: The Presidential Elections of 1974, Howard R. Penniman, ed. (324 pp., $4.50)

The French National Assembly Elections of 1978, Howard R. Penniman, ed. (255 pages, $7.25)

Germany at the Polls: The Bundestag Election of 1976, Karl H. Cerny, ed. (251 pp., $7.25)

India at the Polls: The Parliamentary Elections of 1977, Myron Weiner (150 pp., $6.25)

Ireland at the Polls: The Dáil Elections of 1977, Howard R. Penniman, ed. (199 pp., $6.25)

Israel at the Polls: The Knesset Elections of 1977, Howard R. Penniman, ed. (333 pp., $8.25)

Italy at the Polls: The Parliamentary Elections of 1976, Howard R. Penniman, ed. (386 pp., $5.75)

Japan at the Polls: The House of Councillors Election of 1974, Michael K. Blaker, ed. (157 pp., $3)

A Season of Voting: The Japanese Elections of 1976 and 1977, Herbert Passin, ed. (199 pp., $6.25)

New Zealand at the Polls: The General Election of 1978, Howard R. Penniman, ed. (295 pp., $7.25)

Scandinavia at the Polls: Recent Political Trends in Denmark, Norway, and Sweden, Karl H. Cerny, ed. (304 pp., $5.75)

Studies are forthcoming on the latest national elections in Belgium, Britain, Canada, Colombia, Denmark, Greece, India, Italy, Japan, the Netherlands, Norway, Spain, Sweden, and Switzerland and on the first elections to the European Parliament. Also forthcoming is *Democracy at the Polls*, edited by David Butler, Howard R. Penniman, and Austin Ranney, a comparative examination of the electoral process in a wide range of democratic nations.

SELECTED AEI PUBLICATIONS

Public Opinion, published bimonthly (one year, $12; two years, $22; single copy, $2.50)

How Democratic Is the Constitution? Robert A. Goldwin and William A. Schambra, editors (150 pp., paper $5.25, cloth $12.25)

The Presidential Nominating Process: Can It Be Improved? Jeane J. Kirkpatrick, Michael J. Malbin, Thomas E. Mann, Howard R. Penniman, and Austin Ranney (27 pp., $3.25)

Vital Statistics on Congress, 1980, John F. Bibby, Thomas E. Mann, Norman J. Ornstein (113 pp., paper $5.25, cloth $12.25)

Presidents and Prime Ministers, Richard Rose and Ezra N. Suleiman, eds. (347 pp., $8.25)

Democracy and Mediating Structures: A Theological Inquiry, Michael Novak, ed. (216 pp., paper $7.25, cloth, $13.25)

Future Directions for Public Policy, John Charles Daly, mod. (38 pp., $3.75)

Political Parties in the Eighties, Robert A. Goldwin, ed. (152 pp., paper $5.25, cloth $10.25)

Bureaucrats, Policy Analysts, Statesmen: Who Leads? Robert A. Goldwin, ed. (134 pp., paper $5.25, cloth $10.25)

The French National Assembly Elections of 1978, Howard R. Penniman, ed. (255 pp., $7.25)

Prices subject to change without notice.

AEI ASSOCIATES PROGRAM

The American Enterprise Institute invites your participation in the competition of ideas through its AEI Associates Program. This program has two objectives:

The first is to broaden the distribution of AEI studies, conferences, forums, and reviews, and thereby to extend public familiarity with the issues. AEI Associates receive regular information on AEI research and programs, and they can order publications and cassettes at a savings.

The second objective is to increase the research activity of the American Enterprise Institute and the dissemination of its published materials to policy makers, the academic community, journalists, and others who help shape public attitudes. Your contribution, which in most cases is partly tax deductible, will help ensure that decision makers have the benefit of scholarly research on the practical options to be considered before programs are formulated. The issues studied by AEI include:

- Defense Policy
- Economic Policy
- Energy Policy
- Foreign Policy
- Government Regulation

- Health Policy
- Legal Policy
- Political and Social Processes
- Social Security and Retirement Policy
- Tax Policy

For more information, write to:

AMERICAN ENTERPRISE INSTITUTE
1150 Seventeenth Street, N.W.
Washington, D.C. 20036